Missionary Trainin

C. David Harley

Missionary Training: The History of All Nations Christian College and its Predecessors (1911-1981)

Uitgeverij Boekencentrum, Zoetermeer

Deze uitgave is nummer 27 in de serie Mission (Missiologisch Onderzoek in Nederland), die onder redactie staat van:
Dr. G.J. van Butselaar
Dr. Th. van den End
Prof. dr. J.A.B. Jongeneel
Prof. dr. A.M. Kool
Dr. J.J. Visser

ISBN 90 239 0702 7
NUGI 631

Preface

When my wife and I applied to an Anglican missionary society, we were asked to go to All Nations Missionary College for a year's course of cross-cultural and missiological studies. We were both graduates in theology and I had served for three years as a curate in an Anglican church in North London. We were not sure why we needed to undertake further training before going to Africa as missionaries but we appreciated the opportunity to do so.

Our year at All Nations proved to be of great value and practical relevance to our future ministry. We appreciated the opportunity to reflect theologically on the nature of the church's missionary task and to consider some of the lessons that can be learned from the story of the expansion of the Christian Church. We also appreciated the way in which we were prepared for the cultural shock that might await us in Africa and the practical advice we were given on living, working and raising children in another culture. It is not for us to judge the effectiveness of our ministry in Africa, but we are sure that we would have been far less effective and less able to cope with the challenges of cross-cultural ministry without the benefit of this year's preparation.

After eight years in missionary work, we were invited to join the faculty of ANCC. Since we had been students, the college had merged with two other colleges, Mount Hermon Missionary Training College and Ridgelands Bible College. The college retained its ethos as a community and its emphasis on holistic training, but the curriculum had expanded significantly. We remained on the faculty from 1978 to 1993, and for eight years (1985 to 1995), I had the privilege to be the principal.

Since leaving the college, we have continued to be involved in the training of missionaries. From 1993-1996, we served as missionary training consultants with Crosslinks (an Anglican missionary society) and with the World Evangelical Fellowship Missions Commission. We visited many missionary training institutions in Africa, Asia and Latin America, both to lecture and to discuss with the faculty and church leaders the principles and practice of missionary training. I then served for three years as dean of the Discipleship Training Centre in Singapore, and am currently involved in setting up a missions track at Trinity Theological College, also in Singapore. Both in my teaching in Singapore, and in my continuing work as a missionary training consultant, I am constantly reflecting on the task of missionary preparation and seeking ways of improving training programmes. If the stories of these colleges and the conclusions I have drawn in this dissertation serve as a source of insight and inspiration to others engaged in the same task, I shall be more than satisfied.

During the writing of this dissertation, I have been aware of the advice, help and encouragement of so many people. I would particularly like to express my thanks to Prof. dr. Jan Jongeneel, professor of missions at Utrecht University, for acting as my supervisor for the writing of this dissertation. We met at the Overseas Missionary Study Center, where we were both staying as senior lectures in residence and where the idea for this dissertation was born. I am especially appreciative of the care and thoroughness with which he has guided my research and my writing. I also wish to express my thanks to Dr. G. H. Anderson for inviting me to lecture and study at OMSC. My wife and I thoroughly enjoyed the excellent facilities of the centre and were grateful for the opportunity to use the extensive library of the Yale Divinity School.

My sincere thanks are due also to a host of other people: Prof. dr. A. W. J. Houtepen for his helpful comments and observations on my initial manuscript; Dr J. J. Visser, director of the Hendrik Kraemer Institute, for kindly agreeing to be my co-sponsor; Marja Kerr and Magritha Jongeneel for the translation of the summary into Dutch; Miss Foote, who checked the chapters on Mount Hermon and ANCC; Mrs MacKenzie and Mrs Harman, who gave helpful comments on the chapter on Ridgelands; David Morris, for reading carefully through the ANBC and ANCC material and giving a great deal of advice on the history of the colleges; John Syratt, the bursar of ANCC from 1973 to 1993, who checked the details relating to legal and financial matters; Ron Davies and Martin Goldsmith, who were both present on the staff at the time of the merger and were responsible for drawing up the new syllabus; Tom Paget, the head gardener and warden of ANCC from 1958 to 1990, for providing his reflections on the practical courses; Margaret Cooper, for editing the comments on admissions procedures; Bob Hunt, whose survey of 1993/4 was the most extensive survey ever undertaken of the former students of all four institutions; the students of RBC who filled in the 1997 survey instrument for this dissertation; Stan Bruce, the librarian of ANCC, who allowed me free access to the college archives and checked all the footnotes and bibliography; my wife, Rosemary, who read through the whole manuscript to correct my spelling and punctuation; my daughter, Ruth, who undertook the administration of the survey on RBC alumni; my younger daughter, Catherine, who gave advice on the layout of the illustrations; my son, Andrew, who gave technical advice on the finer points of Microsoft Word; Mike and Stephne Whittles, whose granny flat in rural Hertfordshire provided the ideal setting for working on the final draft of this thesis; Carole Hudson, for faxing archival material out to Singapore and loaning the use of her computer; Ruth McGavin for providing information about her father, Henry Brash Bonsall. Without the help of those mentioned above and many others, this dissertation would never have seen the light of day.

Abbreviations

AACC	All-Africa Conference of Churches
AEF	Africa Evangelical Fellowship
ANBC	All Nations Bible College
ANCC	All Nations Christian College
ANMC	All Nations Missionary College
ANMR	All Nations Missionary Review
ANMRns	All Nations Missionary Review, new series
ANMU	All Nations Missionary Union
AWM	Arab World Ministries
BCC	British Council of Churches
BCMS	Bible Churchmen's Missionary Society
BGEA	Billy Graham Evangelistic Association
BMMF	Bible and Medical Missionary Fellowship
BSPM	Board of Study for the Preparation of Missionaries
CBMS	Conference of British Missionary Societies
CDRS	Certificate and Diploma in Religious Studies
CMS	Church Missionary Society
CNAA	Council for National Academic Awards
CWME	Commission for World Mission and Evangelism
EFMS	Evangelical Foreign Missions Association
ERCDOM	Evangelical Roman Catholic Dialogue on Mission
FIEC	Fellowship of Independent Evangelical Churches
IBMR	International Bulletin of Missionary Research
IFMS	Interdenominational Foreign Missions Association
IMC	International Missionary Council
IRM	International Review of Missions
MHMTC	Mount Hermon Missionary Training College
MRAN	Missionary Review of All Nations
MRANs	Missionary Review of All Nations supplement
MTC	Missionary Training Colony
NAN	News from All Nations
OM	Operation Mobilisation
OMF	Overseas Missionary Fellowship
RBC	Ridgelands Bible College
RCR	Rideglands College Record
SAGM	South Africa General Mission
SAMS	South American Missionary Society
SCM	Student Christian Movement
WBT	Wycliffe Bible Translators
WEF	World Evangelical Fellowship
WCC	World Council of Churches
WMC	World Missionary Conference, Edinburgh 1910
ZBMM	Zenana Bible and Medical Mission

Table of contents

1. Introduction

1.1 Stating the problem

The missionary movement of the Western Protestant churches which had accelerated through the nineteenth century received increased momentum from the World Missionary Conference held in Edinburgh in 1910. The challenge was given to men and women to go out into the mission field since it was confidently expected that the strength of the Western missionary force would treble within thirty years.[1]

At the same time it was recognised that those who were sent must be adequately trained. One of the eight commissions of the Edinburgh conference particularly addressed the matter of missionary training. This commission recognised 'the need for more specialised preparation of missionaries for their work and for their particular mission field', and that conclusion was fully supported by the open discussion before the Conference.[2]

The commission further recommended that, in view of the complexity of the situation, a Board of Missionary Studies should be established to give expert attention, on behalf of missionary societies, to all the factors involved in the adequate preparation of missionaries for their task. Within a year, such Boards had been established on both sides of the Atlantic.[3] At the first annual meeting of the American Board of Missionary Preparation, John R. Mott spoke of the importance of increased efficiency in the training of missionaries for their task:

> I realise today that, in my own thinking, the adequate training of our missionaries seems at least one of the supreme problems, if not the foremost one, faced at the present time by the Christian churches.[4]

Mott was particularly impressed by the fact that the reports of all eight commissions at the Edinburgh Conference emphasised the need for improved missionary preparation.

In the following decades several new chairs of missiology were instituted in Europe and North America. According to O. G. Myklebust, in the ten years after Edinburgh, chairs of Mission were founded at six institutions in the USA, including the Boston University School of Theology, Princeton Theological Seminary, and the Union Theological Seminary in New York.[5] The University of Copenhagen established an associate professorship in the History of Missions in 1923. The Selly

1. S. C. Neill, *A history of Christian missions*, 2nd ed. (1986), p. 333.
2. The World Missionary Conference, *Report of Commission V* (1910), p. 180.
3. The Board of Study for the Preparation of Missionaries was established in Britain and the Board of Missionary Studies in the United States.
4. J. R. Mott, 'The importance of increased efficiency in the training of missionaries for their task', in: *The first and second reports of the Board of Missionary Preparation, 1911-1912*, ed. F. P. Turner and F. K. Sanders (1912), p. 33.
5. Myklebust also points out that in North America in the 1920s full professorships were established in no less than eleven institutions.

Oak Colleges in Birmingham, England, set up a chair of missions in 1936.[6] In 1939, J. H. Bavinck was appointed to the chair of Missions at the Theological College in Kampen and the Free University in Amsterdam. In many other universities, lecture courses on missions-related topics were offered. Summer schools on mission were regularly held. The question of missionary training continued to be raised and discussed at subsequent international missionary conferences.[7]

By the end of the Second World War, the Western missionary enterprise had undergone a radical change. The euphoria that had surrounded the Edinburgh Conference had largely evaporated. Many of the countries of Europe were seeking to recover from the devastation of war. Fewer men and women were offering themselves for missionary service. Many countries in Africa and Asia which had been colonised by Western powers sought and obtained independence. Those missionaries who remained were viewed with suspicion as vestiges of colonialism and were often expelled. At the All-Africa Conference of Churches, held in Lusaka in 1974, Canon Burgess Carr, general secretary of the AACC, called for a moratorium on the receiving of money and personnel from the West. He argued that this was the only way that the African Church could assert itself in its mission to Africa and become a mature partner in the ecumenical world community.

These changed circumstances did not mean an end to the Western missionary endeavour, but they heightened once again the need for thorough selection and preparation. In 1944, a series of articles was published in the *International Review of Missions,*[8] which drew attention to the problems that confronted the new generation of missionaries: communism, nationalism, antagonism towards Western personnel, and a general antipathy towards Western ideas and initiatives. Western missionaries could no longer expect to control the national church in the countries where they served. They would only be welcome as partners, who were willing to serve under local leadership in the upbuilding of the life of the younger churches.[9]

Even before the war, the World Missionary Conference held at Tambaram (1938), had again emphasised the need for further specialised training to enable missionaries to 'enter intelligently and sympathetically' into the service of the national church.[10] Yet, in spite of the insistence at Edinburgh and subsequent international missionary conferences that missionaries needed to be thoroughly prepared for their work, the majority of missionaries continued to be sent out with little or no specialised training.

The experience of the Churches of Christ is typical in this respect. In a review of missionary training in that denomination, Alan Henderson writes: 'Prior to 1936 relatively little practical attention was devoted to the training and preparation of the

6. The first chair of Missions in Britain had been established in Edinburgh in 1867.
7. IMC, *The Jerusalem meeting of the IMC, 1928,* vol. II (1928), pp. 86, 95, 100 etc., *The world mission of the Church: findings and recommendations of the meeting of the IMC, Tambaram, Madras, 1938* (1939), pp. 83-86.
8. J. M. Davis, 'The preparation of missionaries for work in the post-war era', in: *IRM* 33 (1944), pp. 241-253; J. Foster, 'Missionary training in the post-war world', in: *IRM* 33 (1944), pp. 361-367; S. Weddell, 'Missionary training in North America', in: *IRM* 33 (1944), pp. 368-375.
9. IMC, *The world mission of the Church* (1939), p. 83.
10. *Ibid.*

overseas missionary.'[11] He goes on to cite as a typical example the experience of one missionary whose 'specific preparation for foreign missions was limited to the guest lecturers who frequently visited the college to discuss missions.'[12]

A similar situation is reflected in a survey sponsored by the Missionary Research Library in New York to ascertain the rate and causes of missionary turnover. Nearly one thousand missionaries took part in this survey, conducted in 1953. 73.9 percent of those questioned said that they had received no training in the principles, history and methods of mission. 83.2 percent said that they had received no cultural orientation before leaving for the field.[13]

While the Western missionary movement declined, and struggled to find its identity and role, the missionary movement in other parts of the world began to grow. The churches of Africa, Asia and Latin America began to assume more of the responsibility for global evangelism, which for so long had been considered the prerogative of the Western churches. They sent out increasing numbers of evangelists and missionaries not only among their own people and within their own countries, but also to peoples of other cultures and across national and continental boundaries. The most comprehensive survey of this missionary movement was published by Dr. Larry Pate in 1989. He stated that the number of missionaries sent out from African, Asian and Latin American churches had trebled in less than a decade.[14]

The growth of this missionary movement has created its own need for appropriate training. New missionary institutions have been established,[15] but they have not been able to meet the demand. Many new missionaries have been sent out without specialised preparation. Some have not been able to cope with the challenges of cross-cultural ministry and have returned home after only a short period of service.[16] Many church leaders and mission agencies have expressed their concern at the high turnover of personnel, and frequently cite inadequate training as one of the main reasons for this unacceptably high rate of missionary attrition.[17]

John Mott regarded the issue of missionary training as one of the supreme problems that faced the church of his day. Thirty years later, Sue Weddell wrote, 'If there is any one branch of missionary work that can be lifted up into prominence and accented in these days of priorities and major urgencies, surely the adequate preparation of those who carry the Message into the post-war world must claim a

---

11. A. Henderson, 'A historical review of missions and mission training in the Churches of Christ', in: *Restoration Quarterly* 35 (1993), p. 206.
12. Ibid., p. 208.
13. K.E. Moyer, *A study of missionary motivation, training and withdrawal: 1932-1952* (1957), pp. 29-36.
14. L. Pate, 'The dramatic growth of two-thirds world missions', in *Internationalising missionary training* (1991), pp. 27-40. *The directory of the Nigerian Evangelical Missions Association* (1993) detailed 2,180 Nigerian missionaries working with 36 indigenous agencies. *The catalogue of Brazilian mission agencies* (1993) recorded 1,793 Brazilian missionaries serving both inside and outside Brazil. *The Korean missions handbook* (1994) listed 3,272 Korean missionaries serving in different parts of the world.
15. *The world directory of missionary training programs* (1995) lists more than 500 institutions around the world that offer some level of missionary training. Many of these were established since 1970.
16. SEPAL, *Catalogue of Brazilian boards, missions and agencies* (1993), p. 97.
17. See W.D. Taylor, *Too valuable to lose: exploring the causes and cures of missionary attrition* (1997).

high place.'[18] The situation today is no less urgent. The consequences of inadequate preparation can be grave for the missionaries and their families, and disastrous for their ministry.

The purpose of this dissertation is to study the unity and variety of missionary training as it was offered at four colleges in Britain between 1911 and 1981. The context for this study will be the transition from colonialism to post-colonialism and the growing antipathy between evangelicals and the ecumenical movement.

1.2 THE RATIONALE OF THE STUDY

The colleges considered in this study were initially established in the first quarter of the twentieth century in the south-east of England. They were all evangelical, interdenominational colleges founded with the purpose of training men and women for missionary service. They all had close associations with the Keswick Convention[19] and were influenced by its teaching. They all had strong links with faith missions and trained many of their missionary candidates. In 1971, these colleges merged to form one larger college, All Nations Christian College.

This dissertation addresses four issues. The first relates to the nature of the training these colleges offered. How did they train their candidates? What was the level and content of their academic courses? What practical instruction was given? How were students prepared emotionally and spiritually for their future work? What lessons do these institutions provide which might help to reduce the level of missionary attrition today?

The second issue relates to the doctrinal stance of these colleges. As evangelical institutions, what was their attitude towards the mainline denominations? How did they relate to the emerging ecumenical movement? How far were they involved in the conferences of the International Missionary Council or the Commission on World Mission and Evangelism? How far did they engage with the questions discussed at those conferences about the nature and practice of mission? What was their own understanding of the missionary task and how did they prepare their students for that task?

The third issue relates to the historical context of these colleges. The period under consideration (1911-1981) saw enormous political changes taking place which profoundly affected the British missionary movement. The empire ceased to exist, as one former colony after another was granted independence. How far did these colleges adapt to these changes? In what ways did they prepare their students to minister in a post-colonial world?

The final question addressed relates to the successful transition that was made from three small institutions to one united institution. When the colleges merged in

18. S. Weddell, 'Missionary training in North America', in: *IRM* 33 (1944), p. 369.
19. The annual convention 'for the promotion of Scriptural holiness', which was founded in 1875 in the English Lake District and attracted evangelicals from a wide variety of Protestent denominations. See J. Pollock, 'Keswick Convention', in *The Concise Dictionary of Christian World Mission* eds., S. Neill, G. Anderson & J.Goodwin (1970), p. 322.

1971, it was not an auspicious time to start a new missionary project of this scale. Many thought the project was doomed to failure. The number of British missionaries was in decline. Only a few years before the merger, one of the colleges had been reduced to thirteen students. In the event, the pessimists were proved wrong. The college quickly grew in size, and gained an international reputation for the quality of its training. The question needs to be asked why the college succeeded when it could easily have failed. What facilitated the transition from three independent colleges to one united college? Why did an increasing number of individuals, and mission organisations, opt for All Nations Christian College for missionary training? What lessons can be learned about the development of an effective training programme?

1.3 THE LIMITATIONS OF THE STUDY

Mount Hermon Missionary Training College (MHMTC), was established in 1911 to train women for overseas ministry. A few years later (1919), a second college, Ridgelands Bible College (RBC), was founded to educate women for Christian service on the mission field. In 1923, All Nations Bible College (ANBC), was opened as 'an interdenominational training college for men, especially for the foreign missions field.'[20]

Initially these colleges developed separately, though Mount Hermon and All Nations were situated in close proximity to one another and for twelve years (1927 to 1939) were administered by the same Board and Trustees, the All Nations Missionary Union (Inc.). In each case their work was interrupted by the Second World War but resumed after a few years.

In 1962, ANBC appointed a former missionary, David Morris, as principal. He was to play a major role in the re-shaping and development of the college. His experience, both in the war and as a missionary in Africa, convinced him of the need for a programme of training that would prepare missionaries for relevant, effective and culturally sensitive ministry in the post-war world. He sharpened the missionary focus of the syllabus, and changed the name of the institution to All Nations Missionary College (ANMC). He was also convinced that men and women should be trained together, and, in the case of married couples, both husbands and wives needed a full course of preparation. In 1971, he persuaded the governing bodies of the three colleges, ANMC, MHMTC and RBC, to form one united college, to be called All Nations Christian College (ANCC).

The college grew from 120 to 150 in the next five years. In 1981, ill-health forced Morris to retire prematurely. By then All Nations Christian College had gained considerable recognition in the United Kingdom, and further afield, for the standard and quality of its missionary training.

The scope of this dissertation is to study the first seventy years in the history of these colleges from the foundation of Mount Hermon in 1911 to the retirement of Morris in 1981.

20. All Nations Bible College, *Prospectus* (1926), p. 2.

ANCC and its antecedent colleges were evangelical institutions situated in the home counties of southern England. They do not represent the training that was given at ecumenical institutions, such as the Selly Oak Colleges in Birmingham, or Roman Catholic colleges such as the Missionary Institute in London. They are not necessarily typical of other Bible colleges in the United Kingdom. It may, however, be reasonably assumed that they give some indication of evangelical missionary thinking and practice during this period.

1.4 THE DEFINITION OF TERMS

The terms 'evangelical' and 'ecumenical' are used in their contemporary meaning.[21] The term 'missionary training' can be understood in a number of ways and does need some elucidation.'[22] A lengthy discussion on the topic was contained in the report of Commission V of the Edinburgh Conference. Since then a great many articles and books have been written on the subject.[23]

Edinburgh 1910 identified four essential components of missionary training. Of these *spiritual training* was regarded as being of primary importance. 'All missionary societies are agreed that there must be genuine spiritual life, thorough consecration to missionary work.'[24] Douglas Webster, writing some forty years later, expressed the view that 'the basic preparation of missionaries is a spiritual one, for the missionary vocation has strains and temptations of its own.'[25]

Side by side with the necessity for training to encourage a deeply rooted independent spiritual life, the Edinburgh conference also stressed the importance of *moral training,* and the development of such qualities as docility, gentleness and sympathy. In 1952, the Willingen Meeting of the IMC spoke of the need to

21. Evangelicals in Britain were committed to evangelism and upheld the final authority of Scripture. Most did not adopt the highly critical attitude towards other Christians that typified fundamentalism in North America or insist on separation from all those whose views differed from their own. For a fuller distinction between evangelicals and fundamentalists, see D.J. Tidball *Who are the evangelicals?* (1994), p. 17.
22. The term 'missionary training' has been in use for at least one hundred years. Several colleges incorporated it in their title, such as the Nyack Missionary Training College, founded in 1882. A series of booklets were published by the Missionary Training School in 1905. Commission V of the Edinburgh Conference (1910) constantly refers to missionary training (e.g. pages 34, 56). However in lectures, articles and other publications the phrase 'missionary preparation' seemed to have been preferred until 1940 when an article on 'The missionary training of medical missionaries' by J. Welch appeared in *IRM* 29 (1940), p. 262-269. Since that date the terms 'missionary training' and 'missionary preparation' have enjoyed equal popularity and appear to have been regarded as synonymous.
23. International Missionary Council *The world mission of the church* (1939), esp. pp. 83-86. Apart from numerous articles in *IRM*, many of which have already been cited, see also R. Hogben, *In training* (1946), D.S. Sargent, *The making of a missionary* (1960), A.T. Houghton, *Preparing to be a missionary* (1956). In recent years the three most significant works to have been published in this field are: H.M. Conn and S.M. Rowen, eds., *Missions and theological education in world perspective* (1984); W.D. Taylor, ed., *Internationalising missionary training* (1991); and R.W. Ferris, ed., *Establishing missionary training* (1995).
24. World Missionary Conference 1910, *Report of Commission V* (1910), p. 19.
25. S. Neill, G. Anderson, J. Goodwin, eds., *The concise dictionary of the Christian world mission*, (1971), p. 494.

foster within missionaries sensitivity, flexibility and alertness as essential qualities for incarnational ministry.[26] Douglas Sargent, principal of the Church Missionary Society Men's Training College, wrote in 1960, 'We are much more concerned with what the student is to be than what he is to know. It is the ability to live together that we would foster rather than the capacity to pass examinations.'[27]

Intellectual training was also included by the 1910 conference in its analysis of missionary training.[28] The report cites five departments of study 'which no missionary candidate, man or woman, could afford to neglect.' These were the science and history of missions, the religions of the world, sociology; pedagogy, and the science of languages.[29]

Over the years many suggestions have been put forward for inclusion within the academic timetable of training programmes.[30] It would be impossible to include them all here but it is worth referring to the curriculum which was drawn up by a distinguished panel of missiologists meeting at Milligan College, Tennessee, in 1974. Their curriculum was designed to be 'suitable for the training of missionaries in cross-cultural understanding.'[31]

Finally, reference was also made at Edinburgh to the need for *practical training*. In particular, the value of training in elementary medicine and hygiene, photography and typewriting was noted.[32] Over the years a host of other suggestions have been put forward, including book-keeping, motor mechanics, building,[33] agriculture, music, and even cobbling.[34] A survey of contemporary missionary colleges reveals a diversity of practical training that reflects the context of each school and the kind of ministries their candidates expect to pursue.[35]

For the purposes of this study, the term 'missionary training' will be understood as embracing every aspect of the pre-field preparation of cross-cultural missionaries. It will be taken to include their spiritual preparation, character development, academic training, and practical instruction.

26. N. Goodall, ed., *Missions under the cross* (1953), p. 213.
27. D. Sargent, *The making of a missionary* (1960), pp. 138f.
28. For a contrary view see H.D. Northfield 'The training of men missionaries.' in *IRM* 46 (1957), pp. 59-67, who argues that missionary training should concentrate on the practical application of the gospel to persons and human situations rather than on elaborate academic study.
29. *Ibid.*, pp. 161f.
30. e.g. C.A. Taber 'The training of missionaries', in: *Practical Anthropology* 14 (1967), pp. 267-274, and quoted in *Missions and theological education in world perspective* (1984), p.321-332. He identified three areas where every missionary needs knowledge and competence: biblical, theological and historical studies; socio-cultural studies; studies in communications and linguistics.
31. The panel was set up by the administrators of the William S. Carter Symposium, held at Milligan College, Tennessee, in April 1974, and consisted of G.H. Anderson, C. Forman, L. Barney, T. Yamamori and A. Tippett. The report of that committee was published in *Milligan Missiogram* 1:3 (1968), pp. 7-19, and in *Missions and theological education in world perspective* (1984), pp. 405-408.
32. World Missionary Conference, *Report of Commission V* (1910), pp. 112-114 and 160.
33. H.D. Northfield, 'The training of men missionaries.' in: *IRM* 46 (1957), p. 64.
34. R. Hogben, *In training* (1946), p. 133.
35. D. Harley, *Preparing to serve* (1995), p. 135.

1.5 THE STRUCTURE OF THE STUDY

This study begins with an historical survey of missionary training in the United kingdom during the present century, to provide the background against which the development of the four colleges can be considered. It surveys the international conferences, both ecumenical and evangelical, which impacted the thinking about mission and missionary training in the United Kingdom. It analyses the work of the Conference of British Missionary Societies, and the Board of Study for the Preparation of Missionaries. It examines a number of training colleges, which represent a cross-section of style and approach to missionary training in Britain during this time. These include the Edinburgh Missionary College, the Missionary Training Colony, Tyndale Hall and Dalton House, and the Selly Oak Colleges in Birmingham. The chapter concludes with a review of the writings of two women and one man, who served as principals of missionary training institutions – Florence Allshorn (Foxbury), Edmund Morgan (College of the Ascension), Gwenyth Hubble (Carey Hall).

Chapters three to five consider the development of the three separate colleges – Mount Hermon Missionary Training College, Ridgelands Bible College and All Nations Bible College – from their foundation to their amalgamation in 1971. Each institution is examined to ascertain its distinctive character and the nature of the missionary training it offered. The same structure is adopted, and the same questions are raised in each case.

1. *Foundation and history*. What was the historical background behind the foundation of the institution? What was the distinctive contribution made by each principal in its development? What were the critical issues in that development and what were the crises that the college encountered during its history?
2. *Doctrinal basis and character*. What was the doctrinal position of the institution, and the purpose for which it was founded? What were its stated aims and objectives? How far have those been maintained or altered? What were the distinctive characteristics of the institution, and in what ways did it differ from other similar colleges? What was its attitude towards Christians of other traditions and what was its stance towards the ecumenical movement?
3. *The training programme*. What were the components of the training programme? In what ways did the college seek to provide spiritual, moral, academic, and practical preparation? To what extent did the college show a willingness to adapt to the changing political situation on the global scene, and how far did it prepare its students to serve in countries which had achieved independence?
4. *Students*. Who were the students in each institution? What were their nationalities and denominational affiliations? On what basis were they accepted? What level of training, academic, or otherwise, had they already received? What were their professions? Where did they go to serve after their period of training and with which missionary agency?

Chapter six concentrates on the history of All Nations Christian College from 1971 to 1981. The same basic structure is used as in the previous chapters, but the examination is carried out in greater detail. A number of additional questions are also raised: How significant was the role played by David Morris? What were the key factors that led to the growth of the college at a time when the Western missionary enterprise was in decline? What were the critical issues at the time of the amalgamation of the three colleges, and how were they resolved? How did the college develop after the amalgamation? How successfully did it address the issues of post-colonial mission? Did it change its stance towards the ecumenical movement? How was the course evaluated by its students?

In the final chapter, the missionary training, given at All Nations and its antecedent colleges, is evaluated against the background of the political, theological, ecumenical, and missiological contexts in which they were founded and developed. Their strengths and weaknesses are described, and lessons are drawn that could be applied to the training of missionaries in the future. The challenges which faced the college, after Morris's retirement, are also examined.

1.6 The methodology of the study

In the second chapter the historical method is used. This involves an examination of published reports and papers of international missionary conferences, a review of the work of the Conference of British Missionary societies, and a study of colleges in the United Kingdom established primarily for the training of overseas missionaries. A review is also given of the writings of three experienced missionary trainers, who were involved in the preparation of British missionaries during this period.

Chapters three to five also adopt the historical method, examining relevant published and unpublished material. A systematic study is made of each college. The comparative method is employed to contrast the distinctive features of each college. In the case of Ridgelands Bible College, the extant archival material was supplemented by the use of a survey instrument completed by seventy alumnae.

In chapter six, research is carried out on published and unpublished material relating to the college during the years 1971-1981. Use is also made of oral history through personal interviews with former principals and staff who worked at the college during this period. A systematic analysis is made of the training that was offered by the college.

1.7 The sources of the study

The primary sources for this study are: (1) the unpublished archives of each institution, including the minutes of the Council and committees of each college, the minutes of the Joint Working Committee which drew up the constitution of the combined colleges, the syllabi with course descriptions and notes, the documents submitted to the Council for National Academic Awards for the accreditation of All Nations Christian College; (2) publications produced by the college, books and articles written by members of the faculty; (3) interviews with, and correspondence from, past members of staff and members of the governing council.

Secondary sources include books and articles written by others about the three colleges and the combined college.

Tertiary sources provide the background information and detail for the whole of this study, and for chapter two in particular. Extensive reference is made to the reports of the International Missionary Council, the Commission on World Mission and Evangelism, and the Board of Study for the Preparation of Missionaries. A number of works dealing with the history and theology of mission have also been consulted. These include: R. C. Bassham *Mission theology 1948-1975: years of world-wide creative tension, ecumenical, evangelical and catholic* (1979); D. J. Bosch *Witness to the world* (1980) and *Transforming mission: paradigm shifts in theology of mission* (1991); K. Fiedler *The story of faith missions* (1994); J. A. B. Jongeneel *Philosophy, science, and theology of mission in the 19th and 20th centuries* 2 vols. (1995 and 1997); O. G. Myklebust *The study of mission in theological education* 2 vols. (1955 and 1957); D. J. Tidball *Who are the evangelicals?* (1994); J. Verkuyl *Contemporary missiology: an introduction* (1978); T. Yates *Mission in the twentieth century* (1996) Material on individual training institutions is drawn from such works as M. Stewart *Training in mission: St Colm's College, Church of Scotland* (1927), J. H. Oldham *Florence Allshorn*, W. S. Hooton and J. S. Wright's chapter on 'The colleges' in: *The first twenty-five years of the Bible Churchman's Missionary Society* (1947). Use has also been made of unpublished archival material of the Missionary Training Colony. The following works on missionary training were also consulted: J. H. Oldham *The world and the gospel* (1916); G. A. Gollock 'The making of a missionary', in: *IRM* 6 (1917) pp. 437-439; E. R. Morgan 'Missionary vocation and training', in: *Essays catholic and missionary* (1928), pp. 233-252; R. Hogben *In training* (1946); D. Webster *What is a missionary* (1955); A. T. Houghton *Preparing to be a missionary* (1956); D. N. Sargent *The making of a missionary* (1960); G. Hubble 'Reasons for missionary training', in: *IRM* 52 (1963), pp. 257-265.

2. Missionary Training in the United Kingdom (1910-1981)

2.1 Introduction

The aim of this chapter is to describe the background and context in which the three colleges, which later united as All Nations Christian College (ANCC), were established and in which they developed. It covers the period from the Edinburgh Conference of 1910, which took place one year before the founding of the first of those three colleges, Mount Hermon Missionary Training College (MHMTC), to the retirement of David Morris, the first principal of ANCC in 1981. It reviews those international missionary conferences which had considerable impact on thinking about mission and missionary training in the twentieth century (2.2). It appraises the work of the Board of Study for the Preparation of Missionaries that was set up in Britain as a direct consequence of the Edinburgh Conference (2.3). It examines those training institutions whose foundations represented significant progress in the advancement of missionary preparation in this country (2.4). Finally, it reviews the writings of three British educationalists who were involved in the field of missionary training (2.5).

2.2 International missionary organisations and conferences

The twentieth century has witnessed a multiplication of international missionary conferences. Following the Edinburgh conference of 1910, there was a succession of conferences that were organised by the International Missionary Council. After the integration of the International Missionary Council with the World Council of Churches in 1961, several assemblies were arranged by the Commission on World Mission and Evangelism (CWME). Finally, towards the end of our period there were a number of evangelical conferences that were motivated, at least in part, by a reaction to the perceived liberalism of the conciliar movement.

2.2.1 Edinburgh conference (1910)

The report of Commission V of the Edinburgh Conference is probably the most thorough report on missionary training that has ever been produced. The members of the commission began their work two years before the conference convened in Scotland. The British participants, whose twelve members made up the largest national group in the commission, were particularly thorough in their groundwork. They met on ten separate occasions to review their subject, to agree on a general procedure and prepare for the conference.[1] They conducted a survey among mis-

1. 9th December, 1908; 11th January, 13th March, 14th May, 5th, 12th, 14th and 15th June, 4th-7th October, 18th November, 1909; 18th and 19th March, 15th and 16th April, 1910.

sionary societies, colleges and training institutions, and consulted a cross section of missionaries who represented different denominations, agencies and types of missionary work. Having collated the responses, they invited a 'large number of qualified persons – missionaries, heads of training institutions, and missionary officials – to give evidence before them.'[2]

The report acknowledged the problem of making generalisations about missionary preparation. First, there was wide diversity among those who could be called missionaries: there were ordained missionaries, medical missionaries, educational missionaries, industrial teachers, secretaries and business agents. Secondly, there were enormous differences between the mission fields to which these missionaries were sent. It was understood that 'the same kinds of training are not necessary for those who are going to Central Africa, to a tribe among whom no white man has lived, as for those who are going to work in Bombay or Peking or Tokyo.'[3] Thirdly, it was recognised that missionary societies differed greatly as to the expectations they put on their candidates and the training they required of them.

The early chapters of the report considered current practices in the selection and training of missionary candidates. Chapter four examined the general preparation that was required of different categories of missionaries.

Missionaries who were to be ordained within the Church of England received their theological training at university, at an Anglican theological college, or at a missionary training institution. Most missionary graduates came from Oxford, Cambridge and Durham. Those who were less able or had less financial resources spent two years at a theological college. In neither case did these ordinands receive much specialised training in missionary subjects in the course of their theological studies.

The Church Missionary Society provided a probationary year at their Preparatory Institution at Blackheath to prepare ordination candidates for the entrance examination to the CMS Missionary Training College at Islington. This probationary year proved of value both as an introduction to theological study for the students and as an opportunity for the staff to assess 'the character and intellectual ability' of the candidates.[4] Those who passed the Islington entrance examination and 'concerning whose suitability for missionary work in other respects the Committee have sufficient evidence'[5] began a three year course of theological study. Prior to their ordination they were required to pass the preliminary examination of candidates for Holy Orders and, as a general rule, the Bishop of London's examination for Deacon's Orders.

While it was evident that missionary ordinands received substantial theological education, the same was not the case when it came to the matter of specialised missionary training. One of the questions that was put to missionary societies was: 'Do you give your theological candidates any special 'missionary training' (i.e. in such matters as the language, history, religion and customs of the people to whom

2. World Missionary Conference, *Report of Commission V* (1910), p. 2.
3. *Ibid.*, p. 13.
4. *Ibid.*, p. 35.
5. *Ibid.*, p. 36.

they are going)?'[6] The answers which were received by the commission left a general impression of vagueness and inadequacy. Most mission boards were dissatisfied with the low status which missionary education received in theological colleges. At the same time, they also knew that missionary candidates formed only a small minority in such colleges and the curriculum was already overloaded. There appeared to be a general resignation that not much could be done to change the situation.

When it came to educational missionary candidates, some societies advised them to procure 'missionary' training, but few societies made provision for it. One society provided no training for men, but insisted that women should do a year or two at a missionary training institution.[7]

A similar situation pertained to medical missionaries. A few mission boards recommended doctors to undergo missionary training. Most did not. Some societies considered that the urgent needs of the field compelled them to send out doctors as soon as possible even though they would prefer them to undergo additional missionary training. One agency felt that all that was required was for the doctor to have ' a real missionary spirit.'[8] Most nurses were required to take a course of missionary preparation, but some 'missionary-hearted nurses' were sent out with no special training at all.

A number of missions sent out industrial missionaries to use their technical skills in developing the local economy and training national workers in various skills. These missionaries were often expected to play a full part in the evangelistic work of the mission, to lead Bible studies, or even to pastor churches. Yet they were given little or no preparation to equip them for this aspect of their work. 'Although they were expected to assist in the spiritual side of the work and although they tend, when on the field, to claim an increasing share in it, they receive no training for it. Societies are apparently satisfied with technical efficiency and with general assurances as to Christian character.'[9]

Chapter five of the report looks more closely at specialised missionary preparation, which is defined as 'the training which is given . . . in those subjects which are not taught in the usual theological curriculum or in the ordinary training for medicine, nursing, teaching, etc., but are concerned solely with the mission field.'[10]

In the survey which was sent to missionary societies, the commission listed the subjects that might be included in a programme of preparation: the missionary aim and its relation to the Gospel, the history of missions, comparative religion, the various forms of missionary activity, their functions and importance, the history, religious beliefs, social customs and practices, and the specific problems of the candidate's prospective field.

The response of the societies appeared most discouraging. One 'honoured' society attached little importance to specific preparation at home for the field. Another

6. *Ibid.*, p. 222.
7. *Ibid.*, p. 41.
8. *Ibid.*, p. 43.
9. *Ibid.*, pp. 46f.
10. *Ibid.*, p. 49.

'large' society regarded these subjects as 'of much less importance before going abroad than the study of Biblical languages, exegesis, etc.'[11]

The members of the commission acknowledged the difficulties of providing adequate and comprehensive training for missionary candidates. They recognised that many individual missions lacked sufficient resources for such an undertaking and proposed the setting up of co-operative ventures in missionary training. Towards the end of the report, the commission recommended the establishment of central institutions, at home and in the mission field, for special missionary preparation.[12]

By 1910 a number of missionary training institutions had already been founded on both sides of the Atlantic.[13] These colleges were primarily intended for lay evangelists and for women who were not accepted into theological colleges. The relative strengths and weaknesses of these colleges is assessed in the report. Their greatest strength seemed to be in the way they developed the character and the spiritual life of candidates. Those who trained in such institutions appeared to demonstrate 'greater consideration for others, more sweetness of disposition and thoughtfulness . . . and new workers get on better with those from whom they differ.'[14] They were also considered to be more zealous and effective in evangelism.

On the other hand, a number of criticisms were made of these colleges. They tended to produce a certain type of missionary. The training they offered was often meagre academically and far below the standard of a university education. 'Speaking generally, the intellectual standard is not yet sufficiently high, nor the teaching sufficiently related to the specific requirements of the case.'[15] It was felt that some of these faults could be remedied by closer contact with missionary societies and wider knowledge of the situation in the field.

These criticism were not valid for all missionary institutions. The Women's Missionary College in Edinburgh, in particular, was praised for its training programme which seemed to exemplify many of the methods which had commended themselves to the commission.[16]

The survey which the members of the commission conducted in the two years prior to the World Missionary Conference convinced them of the seriousness of the situation. 'Nearly every board has admitted its failure to reach its own ideals. And there is widespread recognition of what we may call relative failure felt both by missionaries themselves and by sympathetic observers of mission work. Earnest men have been willing to confess that they could see how and where their work was weak. And again and again they see the cause of their weakness in defective preparation.'[17]

The major part of the report of the commission examined the principles of missionary preparation and their implementation. The members of the commission de-

11. *Ibid.*, p. 50.
12. *Ibid.*, pp. 180-192.
13. A list of the missionary training institutions that responded to the commission's survey is given in appendix III of the report, pp. 236-237.
14. World Missionary Conference, *Report of Commission V* (1910), p. 54.
15. *Ibid.*, p. 89.
16. *Ibid.*, pp. 87f.
17. *Ibid.*, p. 97.

scribed the missionary task as the presentation of the Christian message, the manifestation of the Christian life, and the organisation of a Christian church and nation. In their deliberation about how missionaries were to be prepared adequately for that task, they identified four areas which must be addressed in any programme of training: the spiritual, the moral, the intellectual and the physical.

The members of the commission acknowledged that God alone was the source of spiritual life and that no amount of training could create the love, faith and hope, which alone are found in Him. However, it was felt that a period of training might remove some obstacles that hinder the growth of that spiritual life and might also prepare the missionaries for the spiritual dangers and temptations which they may encounter. 'He has to be ready in case of necessity to face the tremendous spiritual dangers of isolation among heathen surroundings. He must know how to face great strain and heavy responsibility without the support of visible Christian fellowship, and how to maintain a high level of spiritual life without the continual renewing which is supplied under normal conditions by the ordinances of common worship.'[18]

Side by side with the necessity for a strong independent spiritual life, the report identified four elements of moral character that an aspiring missionary should seek to acquire. The first of these was 'docility' or a teachable spirit. The attitude of a new missionary must be 'that of a learner, not only, as is necessarily the case, with regard to language, but also to manners, customs, modes of thought, standards of morals, religions, institutions of the country ... He should be encouraged constantly to seek counsel from his senior colleagues and also, as soon as his language allows, from the officers and leaders of the native church, who are so competent to teach and help him.'[19]

A second quality that was recognised as being highly desirable in a missionary was that of 'gentleness' or 'sweet reasonableness', that spirit of adaptability and courtesy which issues in a right relationship with peoples of other cultures and backgrounds. One of the problems acknowledged by the report was the incipient racial prejudice and arrogance that characterised many missionaries. 'The white man so instinctively feels that he is lord of creation, that it is hard for him, no matter how Christian he may be, to get over the idea that men of a different colour are his inferiors. He is apt to be brusque and peremptory. He is always in a hurry and impatient of delays.'[20] Unless a missionary can show greater patience and humility he stands little chance of exerting much spiritual influence in his ministry.

Missionaries must also demonstrate that quality of sympathy with different peoples that characterised the ministry of the apostle Paul. It was his ability to draw alongside others, whatever their religious or cultural background, that created an effective bridge for the communication of the gospel. Like Paul, the missionary of twentieth century, must learn to love those to whom he goes, to appreciate the glories of their civilisation and culture, to understand what is important to them and what is revered and honoured among them.

18. *Ibid.*, p. 100.
19. *Ibid.*, p. 102.
20. *Ibid.*, p. 103.

The final quality that was listed under desirable moral characteristics of a missionary was the capacity to lead. Again and again the responses to the survey that was sent to missionaries on the field included a plea for men who could lead. 'We only want men in China who have capacity to lead.' 'We especially need men who have the ability to lead, organise, teach.' 'The greatest need of the ministerial body in China today, next to Christian character, is for great leaders.'[21]

The report devoted several pages to a consideration of those subjects that should form the basis of the intellectual training of missionaries. These included a good grounding in biblical literature and Christian doctrine. At the same time the missionary candidates must recognise that they could not simply transplant doctrinal statements, that were formulated thousands of miles away and several centuries before, and expect them to meet the religious needs of a very different people. They must learn to reapply 'the inexhaustible riches of wisdom and knowledge that are stored in Christ.'[22]

In the area of 'special missionary training' the report specified five areas that should be covered in the training curriculum.[23] It lamented the fact that so often missionaries had been given little opportunity to study in these areas.[24] One missionary with forty years experience said he had 'never met a missionary who had studied the science of missions.' Another wrote 'I went forth without any knowledge practically of the people I was among. I was obliged to pick up anything I learned by degrees. . . . I have always felt this was a great disadvantage.'[25]

Although Edinburgh 1910 is rightly regarded as a major milestone in the development of the modern missionary movement,[26] there were fundamental weaknesses. It represented an almost exclusively western perspective on mission. There were very few Asian or African delegates and, although significant contributions were made by Cheng Ching Ye of China and V. S. Azariah of India, the vast majority of speeches were presented by Europeans or North Americans. Commission V had no representative from the Third World, although a number of national church leaders had been consulted prior to the conference. The comments in the report were given from an Anglo-saxon viewpoint. The assumption appears to have been made that most missionaries would be white and Western.

Nearly all the Western delegates came as representatives of missionary societies.[27] Only societies which had missionaries in the field were eligible to send representatives and the size of each delegation was in proportion to the number of missionaries in active service. Many agencies were the official missionary organisation of their denomination, but they could only speak in the name of the mission and not in the name of their church. Edinburgh was 'a conference of societies and

21. *Ibid.*, p. 105. These are quotations from three missionaries who responded to the survey sent out by the commission.
22. *Ibid.*, p. 110.
23. These have been cited already in the first chapter. They are: (1) the science and history of missions; (2) the religions of the world; (3) sociology; (4) pedagogy; and (5) the science of languages.
24. *Ibid.*, p. 162.
25. *Ibid.*, p. 165.
26. W.R. Hogg, *Ecumenical foundations* (1952), p. 134.
27. A few places were reserved for special nominations by the Executive Committee.

not a council of churches.'[28] After the conference, it was uncertain what impact it would have on the wider church. The clear call to world evangelisation had sounded from Edinburgh, but would it be heard? Would the representatives of the different mission agencies be able to persuade their various constituencies to implement the resolutions that had been made? Although the Edinburgh conference demonstrated the importance of thorough missionary training and laid down the foundational principles for that training, the question that remained after Edinburgh was whether or not its recommendations would be implemented.

2.2.2 International Missionary Council (1921-1961)

Within four years of the Edinburgh conference, the world was at war. The committee that was given the responsibility of continuing the work of the conference was unable to take much action until 1918. Once the war had ended, the officers of that committee initiated steps that led to the formation of the International Missionary Council. This body was formally constituted at a conference held at Lake Mohonk, New York in 1921. Whereas the authority of the continuing committee of the Edinburgh conference derived solely from that gathering, the new body received its authority from the various national Christian Councils. In the succeeding decades, the International Missionary Council would make an incalculable contribution to global mission and to the cause of missionary training through the publication of the International Review of Mission and through the organising of a succession of significant missionary conferences.

John Mott, who was to serve as the first chairman of the International Missionary Council, prepared a paper for consideration at that inaugural meeting at Lake Mohonk. He argued the case for the maximum degree of international co-operation in the missionary task. He suggested spheres in which such co-operation was both desirable and practicable, and he included among them the area of missionary preparation. He urged training schools in the home countries and language schools on the field to work as closely together as possible. He recognised that the new generation of missionaries would face greater challenges than ever before. He believed that 'far better men and women will be required to meet the situation', and added that 'they will do their work in an international age. It is supremely important that they produce an international outlook.'[29] He believed that the internationalising of mission training would create that outlook, as students were enriched by those of 'different national streams of experience and different national outlooks on life.'[30]

Jerusalem (1928)

The next international missionary conference was held on the Mount of Olives in Jerusalem in 1928. The mood of the conference was very different from that which pertained eighteen years before. The optimism which characterised the Edinburgh

---

28. R. Rouse and S.C. Neill (eds.), *History of the ecumenical movement, 1517-1948* (1967), p. 357.
29. J.R. Mott, *International cooperation: its possibilities, its costs and its realisation* (1921), p. 20.
30. *Ibid.*

conference had largely evaporated. As D. Bosch observed in his book *Witness to the world* (1980):

> Between Edinburgh and Jerusalem lay the first World War (1914-18) and the Russian Revolution of 1917. Edinburgh's confidence of sure victory was shattered. Western civilisation had proved itself to be bankrupt. The question was no longer: How do we let the non-Christian world share in everything we have to offer? But, rather: How do we salvage Jesus Christ from the ruins of Western civilisation?[31]

The scope of the Jerusalem meeting was much wider than at Edinburgh. It tackled problems of secularism, race, industrialisation and rural poverty. The younger Churches were more widely represented at Jerusalem than they had been at Edinburgh. Of the 250 delegates, more than fifty came from the non-western world. The relationship between the younger and older churches was one of the prominent issues of debate. According to K. S. Latourette, this reflected 'the rising tide of resentment throughout the non-western world against domination by the West.'[32]

Special attention was given at the conference to the training of rural missionaries and a recommendation was made that the training currently given at seminaries in the United States for rural workers could be profitably adapted to work in China.[33] In view of the growing dissatisfaction with seminary education in North America during this period this seems a strange suggestion, demonstrating a remarkable lack of understanding as to what would really be appropriate in rural China.

The conference report also encouraged interdenominational co-operation in the training of missionaries, both at the home base and in the field. It cited examples of co-operative ventures in Peking, Tokyo, Bangalore and Cairo.[34]

The conference exhorted would-be missionaries to examine the reasons why they wished to go abroad. They should take care lest they were drawn by self-interest and attracted by the greater opportunities for leadership and promotion that the foreign field could proffer.[35] They were also strongly advised to take their preparation seriously. They should not allow their eagerness to begin their work to curtail their period of training. One of the dangers to be avoided was that of supposing there were any short-cuts in the preparation of those who undertake Christian service, least of all among those who were intending to serve in a country that was not their own.[36]

The Jerusalem meeting of the International Missionary Council was not without its difficulties. There were no Germans present, partly because of the First World

31. D.J. Bosch, *Witness to the world: the Christian mission in theological perspective* (London, Marshall, Morgan and Scott, 1980), p. 161.
32. K.S. Latourette 'Ecumenical bearings of the missionary movement and the International Missionary Council', in: *The history of the ecumenical movement 1517-1948*, R. Rouse and S.C. Neill (eds.) (1967), p. 369.
33. IMC, *The Jerusalem meeting of the IMC*, VI (1928), p. 175.
34. IMC, *The Jerusalem meeting of the IMC* VII (London, Edinburgh House, 1928), p. 23.
35. IMC, *The Jerusalem meeting of the IMC*, III (1928), pp. 21, 167.
36. IMC, *The Jerusalem meeting of the IMC*, II (1928), pp. 86, 95, 100.

War and partly from disquiet about the social content of the programme. Some of the delegates from other nations also expressed strong reservations about the emphasis on a social gospel and the hint of syncretism that was perceived to be present in some of the papers. In the event the conference was held together by a magisterial statement produced by William Temple that was acceptable to both sides. But fundamental issues had been raised and in time they would cause further divisions and would lead to an increasing disillusionment with the conciliar movement among evangelicals.

Tambaram (1938)

By the time of the next conference of the International Missionary Council, which was held at Tambaram, Madras in 1938, a significant change had taken place in the relationship between the older 'sending' churches of the West and the 'receiving' churches of Asia and Africa. Leaders of the Western churches realised that they could not, and should not, expect their missionaries to continue in positions of leadership in national churches when those churches were well established and more than able to provide their own indigenous leadership.

Missionaries were still being requested, but they had to be willing to work under the direction of national leaders. The function of missionaries for the next decade was stated by the Tambaram conference in the following terms:

1. to be a colleague and friendly helper in up-building the younger churches;
2. to carry the gospel to unreached areas and develop new lines of approach;
3. to witness against all the varied forms of secularised and materialistic life in the society in which he lives, particularly that which derives from his own country;
4. to embody the experience of the universal church; and
5. to build bridges of Christian understanding and co-operation between classes, races and nations.[37]

These goals had inevitable implications for the training of missionaries. They had to be free from any sense of racial, cultural, spiritual superiority, and denominational narrowness. They needed to develop a sensitive understanding of the changing currents of political, economic, social and religious life, and to cultivate the capacity to discern and appreciate the aspirations of other people. The focus of preparation had begun to shift from training for leadership to training for partnership.[38]

The ideals that were expressed at Tambaram were commendable, even if the language remained somewhat paternalistic. The problem was that these ideals were very difficult to put into practice. In the eyes of many, little seemed to change after Tambaram. The lifestyle of many missionaries seemed to reflect rather than challenge the materialism of the society from which they came. They still expected to be in charge. Mission societies still maintained their separate identity in the receiv-

37. IMC, *The world mission of the church* (1938), pp. 83f.
38. *Ibid.*, pp. 83f.

ing country even though they supported the ideal of the indigenous national church. Anglo-Saxon bishops were still often appointed in preference to nationals.

Whitby (1947)

The next meeting of the International Missionary Council, was held at Whitby, Ontario, in 1947 under the general theme 'Christian witness in a revolutionary world.' The world was still seeking to recover from the convulsions of the Second World War, but it was not yet obvious what effect that war would have on the world as a whole, on the Western colonial powers, or on the reputation and standing of the Christian church.

In spite of the enforced separation experienced by many Christians during the war, delegates at Whitby recognised their essential oneness in Christ. They were united in their relationship with Christ and in their loyalty to his kingdom. They were also called to be united in their mission to extend his kingdom in the world. They spoke of the 'supernationality of missions.'[39]

Since the task of mission was the task of the universal church, it was recommended that the spirit of missionary concern should be fostered in the younger churches, and their members should be trained for evangelism, so the whole people of God could reach out together in 'pioneer work in all those parts of the world in which the gospel has not yet been preached and the church not yet taken root.'[40] Responsibility for missionary work was no longer to be seen as the prerogative of white, Western Christians. Missionaries might be of any colour and originate from any corner of the globe. They might be British or American. They might also be Chinese.[41] Missionaries of every description, from every part of the world church and with the most varied qualifications, were still required. What mattered was not their nationality or their colour, but their character and spiritual quality. They needed both a humility that loves to lead by serving, and a limitless capacity for adaptation.[42]

Willingen (1952)

The theme of unity appeared again at the IMC conference held at Willingen in 1952. The younger churches expressed their concern at the disunity of the church: 'We believe that the unity of the church is an essential condition of effective witness and advance. In the lands of the younger churches a divided witness is a crippling handicap.'[43] Five years previously, the Church of South India had come into existence. This was a concrete example of this co-operative spirit and desire for unity, which neither denominations nor mission agencies in the West were quick to emulate. So far as the training of missionaries was concerned, the views which had been expressed at Whitby and Willingen provided sound reasons for providing missionary training in an interdenominational rather than a denominational context.

39. S.K. Latourette and W.R. Hogg, *Tomorrow is here* (1948), p. 220.
40. C.W. Ransom, *Renewal and advance* (1948), p. 175.
41. S.K. Latourette and W.R. Hogg, *Tomorrow is here* (1948), pp. 116-118.
42. C.W. Ransom, *Renewal and advance* (1948), p. 202.
43. Willingen report, *The missionary obligation of the church* (1952), p. 40.

At Willingen, one group of delegates was given the responsibility of considering the vocation and training of missionaries in the contemporary world. This group presented a statement, which was subsequently adopted by the enlarged assembly. This statement recognised that it was impossible to prepare missionaries for every eventuality they might encounter anywhere in the world. What was possible was to provide the opportunity for them to grow and 'become the kind of people who will, through the resources which are in God, be adequate in any situation and be able to meet others on a level of Christian level of relationships.'[44]

Having defined the three component parts of training,[45]the statement went on to suggest several elements that should be incorporated into any comprehensive programme in order that the candidates should be adequately equipped for ministry in the modern world. A study of the ecumenical movement and experience in ecumenical projects would broaden the students' horizons, making them aware of the importance and the potential of interdenominational co-operation. Some knowledge of differing political systems and revolutionary movements would prepare them for ministry in a revolutionary world. Emphasis was also laid on the developing of interpersonal skills to 'help students to enter into genuine and vital relationships with persons.'[46] The statement also underscored the importance of sensitivity, flexibility and alertness as essential characteristics of those who seek to identify with the people to whom they go.

What was seen by some as significant progress at the Willingen conference was viewed by evangelicals with growing alarm. The IMC seemed to be adopting an increasingly political agenda with a growing emphasis on ecumenical co-operation. To many evangelicals this threatened their independence and was perceived as taking them further away from the priority of evangelism.

Ghana (1957/8)

At the Ghana meeting of the International Missionary Council (1957/8), questions were raised about the legitimacy of the missionary movement. Should missionaries be sent at all? The discussions that took place in Ghana heralded dramatic changes in the patterns of world mission. In the decades that followed, drastic reductions were made in the number of missionary personnel who were sent out by main-line denominations in the West.

The concern which evangelicals had felt at earlier IMC conferences increased. The suggestion of a missionary moratorium seemed to fly in the face of the great commission (Matthew 28:16-20). Eight years later, evangelicals held two international conferences of their own.[47] Both of these were marked, as Timothy Yates has observed, by 'growing mistrust, even hostility, towards the WCC among evangelicals.'[48]

44. N. Goodall, ed., *Missions under the cross* (1953), p. 212.
45. (1) pre-field; (2) first term; (3) first furlough. See chapter 1.
46. *Ibid.*, p. 213.
47. The first of these was the Berlin Congress on Evangelism (1966).
48. T. Yates, *Christian mission in the twentieth century* (1994), p. 195.

The Ghana consultation did not recommend a total moratorium of missionary personnel from the West, but it did insist on a more stringent selection process. It was agreed that no missionaries should be sent if they are 'almost untrained to understand the spiritual tradition of the special area.'[49] Gwenyth Hubble, reporting from a group discussion to the general assembly, commented that 'the missionary will be welcome if he does not wish to dominate, if he is able to be truly Christian in his relationships even if he is not given as much opportunity for activism as his predecessors.'[50] Mission boards had the responsibility of carefully selecting new missionaries and preparing them for the situation they would face and for becoming the kind of people they needed to be.

The call from Ghana for the more thorough screening of candidates was both appropriate and timely. It is uncertain how far its recommendations were ever implemented by the denominations it claimed to represent. The number of training institutions which could guide mission agencies in their selection, or provide courses in cultural sensitisation, remained few and far between. Yet the number of missionaries, coming from the evangelical constituency in the West, continued to escalate.

John V. Taylor argued that the geographical concept of the missionary task was largely out of date. Mission is not from the West to the rest; it is from the church to the world. 'If the phrase 'foreign missionary' has a significance that needs to be preserved, it must include those who are sent forth from the churches in Asia and Africa.'[51]

Taylor's point was well made but it largely fell on deaf ears. Within those Western churches which continued to send out missionaries, the dominant understanding remained that missionary work was the task of the Western churches. Evangelicals slowly came to the realisation of the truth, that had been stated at Ghana, that it was the responsibility of the whole church to take the whole gospel to the whole world.

As large evangelical mission agencies began to realise the importance of developing truly international mission teams, they started to welcome partners from Asia, Africa and Latin America. Even so the Overseas Missionary Fellowship (OMF), which had a missionary force of over 900 workers and was highly regarded among evangelical missions, did not receive its first Asian missionary until 1966.[52]

2.2.3 Commission on World Mission and Evangelism (1961-1980)[53]

Ghana was to be the last meeting to be organised under the aegis of the IMC and the WCC and, as Yates suggests, it may have been the turning point in the divergence

49. W. Freytag, 'Changes in the pattern of Western missions' in: R.K. Orchard, ed., *The Ghana assembly of the IMC* (1958), p. 144.
50. R.K. Orchard, ed., *The Ghana assembly of the IMC* (1958), p. 178f.
51. J.V. Taylor, 'The place and function of the missionary', in: R.K. Orchard, ed., *The Ghana assembly of the IMC* (1958), p. 29.
52. W.R. Beattie, *The theology of mission of OMF International: an assessment of the impact of internationalisation and interactions with the Korean missionary movement from 1964 to 1998* (M.Sc. dissertation, University of Edinburgh, 1998), p. 34.
53. Originally it was called the Division for World Mission and Evangelism (DWME).

between the ecumenical movement and the burgeoning evangelical constituency.[54] At the Third Assembly of the World Council of Churches, held in New Delhi in 1961, the International Missionary Council was integrated into the World Council as the Commission on World Mission and Evangelism (CWME).

New Delhi (1961)

Edinburgh had called for a greater commitment both to evangelism and to unity, without which the credibility of the gospel was seriously compromised. The integration of the IMC into the WCC gave visible expression to these objectives. Mission was the task of the whole church and mission was to be carried out by Christians who were united in their task and in their commitment to Christ.

After the amalgamation of the IMC and the WCC, Bishop Stephen Neill wrote: 'This was indeed a momentous moment in Church history. More than two hundred church bodies in all parts of the world, assembled in the persons of their official representatives, had solemnly declared themselves in the presence of God to be responsible for the evangelisation of the whole world.'[55] However, not everyone shared his optimism. There were many like M. A. C. Warren, the General Secretary of the Church Missionary Society, who were apprehensive about this new development. He was aware of the importance of the voluntary principle, and of all that had been achieved through the work of voluntary societies. He feared that the great and free fellowship of missionary societies within the International Missionary Council could easily lose its drive and enthusiasm if regarded simply as a department of the World Council of Churches.

As time went on an increasing number of evangelical voices, such as that of Carl McIntyre, a leading fundamentalist[56] in North America, were raised in strident criticism of the WCC. Other evangelical leaders, like John Stott and Andrew Kirk, were more measured in their comments. Some like Leslie Lyall, a member of the OMF, who wished to create greater convergence between the two groups, produced joint pamphlets with representatives of the WCC.

The New Delhi assembly recognised the increasing number of lay people who were leaving their own countries to work in business, industry and government service and were making an important contribution in mission. The assembly urged member councils to provide training for such 'non-professional missionaries.'[57]

Mexico (1963)

The meeting of the CWME, held in Mexico (1963), paid particular attention to the question of dialogue with and appropriate witness to adherents of other religions. 'The witness of Christians to men of other faiths' report stated that 'the Christian attitude towards men of other faiths is basically one of love for all men, respect for

54. T. Yates, *Christian mission in the twentieth century* (1994), p. 196.
55. S. Neill, *The Church and Christian union* (1968), p. 108-9.
56. While fundamentalists and evangelicals hold similar doctrinal positions, one distinctive of fundamentalists is their insistence on separation from any Christians who hold false doctrines. See K. Fiedler, *The story of faith missions* (1994), p. 27.
57. IMC, *Report to the assemblies of the IMC and the WCC* (1961), p. 39.

sincerity wherever found, and patience to search for ways to bear effective witness.'[58] The implications of this for the training of missionaries were clear. Those who were sent out to minister among people of other faiths must be willing to listen to, and learn from, other religious traditions. They must develop an attitude of respect, sensitivity and humility, as they seek to witness to the good news of Jesus Christ.

At the Mexico conference it was recognised that the old 'sending and receiving' pattern of mission belonged to the past, and that mission now took place in six continents and from six continents. It was observed that the churches of Asia were sending missionaries overseas while traditional 'missionary-sending' churches in the West were acknowledging their need to receive missionaries from other countries. This provided further good reason for providing international training centres where candidates from all over the world could train together, learning from each other's perspectives, and preparing one another to work in international teams. It also revealed the necessity not only to prepare Western missionaries to understand the cultures of the non-western world but also to equip Christians from Asia and Africa to minister effectively in Europe and North America.

The conference also noted the growing trend of short-term mission service. 'God will in his mission to the world continue to use many types of 'missionaries', both 'long-term' and 'short-term' and 'the Christian layman abroad in the mission of the church', and in future he may choose increasingly to place the responsibility for mission on those who are not 'long-term missionaries'.[59] The growing recognition of the role of tentmakers and short-term missionaries in world mission had important implications for those concerned with missionary training. New intensive programmes would need to be devised, which could be held at weekends or in the evening, and which would meet the specific needs of these groups.

Uppsala (1968)

When the WCC assembly met at Uppsala in 1968, the world had been rocked by wars, student riots and political assassinations. The themes chosen for the assembly reflected a desire for the church to address these issues. Mission could not be conducted in a vacuum. The church was called to minister to the felt needs of the world. Therefore the world, rather than the church, should set the agenda for mission . Two of the six sections of the assembly were devoted to 'World economic and social development' and 'Towards justice and peace.'

To some evangelicals, Uppsala appeared to devalue the role of the church in mission, and to reduce concern for world evangelisation. Donald McGavran raised the question: 'Will Uppsala betray the two billion?'[60] It seemed that the commitment to global evangelism which had characterised the IMC since its inception had

58. R.K. Orchard, ed., *Witness in six continents: records of the meeting of the CWME of the WCC held in Mexico City, 8-19 December 1963* (1964), p. 144.
59. R.O. Latham, *God for all men* (1964), p. 68. This statement was first made at a consultation held in Toronto in August 1963 under the chairmanship of Pastor Jacques Rossel, President of the Basel Mission. This report was then endorsed at the Mexico meeting of the CWME.
60. This refers to the estimated number of those who had never heard the gospel.

now been lost. John Stott was also vocal in expressing his concern. Yates sums up Stott's feelings: 'Stott failed to find in the (Uppsala) report any concern for spiritual hunger comparable to that which had been pressed in regard to physical hunger and poverty. The prior concern of the church should be in relation to the millions of people who, being without Christ, are perishing.'[61]

J.V. Taylor sought to win over evangelicals with his assertion that the gospels of personal conversion and of social responsibility could be held together. Visser 't Hooft also argued for a balanced and holistic understanding of mission, which combined 'the vertical interpretation of the gospel as essentially concerned with God's saving action in the life of the individual, and the horizontal interpretation of it as mainly concerned with human relationships in the world.'[62]

Reflecting on the deliberations of the Uppsala meeting, J. Verkuyl called for further theological reflection on collective, institutional and structural sin. He spoke of the need for structural conversion and pointed out that conversion had been confined in evangelical theology 'almost wholly to the inner psychic life of individual persons or to radical change in personal relationships with others individuals.'[63] He argued that the word could also be appropriately applied to nations and societies.

Bangkok (1973)

The theme of the Bangkok Assembly of the CWME (1973) was 'Salvation today.' It sought to address the question: 'What is the form and content of the salvation which Christ offers men in the secular world?' Consensus on a definition of 'salvation' eluded the conference though there was general agreement that the salvation which Christ brings must embrace the whole of human life. Salvation in Jesus Christ was described as his 'liberation of individuals from sin and all its consequences.' [64] That liberation must have a social dimension because 'God's justice manifests itself both in the justification of the sinner and in social and political justice.'[65]

The report of the assembly called for a renewed understanding of the Bible from the viewpoint of the oppressed.[66] Those who were preparing for mission need to comprehend God's preferential option for the poor and his desire to redeem all mankind from everything that keeps it in slavery. The task of missions is to free men and women not only from the sin which is within them, but also from the sin which pervades human societies. 'The scandals of racism, of social injustices, of economic and political oppression ... all these challenge Christians urgently to express in action the salvation of Jesus Christ.'[67]

---

61. T. Yates, *Christian mission in the twentieth century* (1994), p. 198.
62. W.A. Visser 't Hooft, 'The mandate of the ecumenical movement', in: N. Goodall, *The Uppsala report: official report of the fourth assembly of the WCC, Uppsala, July 4-20, 1968* (1968), p.317.
63. J. Verkuyl and H. G. Schulte Nordholf, *Responsible Revolution: the means and ends for transforming society* (Grand Rapids, Eerdmans, 1974), p. 42. This had been previously published in Dutch in 1970.
64. *Bangkok Assembly, 1973. Minutes and report of the Assembly of the CWME of the WCC December 31, 1972 and January 9-12. 1973* (1973), p. 88.
65. *Ibid.*, p. 102.
66. *Ibid.*, p. 23.
67. *Ibid.*, p. 2.

The assembly recommended that mission organisations should evaluate critically the extent to which their patterns of missionary engagement reflected cultural imperialism. Where the presence of Western missionaries was felt to inhibit the local church in the expression of its national identity, serious consideration should be given to a moratorium on the sending of foreign personnel. Western churches that were thus freed from the traditional missionary enterprise could use their resources to develop new approaches to education among their own people. They would also be able 'to give financial support to those struggling for freedom from unjust and dehumanising systems.'[68]

Nairobi (1975)

Bassham views the Fifth Assembly of the WCC, held in Nairobi, Kenya (1973), as one which consolidated the work of previous assemblies.[69] There was a reaffirmation of the churches' responsibility to full engagement with the world in its social, economic and political problems. At the same time, there was a strong call, notably by Bishop Mortimer Arias of the Evangelical Methodist Church in Bolivia, for a renewed commitment to evangelism.[70]

Nairobi understood that it was the vocation of the whole church to bring the whole gospel to the whole person in the whole world. 'The whole church' embraced every member of every congregation. 'The whole gospel' included redemption and liberation. 'The whole person' implied that the church must address every area of human need. 'The whole world' demonstrated that the gospel must be shared with 'every person of every class and race, on every continent, in every culture, in every setting and historical context.'[71]

Melbourne (1980)

The theme of the Melbourne conference of the CWME (1980) was 'Your kingdom come.' As Bangkok had addressed the meaning of 'salvation', so Melbourne examined the meaning of the 'kingdom.' Was the kingdom of God present now, or was it not yet? Was it the task of the church to offer an invitation to the kingdom of the future, or to establish that kingdom on earth through social, political and economic development?

The conference recognised that Christ 'established a visible link between the coming of the kingdom and the proclamation to the poor.'[72] He also identified with the marginalised and oppressed, willingly giving himself to be involved in their struggles and pain. He thus provided a model for Christians to follow. They too were to adopt a 'fundamental option for the economically and politically poor' and to affirm 'that solidarity with these is today a central and crucial aspect of Christian

68. *Ibid.*, p. 24.
69. R.C. Bassham, *Mission theology: 1948-1975* (1979), p. 105.
70. M. Arias, 'That the world may believe', in: *IRM* 65, no.257 (January, 1976), pp. 13-26.
71. C.A. Paton, ed., *Breaking barriers. Nairobi 1975. The official report of the Fifth Assembly of the WCC, Nairobi, 23 November-10 December 1975* (1976), p. 53.
72. N. Lossky et al.,eds., *Dictionary of the ecumencial movement* (1991), p. 334.

mission.'[73] They too should be willing to emulate the pattern of the incarnation and suffer with those who suffer. Authentic evangelism takes place amidst struggles, and evangelism is not possible without true involvement.

Melbourne posed an enormous challenge to those who felt called to serve as mission partners in the global church. Their call was not simply to proclamation, but to incarnation and identification.

2.2.4 Evangelical conferences (1966-1980)

In the 1960s, it seemed almost inevitable that evangelicals would eventually organise their own international conference. There was growing distrust of the WCC and a suspicion that orthodoxy had been replaced by syncretism and the message of new life in Christ by a social gospel. It is now necessary to examine trends and developments in evangelical mission theology during the closing years of the period under discussion.

Early evangelical mission theology

Martin Luther used the term 'evangelical' to describe all Christians who accepted the doctrine of *sola gratia* which he understood as the heart of the gospel (euangelion).[74] In Britain, the term was particularly associated with the religious revivals led by John Wesley and George Whitfield. Evangelicalism was characterised by an insistence on individual conversion, by personal religious piety, moral rectitude, and social concern. In 1846, evangelicals in Britain formed the Evangelical Alliance. Members were asked to sign a doctrinal statement which included the authority of Scripture, the Trinity, the work of Christ, justification by faith, the work of the Holy Spirit, and eschatology. Under the influence of men such as Charles Simeon, Charles Finney and Dwight Moody, many evangelicals became deeply involved in the task of world mission.

Towards the end of the nineteenth century, evangelicals became increasingly disturbed by developments in the fields of biblical criticism and scientific research that appeared to undermine the truth, uniqueness and validity of the Christian faith. They were even more concerned by the way in which some within the church were seeking to relate Christianity to these developments. In North America, this developed into a struggle between 'liberals' and 'fundamentalists', the latter being the name given to those who subscribed to the understanding of biblical Christianity presented in a series of essays entitled *The Fundamentals*.[75]

The period after the Second World War witnessed a revival of life and vitality among evangelicals. Although many agreed with the essential doctrines that were propounded by the fundamentalists, they were unhappy with their negativity and

73. WCC, *Your kingdom come: mission perspectives. Report on the World Conference on Mission and Evangelism (Melbourne, Australia, 12-25 May 1980* (1980), p. 557.
74. P.M. Bassett, 'Evangelicals', in: N. Lossky et al., eds., *Dictionary of the ecumenical movement* (1991), p. 393.
75. Fifteen volumes of essays were edited by A. Dixon and R. A. Torrey and were published between 1910 and 1915 under the title *The Fundamentals: a testimony to the truth*.

their unwillingness to have any association with Christians who held different views. In consequence, these evangelicals began to create new structures for fellowship and co-operation in the fields of mission and evangelism.

Wheaton (1966)

In 1966, the Interdenominational Foreign Missions Association (IFMA, 1917) and the Evangelical Foreign Missions Association (EFMA, 1945) sponsored the Congress on the Church's Worldwide Mission in Wheaton, Illinois. Many reasons were cited for the convening of this congress but, according to Yates, 'the primary factor involved the dissatisfaction evangelicals felt regarding ecumenical mission theology and practice, especially following the integration of the IMC with the WCC in 1961.'[76]

Wheaton reaffirmed the primacy of evangelism and the priority of church-planting above all other forms of missionary activity. The congress was clearly influenced by the teaching of Donald McGavran, who had founded the Institute of Church Growth in 1960. McGavran believed that numerical growth should be the primary goal of the church. He advocated careful research to show what hinders and what promotes that growth. He exhorted churches and missions to devote less time to those activities which, although worthy in themselves, distracted them from this primary task. [77]

Berlin (1966)

Later in the same year, the Billy Graham Evangelistic Association (BGEA) sponsored the Berlin Congress on Evangelism. The congress attracted 1,100 evangelical leaders from more than 100 countries. The central purpose of the conference was to consider the place of evangelism in the church and in the world. The evangelical journal, *Christianity Today*, which co-sponsored the event, explained the distinctive identity of the congress: 'In contrast to other recent ecumenical conferences ..., this congress assumes both the Reformation principle of the final authority of the Bible and the apostolic emphasis on the evangelisation of mankind as the primary mission of the church.'[78]

John Stott presented three Bible studies based on the accounts of the Great Commission as found in the gospels of John, Matthew and Luke. He declared: 'We engage in evangelism today not because we want to or because we choose to, but because we have been told to. The church is under orders. The risen Christ has told us to "go" to "preach," to make "disciples"; and that is enough for us.' [79]

Evangelism was defined in the closing statement of the congress as 'the proclamation of the gospel of the crucified and risen Christ, the only redeemer of men, according to the Scriptures.'[80] This statement emphasised proclamation as the

76. T. Yates, *Christian mission in the twentieth century* (1994), p. 194.
77. D.A. McGavran, *Understanding church growth* (1972), p. 82f.
78. 'Good news for a world in need', in: *Christianity Today* 11:1 (Oct. 14, 1966), p. 34.
79. C.F.H. Henry and W. S. Mooneyham, eds., *One race, one gospel, one task. World Congress on Evangelism, Berlin, 1966* Vol 1 (1967), p. 37.
80. *Ibid.*, p. 6.

means of evangelism, the person of Christ as the focus of that proclamation, and the Bible as the authority for that proclamation.

Frankfurt (1970)

In 1970, Peter Beyerhaus, Professor of Mission at Tübingen, produced the 'Frankfurt Declaration on the Fundamental Crisis in Christian Missions.' He had become deeply concerned by developments within ecumenical mission theology which appeared to have become increasingly anthropocentric, and to have identified salvation with social progress and development. His declaration contained seven affirmations about the nature and content of evangelism, as revealed in Scripture, and rejected the distortions which he perceived in the deliberations that had taken place since the integration of the IMC and the WCC. Beyerhaus was not seeking to encourage evangelicals to leave the WCC, but he was calling the CWME to return to the more biblical understanding of mission that was promulgated at the meetings of the IMC at Whitby and Willingen.

Lausanne (1974)

In 1974, the BGEA sponsored another conference. This was held in Lausanne, Switzerland, and drew together 2,473 participants from all over the world. Again there was a strong emphasis on the verbal communication of the gospel, and a rejection of the relativism and pluralism that seemed to permeate the thinking within conciliar circles. At the same time there was an affirmation of the church's responsibility towards the poor and the oppressed. This represented a significant development in the evangelical understanding of the mission of the church, and reflected the influence of the Bangkok conference of the CWME held in the previous year. The Lausanne Covenant, which was signed by the majority of the participants, and has remained a formative influence in the evangelical world, emphasised that both evangelism and social action were the responsibility of all Christians: 'We affirm that evangelism and socio-political involvement are both part of our Christian duty.'[81]

Although the topic of missionary training was not addressed directly, Bruce Nicholls, professor of theology at Union Biblical Seminary in India, presented an evangelistic strategy paper on *Theological education and evangelisation*. He argued for a radical reappraisal of the way in which men and women were being trained to carry out the mission of the church. He stressed the need for the integration of academic, spiritual and practical training in theological education, and argued that the education of the whole person 'can only be achieved in community.'[82] He proposed a restructuring of curriculum design, in order that students might become mature persons in Christ, effective communicators of the gospel, skilled in church-planting and pastoral care, and sensitive and responsible participants in the various structures of society.

---

81. International Congress on World Evangelisation, *Let the earth hear his voice* (1975), p. 5.
82. B. Nicholls, 'Theological education and evangelism', in: ICWE, *Let the earth hear his voice* (1975), p. 639.

Pattaya (1980)

In 1980, the Lausanne Committee for World Evangelisation (LCWE), which had been formed in 1974 after the Lausanne Congress, sponsored another conference in Pattaya, Thailand. This conference again affirmed the church's responsibility for both evangelism and social action, but went on to say: 'nothing contained in the Lausanne Covenant is beyond our concern, so long as it is clearly related to world evangelisation.' This wording reflected the concern among some evangelicals that the Lausanne Covenant had gone too far in allowing equal status to evangelism and social action. It represented their desire to reaffirm the priority of the former.

From one perspective it can be argued that the LCWE, with its primary concern for world evangelisation, continued the work of the IMC. It rejected the syncretism and universalism that were perceived to dominate the WCC, and affirmed the authority of Scripture and the uniqueness of Christ. Many evangelicals had sought to distance themselves from the conciliar movement, but they recognised that its emphasis on socio-political involvement had strong biblical support. They also recollected that concern for the poor and the disadvantaged had once been a strong component of evangelical Christianity.

2.2.5 Conclusion

It is not possible in a few pages to give anything more than a cursory survey of these major conferences and the evolution of mission theology that they reflect. Some of the major themes that were discussed at these conferences, however, had a direct bearing on the training of missionaries.

The Edinburgh conference of 1910 called for the evangelisation of the world, but recognised that this task could only be carried out effectively if Christians were united in their witness to Christ. The vision of Edinburgh led inexorably to the formation of the WCC and the integration of the IMC and the WCC in 1961. In the words of K. S. Latourette, 'it cannot be said too often or too emphatically that the ecumenical movement arose from the mission movement.'[83]

Missionary candidates needed to be inculcated with this same ecumenical spirit. They needed to have a high doctrine of the church and to be committed to working with Christians from other traditions. They needed to receive instruction in ecumenical studies and would benefit from being trained in an interdenominational environment.

In the decades that followed Edinburgh, the churches in the non-western world grew in strength and confidence. They were eager to assume leadership and responsibility for their own national churches. They were still willing to receive missionaries from the West, providing they were carefully selected and exhibited a willingness to serve as partners. They wanted the kind of missionaries who would work with them and under their leadership.

---

83. K.S. Latourette, 'Ecumenical bearings of the missionary movement', in: R. Rouse and S. C. Neill, *History of the ecumenical movement* (1967), p. 362.

The existence of national churches also raised questions about the relationship between these churches and missionary agencies. Should the mission agency continue to maintain its own identity in a country where the church has been established? Should the leadership, property and resources of the mission be handed over to national Christians? Since mission is the responsibility of the whole church, how far does the continuing existence of mission organisations perpetuate the erroneous idea that mission is actually the task of a minority? These were key issues that needed to be addressed not only by mission executives but also by those involved in the training of missionary candidates.

A constant theme of the whole period was that mission is the task of every Christian. The whole church has the responsibility to take the whole gospel to the whole world. The younger churches no longer wished simply to be recipients of mission, they also wished to play their full part in mission. Mission must take place in six continents, with Christians going from all nations to all nations. In this case, the calling of the missionary was not only to serve under the leadership of the national church, but also to help equip members of that church for mission in the world.

Since the Second World War, a number of terms relating to the mission of the church have been the subject of much discussion, revision and redefinition. The term 'mission' itself was seen to involve much more than verbal proclamation of the gospel. 'Salvation' was viewed as both redemption and liberation. 'The kingdom of God' was described both as an eschatological event to which the Christian community looks forward, and as a present reality which the church must seek to bring about in the world. While there had been no unanimity about the meaning of these terms, it was recognised to be vital for missionary candidates to think through these issues and be made aware of their implications.

A strong emphasis in the later meetings of the CWME was the call to incarnational service. Christ is the model which Christians are to follow. His identification with the poor is one they must emulate and his willingness to bear the cross an example they must copy. Missionary training, therefore, must foster an attitude of self-sacrifice, and prepare candidates for mission in a context of suffering and persecution. In the light of the volatile political situations in so many countries of the world, it was imperative that missionaries were equipped to cope with situations of stress and danger. They also needed to include in their preparation a study of the social and political sciences.

Changing patterns of missionary service were also identified during this period. It was recognised that short-term missionaries, and Christian professionals living in non-western countries, could also make a significant contribution to the task of world mission. This, too, had significant ramifications for those engaged in missionary training, who now faced the challenge of designing new and appropriate courses.

Evangelicals had traditionally viewed mission as being virtually synonymous with evangelism. They had reacted with concern to the liberal tendencies within the ecumenical movement, which emerged in 1968, and objected to its emphasis on the social implications of the gospel. McGavran, through his Church Growth Institute, had reminded them that in the light of the Great Commission the primary goal of the church should be to seek numerical growth through evangelism. Beyerhaus had reiterated the essential components of the evangel. Yet there was a growing recognition among evangelicals that there were solid biblical grounds to support the place of Christian presence and social action in the mission of the church. This was reflected in the Lausanne Covenant, which has had a major impact on evangelical mission theology ever since. Even so, the tendency among evangelicals has been to emphasise the primacy of the proclamation of the Gospel, and to devote much time in their consultations to the practicalities of evangelistic strategy. In consequence, the missionary preparation offered in evangelical colleges and Bible schools tended to concentrate on evangelism and church-planting, rather than on preparation for social action or development work.

The Edinburgh conference drew attention to the fact that most Western missionaries were being sent out with little or no specialist missionary training. It appealed to the wider church to take this issue up as a matter of urgency. It suggested the setting up of specialised training colleges on both sides of the Atlantic, and it recommended the development of training programmes that provided academic, spiritual and moral preparation for missionary candidates. We must now consider the developments which took place within the United Kingdom to provide this training, and examine the extent to which the recommendations of Edinburgh 1910 were implemented.

2.3 THE CONFERENCE OF BRITISH MISSIONARY SOCIETIES (1912-1977)[84]

After a consideration of the broad canvas of international missionary debate, attention must now be focused on developments that occurred in Britain during this period and the steps were taken to implement the recommendations concerning missionary training that came out of the various international conferences.

2.3.1 The Board of Study for the Preparation of Missionaries (1911-1930)

The Conference of Missionary Societies in Great Britain and Ireland[85] was formed in 1912 out of a desire to increase the co-operation, and thereby the effectiveness, of the many British agencies involved in missionary work.

At the first annual meeting of the Conference a report was presented by H. U. Wiebrecht on the Board of Study for the Preparation of Missionaries. The Board of Study had already been set up in the previous year (1911) as a result of the appeal made at Edinburgh 'that men and women should be sent out technically trained for the work of the field, and also ready to win the intellectual sympathy of those at the home base.'[86] The general purpose of the Board was 'to supply guidance rather than assistance to missionary societies in the preparation of missionaries for their

84. After 1977 it became the Conference for World Mission, a division of the British Council of Churches.
85. It is more commonly known as the Conference of British Missionary Societies (CBMS).
86. CBMS, *Report of the first annual conference* (1912), p. 24.

work.'[87] For nearly twenty years the Board of Study carried the main responsibility in Britain and Ireland for the promotion of missionary training. In the view of Kenneth Maclennan, the secretary of the CBMS, 'It has drawn attention to the need for missionary preparation and raised the standard. It has formed public opinion as to the need and the quality and the character of the preparation demanded.'[88]

From its inception, one of the functions of the Board of Study was to supply information and guidance both to those wishing to create and organise departments of missionary training and to those seeking to find such training. Institutions could ask for recommendations about curricula or available teachers.[89] Missionary candidates could receive advice on available training and assistance in 'mapping out a course of studies.'[90] From 1915 to 1917, the Board published a quarterly bulletin, which contained current bibliographies of publications suitable for missionary training, details of courses promoted by the Board of Study, and information about other facilities available for mission studies.[91]

2.3.1.1 Summer schools (1912-1930)

In 1912, the Board of Study held its first summer school for missionary candidates and missionaries on furlough. These summer schools were held every year until 1930 (with the one exception of 1918 when no summer school was held), and were usually of two to four weeks' duration. The first of these was held at Queen's College, Oxford. Subsequent summer schools were usually held either at Oxford or Cambridge. The diversity of the topics covered can be seen in the list of lecture courses. For example, the school held in Oxford in August 1916 included lectures on phonetics, the history of mission, Islam, educational psychology, anthropology, African languages and religion, the religions of China, and Hinduism.[92] As well as providing relevant instruction, these courses were also designed to encourage fellowship among the participants and the deepening of their spiritual lives.

2.3.1.2 Study courses (1914-1930)

The Board of Study was also able to make arrangements for lecture courses to be given in London during university terms. These were held in London, initially at King's College (1914)[93] and subsequently at University College and the School of Oriental Studies. When the latter was opened by King Edward VII in 1917, the director of the school, Dr Ross, stated that 'the governing body of the school are willing to provide instruction in any department of Eastern study for which there is a demand, at such times, and for such length of course, as may best meet the needs of the students.'[94]

87. K. Maclennan, *Twenty years of missionary co-operation* (1927), p. 20.
88. *Ibid.*, p. 77.
89. CBMS, *Report of the annual conference* (1915), p. 37.
90. *Ibid.*
91. CBMS, *Report of the annual conference* (1917), p. 38.
92. CBMS, *Report of the annual conference* (1917), p. 38.
93. CBMS, *Report of the annual conference* (1915), p. 38.
94. *Ibid.*

These courses proved to be so popular that they were soon taking place during each term of the academic year. At one time, courses were being conducted on five afternoons every week.[95] Located in the centre of London, they were accessible primarily to those who lived in or near the city. By 1921, the number of attendees reached 278, most of whom took the three-term course.[96] As the years passed the courses offered became more comprehensive and sophisticated. Subjects included 'An introduction to the study of religion', 'The vital forces of non-Christian religions', 'Lines of approach with the Christian message', 'Racial inter-relationships', 'The psychology of the teaching process', etc.[97]

2.3.1.3 Courses in education (1916-1930)

In 1916, two experienced missionaries, who faced new responsibilities for superintending schools and training teachers, sought help from the Board of Study during their furlough. Under the guidance of the educational adviser, appointed by the board, they were able to attend a specially arranged two-term course and obtain diplomas in Educational Theory and Practice.[98] In the next few years, many more missionary candidates, and missionaries on furlough, took similar specialised courses in education both in London and Cambridge. Secular establishments seemed eager to accommodate them. The Delegacy of Goldsmith's College passed a resolution welcoming candidates, who were recommended by the Board of Study, to use their facilities.[99] The Cambridge Syndicate were willing to adapt their requirements to meet the case of missionary students. By 1927, 202 missionaries had received special training in education through this scheme.[100] In the following years the demand for this specialised course declined. In 1929, the last year that the course was held, only four students took part, all of them candidates of the Church Missionary Society.[101]

Specialist courses were also provided for many years in linguistics (through the services of the School of Oriental Studies)[102] and moral hygiene (in conjunction with the British Social Hygiene Council).[103]

2.3.1.4 Central College of Missionary Studies

One of the issues to which the Board of Study gave early consideration was the establishing of an interdenominational missionary training college. In 1915, it was proposed that such a college should be centrally located, preferably in a 'site close to London, and in a quiet and healthy neighbourhood.'[104] It would provide opportunities for specialised missionary preparation for men and women who had already com-

95. Two at King's College, one at the School of Oriental Studies (on phonetics and language study) and two at the YMCA (on tropical hygiene and physical education).
96. CBMS, *Report of the annual conference* (1921), p. 47.
97. CBMS, *Report of the annual conference* (1923), p. 18.
98. CBMS, *Report of the annual conference* (1917), p. 30.
99. CBMS, *Report of the annual conference* (1917), p. 38.
100. CBMS, *Report of the annual conference* (1927), p. 46.
101. CBMS, *Report of the annual conference* (1929), p. 52.
102. CBMS, *Report of the annual conference* (1926), p. 48.
103. CBMS, *Report of the annual conference* (1931), p. 29.
104. CBMS, *Report of the annual conference* (1915), p. 40.

pleted the courses of general and technical preparation required by their societies. The college was designed to supplement rather than replace the work of institutions of general theological and missionary training. One of the aims of the proposed college would be 'to guide the students to a deeper realisation of the spring, the spirit and the goal of missionary work, and to deepen their sense of consecration to and fellowship in the mission enterprise.'[105] The college would be residential and the course would be of one year's duration. Lectures would be offered on a wide range of subjects, and supplemented with tutorial instruction, essays and discussions.

There was much support for the new college. The college would provide an excellent opportunity for closer co-operation between missionary societies. In 1916, detailed proposals for a Central College of Missionary Studies were presented to the British Conference of Missionary Societies, but the First World War made it impossible to put any plans into effect.[106] After the end of the war the proposals were not brought back to the Conference and the scheme was never implemented.

2.3.1.5 Recommendations of the 1926 committee

In December 1925 the standing committee of the British Conference appointed a sub-committee to consider the future of the Board of Study. The report of this committee, presented to the conference in the following year, strongly endorsed the importance of the work of the board and called for an expansion of its activities. It advocated 'the increased provision of means for the specialised preparation of missionaries.'[107] The members of the committee made this recommendation on the basis of evidence it received from missionaries, educationalists, government officials and national church leaders in Africa and the East. They stated their conviction that missionary training was much more than the passing on of knowledge. It is 'not a question merely of imparting knowledge, but of furnishing outgoing missionaries, in a time of peculiar difficulty and supreme opportunity, with what will aid them to gain access to the hearts and minds of those to whom for the sake of Christ they go.'[108]

Their report contained six proposals: first, that more advanced courses should be made available to meet the needs of missionaries returning on furlough; secondly, that specialised training should be provided for medical and educational missionaries; thirdly, that modern educational methods and the latest technology should be employed in language learning; fourthly, that missionary training should be more closely related to the social and economic conditions in which the missionaries would serve and teach; fifthly, that theological colleges should be encouraged to increase the level of mission education that they provide for future candidates; and sixthly, that serious consideration should be given to the establishment of a non-residential training institution in London, to provide in the capital city the kind of instruction that was already available in Birmingham (through the Selly Oak Colleges), and in Edinburgh (through the Women's Missionary College).

105. *Ibid.*, p. 39.
106. CBMS, *Report of annual conference* (1916), pp. 21-24.
107. CBMS, 'Report of the Special Committee' in: *Report of the annual conference* (1926), pp. 47-52.
108. *Ibid.*

In spite of the thoroughness of this report and the strong case that was given in support of its recommendations, little ever came of it. None of its proposals were implemented. No new funds were made available. Far from marking a new stage in the development of the board's activities, the year 1926 saw the beginning of its decline.

At the 19th annual conference of the CBMS, the future of the board was again the subject of debate. The conference concluded that 'the development of training institutions and of the policy of the societies with regard to the training of missionaries has now reached a point where it is doubtful whether the maintenance of a board with a separate budget can be justified.'[109] By 1931 the Board of Study had ceased to exist.

2.3.2 The Bureau of information (1931-1977)

In 1931, after the demise of the Board of Study, a standing committee of the British Conference entered into an agreement with the Senatus of the Selly Oak Colleges, Birmingham to establish a Bureau of Information. This would continue 'the valuable work done in the past at Edinburgh House in gathering information regarding various kinds of special training, lecture courses and other help available for missionaries and candidates.'[110] The Bureau was to be housed in the Selly Oak Colleges and the costs shared between the British Conference and the Senatus. The functions of the bureau would be: (1) to deal with and follow up inquiries; (2) to maintain an up-to-date list of facilities for special courses of study; (3) to keep in touch with college and other centres where instruction can be obtained; and (4) to compile suitable bibliographies.[111]

During the 1930s, the bureau annually sent out details of the services it provided to more than five thousand missionaries. It answered numerous queries from both missionaries on furlough and candidates. These varied from enquiries about 'methods and principles of teaching', 'psychology' and 'anthropology' to 'methods of exterminating wood lice' and 'how to deal with a plague of bats.'[112] After the Second World War, the bureau continued to circulate information about conferences and short courses that might be of interest to missionaries.[113] After 1961, the bulletin was incorporated into a circular letter, which was sent out by the Professor of Missions at Selly Oak and contained 'information about Selly Oak and missionary affairs generally, with notes on recent books.'[114]

In 1977, the Conference of British Missionary Societies was integrated into the British Council of Churches. The task of providing information about missionary training among the ecumenically-minded churches in Britain devolved largely on the Selly Oak Colleges.

109. CBMS, *Report of the annual conference* (1930), p. 21.
110. CBMS, *Report of the annual conference* (1931), p. 30.
111. *Ibid.*
112. CBMS, *Report of the annual conference* (1935), p. 34.
113. CBMS, *Report of the annual conference* (1958), p. 32.
114. CBMS, *Report of the annual conference* (1961), p. 38.

2.3.3 Conclusion

The participants of the 1912 conference of the CBMS had been inspired by the vision of the evangelisation of the world in their generation. At the same time, they realised the importance of the careful selection and the thorough preparation of missionary candidates. For the next twenty years they gave their full support to the work of the Board of Study.

The various summer schools and study courses, organised by the board, went some way to providing the academic dimension of mission training that been suggested at the Edinburgh conference. They were unable to do a great deal towards the developing of the character and the spiritual life that had been identified at the same conference as being of equal importance.

The failure to establish a central college of missionary studies in or near London was a serious setback to the cause of missionary training in the United Kingdom. The members of the Board of Study had been convinced by the strong recommendation that came out of Edinburgh. They had recognised the importance of establishing such an institution but in the event were unable to realise their ambition. An interdenominational college, supported by the full weight of the CBMS, would have received public recognition and provided the kind of training that had been advocated at Edinburgh. It would now be left to single agencies or denominations to seek to provide the kind of training that the Board of Study had been unable to establish.

2.4 Missionary Training Institutions

Although the Conference of British Missionary Societies was never able to fulfil its dream of setting up a central college for missionary preparation, a number of different groups and individuals did seek to provide that need. The report of Commission V of the Edinburgh conference had already listed nineteen colleges in Britain that were involved to some degree in the training of missionaries in 1910. Some of these institutions were primarily or exclusively concerned with training for the home mission field. Many were extremely small, and several ceased to exist soon after 1910.[115]

Over the next seventy years new colleges were established, either with the exclusive aim of preparing missionaries, or with a deliberate intention of including the training of missionaries among their objectives. The *World Christian Encyclopaedia* (1980) listed twelve Protestant colleges in the United Kingdom that were offering long-term residential missionary training. One of these was All Nations. Six were associated with the Selly Oak Federation, which is considered later in this section. The other five were Emmanuel Bible College, Birkenhead; the Lebanon Missionary Bible College, Berwick-on-Tweed; the Missionary Orientation Centre, Bulstrode; the Missionary Training College, Glasgow; and Redcliffe Missionary Training College, London.[116]

---

115. World Missionary Conference, *Report of Commission V* (1910), pp. 236-7.
116. *World Christian encyclopedia* (1980), p. 1010.

Since it is not possible to examine every college in detail, we will limit ourselves to four that represent a cross-section of missionary training institutions that were operative in the British Isles during this period: the Edinburgh Missionary College, because it was one of the first missionary training centres to be founded in Britain and was well established by 1910; the Missionary Training Colony, because it represented a unique experiment in the preparation of missionaries along the lines of military training; Tyndale Hall and Dalton House because they were examples of denominational missionary training colleges; and the Selly Oak Colleges, because of their world-wide reputation as an ecumenical missionary training federation.

2.4.1 The Edinburgh Missionary College (1887)

The Missionary Training Institute of the Free Church of Scotland was opened in 1887. It was founded by the Women's Foreign Mission Committee who realised the importance of training women who were going to face the demands of missionary work in the closing decades of the nineteenth century.

The first Principal, Anne Hunter Small, was a child of missionaries and had herself gone to India as a missionary at the age of eighteen. 'I started my Indian career', she wrote, 'with one piece of uncommon equipment... I had carried on from childhood a passionate love for India and her people. As between Great Britain and India in their mutual relationship I was on the side of India every time. I criticised hotly our British restlessness, acquisitiveness and self-assertion; our talk of commerce while intending conquest, our attempts to gloss over our not very admirable ambitions with what seemed to my youthful partisanship hypocritical profession for the good of India.'[117]

When she returned to Scotland after seventeen years, she was disillusioned about many aspects of the life and worship of the church. The Scottish Church seemed isolated from the rest of the Christian world. The Sunday services were so dominated by preaching as to exclude other aspects of worship. Women seemed to be relegated to a subordinate rather than a partnership role in the life of the church. 'There were, I found, two parallel working groups in most congregations, the official and the other – mainly composed of women – which supplied the workers.'[118] These reflections, combined with her own experience in India where she was used to partnership and frequent consultation, were to have a profound effect on the way she approached the training of missionaries.

When she became principal there were only three students. As the college grew, larger property was required and in 1908 the foundation stone of a purpose-built campus was laid.[119] In a cavity under the foundation stone were placed 'earth from the grave of St Columba and sand from Martyr's Bay, Iona, symbolising our desire to be within the ancient missionary tradition of our land.'[120]

117. Quoted in M. Stewart, *Training in mission: St Colm's College, Church of Scotland* (1972), p. 2.
118. *Ibid.*, p. 4.
119. The college was then called 'The Women's Missionary College'.
120. *Ibid.*, p. 7.

When the World Missionary Conference was held in Edinburgh, the college was able to welcome such distinguished persons as J. H. Oldham and Bishop V. S. Azariah of India. Miss Small, who had been a member of the Conference Preparatory Committee, was asked to prepare a paper describing her training policy.[121] As a result of giving this paper, she became involved in the development of other missionary training colleges. During the next few years she welcomed several Principals who wanted to visit the college before taking up their own responsibilities for training missionaries.

The training given at the college (which was also known as St Colm's) was an 'integrated, organic programme planned around the vital core of worship, study and personal involvement in practical field work.'[122] The teaching was largely informal and interactive. 'The chief points of method to be marked upon are the small place which lectures hold, and the entire absence of examinations. Nearly all class-work is conversational; and behind it there is always a system of conference among the students themselves.'[123]

Miss Small gave great weight to the value of training through community. It was through the community that 'students grew in living relationships with Christ, maturing through self-discovery, responsibility and challenging involvement, both inside and outside the walls of the college.'[124] Within the novel experience of living in close proximity to others, students were being prepared for the intimate relationships that might be forced upon them by the exigencies of the mission field. They also began to discover themselves, to learn what it meant to be a real person, an 'original' self not a clone of another.

Students also learned from one another as they encountered those from different national and denominational backgrounds within the student body. In the first twenty years of the college's life, candidates were accepted from ten countries and twelve denominations.

Inevitably there were problems. Differences in age, nationality, qualifications, devotional practice and personal routine were bound to cause friction from time to time. Those who answered a call to missionary service often needed a certain ruggedness and determination if they were going to persevere and succeed in their pioneer work, but those characteristics don't always foster harmony in a settled community. But through the conflict emerged 'the life of friendship, exploration and self-discovery that transcends difference. The students experienced the unity of common allegiance which embraces diversity and demands no common uniformity.'[125]

There were few rules at the college. 'The original intention was to create a natural, free and wholesome family life, governed only by the law of mutual loyalty and service.'[126] This free life was deliberately adopted by Miss Small as the best

121. World Missionary Conference, *Report of commission V* (1910), pp. 250-252.
122. *Ibid.*, p. 9.
123. A. H. Small, 'The Women's Missionary College, Edinburgh', in: World Missionary Conference, *Report of Commission V* (1910), p. 251.
124. M. Stewart, *Training in mission: St Colm's College, Church of Scotland* (1972), p. 10.
125. *Ibid.*, pp. 121f.
126. *Ibid.*, p. 122.

way to develop missionaries for the actualities of missionary service. She writes, 'Some have preferred to proceed by imposing a rule from without, under which, in process of time, habits and an instinct of obedience are established. But a missionary student has in view a position of great and new responsibility, where she will be removed from her natural advisers, and be sat down in a circle of men and women often too busy to give her much aid or counsel; what she needs, second only to her private life with God, is the power of judging for herself and acting upon her own judgement, and these things can only come by the enjoyment of considerable independence.'[127]

In 1934, after the union of the Presbyterian Church of Scotland and the United Free Church, the college began to give increasing attention to the training of women for ministry in the home country. It worked closely with Deaconess House and was renamed 'The Church of Scotland's Women's Missionary College: St. Colm's'. It is now known as 'St. Colm's Education Centre and College' and provides a broad range of educational programmes for members of the Church of Scotland and other denominations.

2.4.2 The Missionary Training Colony (1921-1939)

The Missionary Training Colony presents a strong contrast with the Missionary Training College in Edinburgh. It was intended for men rather than women, and was run with the military discipline of an army barracks rather than with the informality of a family home.

The colony was founded by Captain Godfrey Buxton. He was the younger brother of Alfred Buxton, who had joined C. T. Studd in pioneer missionary work in Africa. Godfrey had hoped to go to the mission field in the steps of his brother and his father, Barclay Buxton, who served for many years as a missionary in Japan,[128] but wounds that he had received during the First World War made that impossible.

It was his brother who pointed out the need for practical missionary training for men. He felt that at that time many recruits who came out to Africa were dedicated but lacking in practical training for such demanding work. He suggested to Godfrey 'that he might establish an organisation to provide special training for pioneer work.'[129]

Land was purchased in Norwood, South London. Old army huts were erected and the colony opened in 1921. The living accommodation was basic, the training was rigorous. More than one student was shocked when they first arrived. C. Armitage describes David Adeney's reaction to the Colony: 'When he first arrived he was shocked to find little more than two army huts sitting starkly on a rough piece of ground. The building in which he had to sleep was unfinished, and opposite his bed a gaping hole let in the chilly winter winds. Every day he had to be up with the

127. A.H. Small, 'The Women's Missionary College, Edinburgh', in: World Missionary Conference, *Report of Commission V* (1910), p. 251f.
128. B. Godfrey Buxton, *The reward of faith in the life of Barclay Fowell Buxton: 1860-1946* (1949). This biography of his father is the only substantial work that Godfrey Buxton wrote.
129. D. Morris, *The Story of Easneye* (nd), p. 13.

others at 6:00 am to have a cold bath and then go out for a run around the block to prepare for an hour of prayer and Bible study before breakfast.'[130]

Although the students did find the training to be 'a bit spartan', they still appreciated it. They saw themselves as being trained for service in the army of the supreme commander. They knew something of the difficulties that lay ahead and wanted to be fully prepared. Bishop Jack Dain wrote with appreciation of his own experience at the Missionary Training Colony: 'I believe this type of training undoubtedly contributed to the perseverance by so many Colony men in remaining on the field. We were prepared for hardship and accepted it in a way that I believe many other equally well-meaning and well-intentioned candidates were not.'[131]

Joe Wright, another former student and father of the current principal of ANCC (Chris Wright), also acknowledged the value of the disciplined training at the colony. Although it was hard at times, he wished it had been longer: 'The life and fellowship were full, free, and at times hilarious,'[132] He particularly appreciated Godfrey Buxton himself, his personal kindness and the warmth and care with which he expounded the scriptures. Once a week the Buxtons would invite the students to their home for supper and the reading of 'Mrs Buxton's missionary letters.'

Chores was an integral part of the disciplined training. Every student took part in jobs like laying paths, darning socks, cleaning, washing and cooking. In David Adeney's case, this was no laughing matter as he often produced 'burnt offerings' when it was his turn in the kitchens, and he would collapse onto his bed at night from sheer exhaustion.

The men who trained there came from a wide variety of social and educational backgrounds. That was one of the enriching features of the programme. Those who came from a university background and from a more privileged environment found themselves working and living alongside men who had little formal education and came from a very different section of society. David Adeney was embarrassed by the way some of the men spoke and behaved, but 'he saw the accompanying boldness in evangelism and respected it.'[133] Traditional presuppositions were challenged as men learned to appreciate one another and recognise their equality and brotherhood in Christ.

Every week members of the Colony were sent out to preach at open-air meetings in Hyde Park or Tower Hill. In the summer they took part in 'the trek'. This involved an itinerant preaching ministry around a group of villages. All their gear and the necessary equipment was loaded into carts, which the trainees pulled from one site to the next. They worked in teams of twelve, led by a staff member, and often walked fifteen miles a day.

For the last week of their practical experience, the students were divided into pairs, given half-a-crown (12.5 pence in modern currency), assigned a village and told to go and live there for a week. 'During those days,' wrote David Adeney,' we learned to practice the principles that had been discussed during the Bible study

130. C. Armitage, *Reaching for the goal* (1993), p. 25.
131. C.J. Dain, in a survey of former MTC students (nd), held in the archives of ANCC.
132. J.C. Wright, in a survey of former MTC students (nd), held in the archives of ANCC.
133. C. Armitage, *Reaching for the goal* (1993), p. 25.

periods earlier in the year... We experienced a life of faith, being dependent on the Lord both for material necessities and spiritual power.'[134]

Nearly three hundred men trained at the colony between 1921 and 1939. Each year the intake was rarely more than thirty. In these years that numbers were lower, Godfrey Buxton felt that the training was actually more successful. As the years passed, the MTC knew its fair share of martyrs, among whom were two of the three 'Freds' who were martyred in Amazonia.

After the Second World War, the Colony was not reopened. Instead, Godfrey Buxton became an active member of the council of All Nations Missionary College and was instrumental in its move to Easneye, the family home of the Buxtons in Hertfordshire.

2.4.3 Tyndale Hall and Dalton House

The Bible Churchmen's Missionary Society (BCMS) was founded in 1922 by a group of evangelical Anglicans troubled by the increasing influence of liberal theology within the Church Missionary Society. With its strong emphasis on the authority of the Bible, it was almost inevitable that the society would eventually establish a college where it could train its own missionary candidates.

There were a number of interdenominational training colleges, including All Nations Bible College, to which the society sent its men for training,[135] but these colleges did not provide training in the doctrines and practices of the Church of England. There were also some evangelical Anglican theological colleges, but these were primarily concerned with training for the home ministry and there was no guarantee that they would always accommodate the candidates the society might wish to send to them.

2.4.3.1 Tyndale Hall (1925)

In April 1924, a resolution was passed by the executive committee of the BCMS 'that a training college for male candidates of the society be established as soon as practicable; and that, if and when vacancies occur, those wishing to train for the Home Ministry be admitted on the condition that such pay the full cost of their training.'[136]

Initially it was hoped to procure a property in the vicinity of London, but no suitable premises could be found. When a suitable property became available in Clifton, Bristol in July 1925, the council decided to purchase it for the proposed college. Bristol was easily accessible to London and was already a strong centre of BCMS support. The college was officially opened in November 1925 as 'The Bible Churchmen's Missionary and Bible College'. The General Secretary of BCMS expressed his satisfaction that at last the society had its own college to

---

134. *Ibid.*, p. 26.
135. Reference is made to missionary candidates from BCMS in the *All Nations Bible College Prospectus* (nd), p. 7. An article on the society was published in the *ANMR* 72 (1924), p. 244.
136. W.S. Hooton and J. S. Wright, *The first twenty-five years of the Bible Churchmen's Missionary Society (1922-1947)* (1947), p. 44.

train men for the mission field and for the ministry at home.[137] The property, a fine Victorian residence of grey Bath stone, was named 'Ridley House'. Over the next twelve years a number of other properties were purchased, largely through the generosity of Dame Violet Wills, and they were named 'Latimer', 'Cranmer' and 'Tyndale'. By 1936 the college owned 'five fine houses in an ideal position on the edge of the Downs.'[138] In 1952, the name of the college was changed to 'Tyndale Hall'.[139]

The college was granted recognition as a theological college of the Church of England in 1928. Among the first group to be ordained, one went as a missionary among the Eskimos, another was sent to South East Persia. The college continued to grow, and by 1931 there were 50 students. The following year brought a crisis to the college which resulted in the resignation of both the principal and the staff. They then proceeded to open a new college on the other side of the Downs. This new college, Clifton Theological College, was recognised by the Church of England whereas Tyndale's recognition was withdrawn. It took two years before the college regained its status as an official theological college.[140]

By the beginning of the Second World War, 83 missionaries (65 of them ordained) had been trained and sent out from Tyndale. During the same period 146 had been prepared for the ordained ministry in the Church of England. After the war the college continued to train men for ministry at home and overseas.

2.4.3.2 Dalton House (1930)

For some years after the founding of BCMS, there was no college for the training of women missionaries. Some candidates were sent to Mount Hermon and Carfax – 'two most excellent and wholly reliable training centres, to which the society is much indebted.'[141] But when it was discovered that the purpose of Carfax was about to be changed, and that 'instead of continuing as a training ground for missionary candidates it was to become a Home of Rest for missionaries on furlough',[142] it was felt that the time had come for the society to establish its own college for women.

In 1930, a large house, Park House, Kingsdown, Bristol, was left to BCMS in the will of Mrs Richard Dalton. This was to be used for 'the training of men or women destined for the mission field.'[143] Mrs Dalton also left an endowment of £23,000. The college was formerly opened by Dame Violet Wills and given the name 'Dalton House.'[144]

The curriculum at Dalton was not restricted by the demands of the General Ordination Examination. More attention could be given to biblical and doctrinal stud-

137. S.F. Russell, *Full fifty years: the BCMS story* (1972), p. 69.
138. *Ibid.*, p. 45.
139. S.F. Russell, *Full fifty years: the BCMS story* (1972), p. 70.
140. In 1972 the two colleges, together with Dalton house, merged to form Trinity Theological College.
141. *Bible Churchmen's Missionary Messenger* VIII (1930), p. 156.
142. *Ibid.*
143. W.S. Hooton and J.S. Wright, *The first twenty-five years* (1947), p. 51.
144. In 1955 the college moved into a big house in Durdham Down that had been known for many years as Carfax.

ies and to subjects particularly relevant for work overseas, such as health, first-aid, tropical medicine and book-keeping. The training was also practical. The students were expected to do the washing up, dig the garden and clean out the drains.[145] All the unpleasant tasks they were requested to perform were considered to be valuable preparation for the future. They were pronounced to be 'G.M.T.' – good missionary training. That, in theory, made them more bearable! One of the enriching components of life at Dalton was the presence of missionaries. When the college reopened after the Second World War, the new principal, Miss Weeks, felt it would be valuable for the students to meet people, who could share what it was like to work in Africa or Asia. So, she invited missionaries on furlough to spend a term in residence in the college so that they could interact with the students and lecture on their particular fields and the religious systems they had encountered. Among those who brought their first-hand experience were Doris Benson from Ethiopia, Lillian Cooke from Burma and Iris Critchell from China.

In 1968, a significant development took place at Dalton. It was joined by St Michael's House, a college that had been founded by Church Society in Oxford. The two colleges combined their resources to form 'Dalton House with St Michael's' to provide training for women both for home and overseas. In 1972, the merged colleges joined with the two men's colleges (Tyndale and Clifton) to form Trinity Theological College.

2.4.3.3 Missionary training and accreditation

Tyndale Hall and Dalton House provide an interesting example of denominational missionary training. They were both set up by a denominational society that represented one wing of its denomination, in this case the conservative evangelical wing of the Church of England. In the case of Tyndale Hall, it was clear from the outset that two factors dominated the thinking of the council: the need for episcopal recognition and the desire for accreditation. In the pursuit of these objectives, the course inevitably became more academic, whereas, by contrast, the training at Dalton House was more practical.

Every ministerial training programme has to maintain the right balance between the academic and the practical, between academic excellence and vocational preparation. The quest for accreditation usually raises educational standards, but it does not necessarily provide more relevant and practical preparation for future ministry.

Tyndale was founded for the training of missionary candidates, but it was also evident from the beginning that men would be trained for ministry at home as well as overseas. In a relatively short space of time it was the former that dominated. In the first 25 years, almost twice as many Tyndale men were trained for ministry in Britain as for other parts of the world. After fifty years, S. F. Russell could write, 'Men have gone out from Tyndale all over the world; an even larger number have brought strength and blessing to the church at home.'[146]

---

145. For an entertaining account of cleaning college drains, see R. Taylor, *Who'd be a missionary?* (1973), p. 20.
146. S.F. Russell, *Full fifty years* (1972), p. 71.

There is no doubt that Tyndale Hall made a very significant contribution to the life of the Church of England.[147] At the same time, it is also possible to observe that the college moved away from its original purpose. What has driven the agenda of the college and dictated its priorities was not so much the needs of the mission field but the demands of the home ministry and the requirements of the General Ordination Examination.

These comments are not made in any spirit of criticism about what happened. They are simply given as observations of what occurred at Tyndale and could be paralleled in the history of many institutions which started life as missionary training colleges. Two observations may be made. First, colleges that seek accreditation raise their academic standards but become less practical and task-orientated. Secondly, colleges that start with the dual focus of training for home and overseas ministry often end up concentrating on the former to the neglect of the latter.

2.4.4 The Selly Oak Colleges

Today the Selly Oak Colleges in Birmingham are known throughout the world as an ecumenical centre for mission studies. What is less well-known is the key role that was played by the Society of Friends in the development of the federation of colleges. Writing of the early history of Selly Oak, D. E. H. Mole states that 'it was Quaker initiative which founded the first four colleges[148]... It was Quaker money which enabled the federation to come about and sustained it during its early years. ... It was Quaker hostility to legalism and binding documentation which gave the Selly Oak Colleges the freedom to develop and grow.'[149]

The first college, Woodbrooke, was founded in 1903, not to prepare overseas missionaries, but to train good leaders in the Society of Friends. Two years later, another college, Kingsmead, was established as a missionary training college. Although it was owned and supported by the Friends' Foreign Missions Association, it was not intended to be exclusive. 'The great thing to avoid,' wrote the first principal, J. W. Hoyland,' is a Quaker stewpot. Our function is to give of what we have and are to others. Intensive stewing is bad and should not be indulged in continuously.'[150] In time missionary candidates from other denominations came to study and the women's department of the Methodist Missionary Society began to use the facilities and share in the management of the college.

The third college, Westhill (1907), was originally 'intended for the ordinary church leader by encouraging higher standards in the conducting of Sunday School.'[151] Subsequently, it concentrated on the training of schoolteachers. Fircroft (1909) was established as a college for working men to provide second chance adult education.

147. Russell lists some of those eminent churchmen who studied at Tyndale: Colin Brown, Colin Buchanan, Geoffrey Bromiley, Frank Colquhoun, Dick France, Stafford Wright, George Duncan, Herbert Cragg.
148. Woodcote (1903), Kingsmead (1905), Westhill (1907) and Fircroft (1909).
149. D.E.H. Mole, 'The Selly Oak tradition' in: *Selly Oak Journal* 1 (1984), p. 3.
150. *Ibid.*, pp. 5-6.
151. *Ibid.*, p. 6.

In 1912, three missionary societies – the Baptist Missionary Society, the London Missionary Society and the women's missionary association of the Presbyterian Church of England – decided to establish Carey Hall, as a missionary training institution, in close proximity to Kingsmead. The students, studying at the new college could benefit from lectures on mission at Kingsmead, biblical studies at Woodbrooke and educational methodology at Westhill.[152]

The proximity of several colleges made further co-operation practicable and desirable. In 1919, the colleges appointed a representative central council to arrange common lectures and seminars. The Senatus of the colleges carried the responsibility for academic affairs and the appointment of visiting specialists and overseas lecturers.[153]

With the advent of Carey Hall, the ethos of the Selly Oak colleges shifted from being predominantly Quaker in orientation to being more broadly representative of the Free Churches. In 1923, the ecumenical character of the federation was developed further when the College of the Ascension was founded by the Society for the Propagation of the Gospel, which represented the anglo-catholic-Catholic tradition within the Church of England. The first principal was Edmund Morgan.

Further developments occurred in 1966, when Carey Hall was combined with St Andrew's College, which had been founded in 1946, to form St Andrew's Hall 'for the preparation of men and women together for Christian Mission.'[154] In 1969, Crowther Hall was established by the Church Missionary Society, representing the evangelical wing of the Anglican Church.[155] Prospect Hall was established as a training centre for physically handicapped people and finally the Fellowship of Churches of Christ Theological College was founded in 1981. Thus the Selly Oak Colleges became a federation of nine institutions.

The Selly Oak Federation of colleges are a remarkable example of ecumenicity and interdenominational co-operation. While they exist in close proximity and share so much in common, each college maintains its own identity and ethos.

2.4.4.1 The Selly Oak Conferences

The federation maintained close links with the Conference of British Missionary Societies and, as already noted, shared responsibility with the conference for the running of the Bureau of Information. From time to time one or other of the colleges hosted a conference on missionary training.

152. This had been founded as a 'Training Institute for Sunday School Workers' in 1907.
153. E. Cadbury, 'The Selly Oak Colleges', in: *IRM* 26 (1937), pp. 119-121.
154. CBMS, *Report of the annual conference* (1966), p. 27.
155. The CMS had originally trained its male candidates at the Islington Institute, founded in 1825. In 1937, the society considered opening a new college in Selly Oak but opted to seek a site in London as it 'provided better facilities for special lectures, better opportunities than elsewhere for training in pastoral skills, and preparation courses of a range and quality not found elsewhere.' (G. Hewitt, *The History of the Church Missionary Society* Vol 1 [1958], p. 456). In 1946, Liskeard Lodge, in Blackheath, was purchased by the society and the name was retained when the college was moved to Chislehurst in 1952. The women missionaries were trained at St Andrew's Hall and Kennaway Hall, but, in 1938, Florence Allshorn instituted a move of the combined colleges to Foxbury, in Chislehurst.

In April 1924, such a conference was convened at Kingsmead to collate the thought and experience of the Western Christian nations in regard to the preparation of missionaries. Seventy delegates represented the major mission organisations from Britain and on the continent. The conference focused on the changes that were taking place in the contemporary world and the repercussions they would have on missionary training. J. H. Oldham, speaking as chairman, drew the attention of the delegates to the growth of the church, the growth of nationalism 'which makes men sensitive and unready to welcome work done by foreigners'[156] and the rapid development of government schools which may challenge the standards of some mission schools.

Another missionary training conference was held at Woodbrooke College in April 1939. The delegates included candidate secretaries of missionary societies, staff of theological colleges and missionary training institutions, and a number of specially co-opted members. The Tambaram meeting of the International Missionary Council had taken place less than a year before and its influence was evident in the papers and discussions at Woodbroke. The theme that dominated the conference was the relationship between the missionary and the church. The view was expressed that missionaries must develop ' a strong sense of the centrality of the church.'[157] They should not forget their ecclesiastical roots when they go overseas, or act as if they had no church affiliation. Those who were ordained should make sure that they obtained some parish experience in their home country before proceeding overseas. Secondly, missionaries should be 'ecumenically-minded' (a phrase taken from Tambaram). They should be able to work alongside other Christian workers, whatever their ecclesiastical tradition. To this end it was suggested that missionary training was best conducted in an ecumenical setting. Thirdly, missionaries should have a clear understanding of, and commitment to, the universal church. They were going out to serve with, and under the guidance of the national church and, as the delegates of the younger churches pointed out at the Tambaram conference, the leaders of the national church would wish to have a major say in the selection, training and direction of any ex-patriate personnel who offered to work with them. In the words of the conference report, 'A candidate needs in these days to be prepared for colleagueship, including serving with, and under, the nationals of the country to which he goes.'[158]

2.4.4.2 The Selly Oak Library

By 1967, the Selly Oak library contained over 60,000 volumes, chiefly in the fields of theology, comparative religion, social studies and education. The missions section was particularly strong on Protestant missions in those areas of the world to which British missionaries were traditionally sent (i.e. Africa and India). A selection of the more important missiological writings of Roman Catholic authors was included, and attempts were being made to procure complete sets of the periodicals of the major British missionary societies.[159]

156. G.A. Gollock, 'The present outlook on the preparation of missionaries', in: *IRM* 13 (1924), p. 391.
157. CBMS, *Report of the annual conference* (1939), p. 32.
158. CBMS, *Report of the annual conference* (1939), p. 35.
159. *The encyclopedia of modern Christian mission* (1967), p. 582.

2.4.4.3 The department of mission.
A chair of missions had already been established at Selly Oak in 1936 with the Rev. Godfrey E. Phillips as the first professor. In March 1970, the council of the Selly Oak Colleges together with the University of Birmingham signed an agreement to set up a chair in the field of mission studies at the University. Walter J. Hollenweger was invited to become the first holder of this chair.[160] He had previously worked in the missions department of the World Council of Churches. The missionary organisations supporting the various colleges also agreed to establish and sponsor a department of mission with its own dean and central programme. The department would include two representatives of the churches of Asia and Africa, who would hold fellowships on an annual basis. Further courses would be supplied by the staff of the individual colleges.

The courses that were offered at Selly Oak followed the traditional curriculum of missionary training, with a strong emphasis on biblical, missiological and ecumenical studies. The Federation also responded to the resurgence of many non-Christian religions and the immigration into Britain of large numbers of Muslims and Hindus. A centre was established for the study of Islam and Christian-Muslim relations, so that Christians and Muslims could study the faith of the other in an atmosphere of friendship and mutual respect.

Subsequently, the study of other faiths was extended by 'the founding of a multi-faith resource centre, by the arrival of Harold Rowland's resources for the study of new religions in primal societies and by the creation of a lectureship in Jewish studies.'[161]

2.4.5 Conclusion

Although St. Colm's was founded more than a decade before the Edinburgh Conference, it anticipated many of the recommendations that were made both at that conference and later at meetings of the IMC. It provided an integrated organic programme that combined worship, study and personal involvement. It laid emphasis on the development of character. It saw communal living with a minimum of rules as the best context in which to encourage personal responsibility and maturity. Although it was strong on developing cultural sensitivity among its students, it was limited in the academic level of its courses. It is to be regretted that such training was only available for women at the college, and that other institutions did not follow the model which it had developed. It is also disappointing that over the years St Colm's itself lost is exclusive focus on missionary training.

The Missionary Training Colony could hardly provide a stronger contrast. It was for men rather than women. It was held in old army barracks rather than a family home. It was run on military lines rather than as an informal community. If the students at St Colm's were trained to be sensitive and to discover themselves, the students at MTC were trained to be tough and to persevere. At the same time

160. W.J. Hollenweger, 'The chair of missions at the University of Birmingham', in: *Selly Oak Journal* 4 (1986), p. 13.
161. D.E.H. Mole, 'The Selly Oak tradition' in: *Selly Oak Journal* 1 (1984), p. 12.

there were a number of parallels between the two institutions. Both gave greater emphasis to moral and spiritual development than to academic learning. Both recognised the value of communal living in affecting that development. The spartan military conditions that pertained at MTC may have been appropriate in the period between the two world wars when men were still being sent out to extremely primitive conditions. It is interesting to observe that it did not reopen after the war and one wonders whether the same level of strict discipline and tough training would have been acceptable in the second half of the twentieth century.

Tyndale Hall and Dalton House were founded by the same denominational mission agency to train men and women for ministry at home and overseas. Once Tyndale Hall achieved recognition as an Anglican theological college, the requirements imposed by the General Ordination Examination of the Church of England tended to dictate the syllabus of the college. Inevitably less time could be devoted to those subjects that were of particular relevance to those going to the mission field. Dalton House on the other hand was not subject to the same requirements and was able to devote more time to practical preparation for overseas ministry. Over the passage of time both institutions found it increasingly difficult to offer effective training both for the mission field and home ministry. As was the case in many similar institutions, it was the latter that took precedence. The Selly Oak Federation was a good example of the kind of interdenominational co-operation that was advocated at successive conferences of the IMC. It had a strong affinity with the burgeoning conciliar movement. Members of the faculty were regular participants at ecumenical gatherings and contributors to the *International Review of Missions.* They were actively engaged in the current debates on the theology of mission, and they identified with the issues and concerns that were raised at meetings of the IMC and the CWME. The academic standard of the courses that were offered was high and the Federation rapidly gained an international reputation as a centre for missiological studies. It enjoyed a close relationship with the Conference of British Missionary Societies and, as has been noted, it continued some of the work of the Board of Study for the Preparation of Missionaries. The group of nine colleges, federated by a central council, inevitably faced a number of logistical and administrative problems. The strength of the federation lay in the fact that each college, though small in itself, could benefit from sharing the resources of a residential faculty, visiting lecturers and an extensive missiological library.

2.5 Missionary training in British literature

The impact of Edinburgh was evident on those in Britain who were committed to and involved in the missionary task of the church. It was also seen in the official statements of main-line churches and in the writings of a number of eminent theologians. In England, the Archbishops' Commission on the Training for the Ministry (1941) asserted that 'it is the vocation of the church to preach the gospel to all nations.'[162]

---

162. O.G. Myklebust, *The study of missions in theological education,* vol. II (1957), p. 30.

In Scotland, a special commission, set up by the General Assembly of the Church of Scotland, affirmed the responsibility of all believers to spread the gospel throughout the world. In a statement on the universal mission of the Church, it affirmed: 'To the Church, which is Christ's Body, is now given the Holy Spirit from whom its members receive . . . inexhaustible opportunities of militant service in sharing with others what they themselves have received.'[163]

Many non-conformist and Anglican theologians emphasised the universal relevance of the gospel and the missionary responsibility of the church. A. E. Garvie argued that 'Christianity alone can be the religion of mankind.'[164] C. F. Raven wrote of the simplicity and universality of the message of Jesus and the responsibility of his disciples to share it with others.[165] Writing in 1938, O. C. Quick conceded that the church was entering a new dark age but saw 'no reason why we should abate for one moment the strenuousness of our missionary efforts.'[166]

A large quantity of literature on missionary training was published by British authors during the period under consideration.[167] Rather than giving a superficial summary of the whole corpus, it seems preferable to consider significant and representative material. We have therefore chosen the writings of three people, who all served as principals of missionary training colleges but represent different traditions. Florence Allshorn was principal of the CMS college for women, which accepted candidates from the evangelical wing of the Anglican Church. Edmund Morgan came from an anglo-catholic background and served as principal of the College of the Ascension. Gwyneth Hubble was principal of Carey Hall, a college founded by the Baptist Missionary Society, the London Mission Society and the Presbyterian Church of England.

2.5.1 Florence Allshorn[168]

Florence Allshorn served as a missionary in Uganda with the Church Missionary Society from 1920 to 1925. When she returned home for furlough, she was found to have a cavity in her lung and had to undergo a prolonged period of convalescence. In 1928, the society unexpectedly asked her to take temporary charge of St An-

163. General Assembly of the Church of Scotland, *God's will for Church and nations* (1946), p. 32.
164. A.E. Garvie, 'The Christian challenge to other faiths', in: *IRM* 1 (1912), p. 580.
165. C.F. Raven, 'The teaching method of Jesus', in: *IRM* 17 (1928), p. 581.
166. O.C. Quick, 'The present situation in Christian theology', in: *IRM* 27 (1938), p. 580. See also his article on 'The Jerusalem meeting and the Christian message' in *IRM* 17 (1928), pp. 445-454.
167. e.g. G. A. Gollock, 'The present outlook on the preparation of missionaries', in *IRM* 13 (1924), pp. 383-402; R. Hogben, *In training* (1946); A.T. Houghton, *Preparing to be a missionary* (1956); D.N. Sargent, *The making of a missionary* (1960); D. Webster, *What is a missionary?* (1955). For a broader selection of books on missionary training, see J.A.B. Jongeneel, *Philosophy, science and theology of mission in the 19th and 20th Centuries Part 11* (1997), pp.169ff.
168. Florence Allshorn only published one article, 'Corporate life on the mission field', in: *IRM* 23 (1934), pp. 497-511, but her approach to missionary training can also be seen in her personal letters and in her biography by J.H. Oldham, entitled *Florence Allshorn: and the story of St Julian's* (1951). She is included in this study because she was responsible for the training of women missionary candidates for the CMS for 12 years and she made a considerable impact on the way missionaries were trained in Britain.

drew's Hall, one of their small missionary training colleges for women missionaries. She had no idea how to run a place like St Andrew's since she had never had any specialised training herself. She also lacked the normal qualifications for such a post, but she believed that she had learned from her years in Africa and she was aware of the particular problems facing women on the mission field.

Initially, some of the council members of the society were shocked by her unorthodox approach to missionary training. She might have been dismissed from her post had it not been for a number of the secretaries of the society who recognised her rare qualities. In time, the fears of doubters were allayed and she was allowed to continue. In 1934, when the two women's colleges of St Andrew's and Kennaway Hall were combined, she was asked to become the new principal. In 1938, she successfully initiated and completed a move of the college to Foxbury, in Chislehurst, where there was accommodation for forty students.

What characterised her distinctive approach to missionary training was her understanding of the essential purpose of that training. For Florence Allshorn, the most important function of a period of missionary preparation was to teach the students to be real; real about their faith in God, genuine in their relationships with one another, open in their appreciation of the world. She could not stand hypocrisy. 'Pious words in chapel followed by complacent or contemptuous attitudes in conversation would meet her quick challenge; lofty sentiments about beauty would be held up against sloppy standards of practical work.'[169]

During her own missionary experience, she had encountered a great deal of 'Christian living' which was anything but real. She had witnessed the poverty of conventional Christianity. She had seen 'the 'silent disasters' that went on in many missionary lives underneath all the hard work and the building up of successful institutions: the loss of vision, the hardening of attitudes, the acceptance of mediocre standards.'[170]

She wanted to do all in her power to prevent such tragedies being repeated in the lives of those for whom she had temporary responsibility. 'We must see that the failure is not repeated. We have made one great mistake in our training. We have spent much time in educating the girl in her spiritual life and preparing her for her work, but her emotional life we have left largely to take care of itself.'[171]

She recognised the strange mixture of emotions that lurk inside every human being and are often completely untouched by our spiritual lives: 'the anxieties, timidities, antagonisms, self-deceptions, inferiorities, revenge attacks, superiorities and withdrawals which somehow our spiritual life does not go deep enough to touch, where all the fighting and friction and the wreckage begin and end.'[172]

At the same time, she knew also that the length of training was very short (a year and a half) and so there were limitations to what could be achieved. 'You really cannot do much in the initial training,' she wrote to a colleague. 'They have not come to the end of themselves; you can only gently try to make them more real.'[173]

169. E. Brown, 'Florence Allshorn', in: *Mission legacies* (1995), p. 113.
170. *Ibid.*
171. F. Allshorn, 'Corporate life on a mission station', in: *IRM* 23 (1934), p. 506.
172. *Ibid.*
173. E. Brown, 'Florence Allshorn', in: *Mission legacies* (1995), p. 114.

She had the capacity to perceive the potential in each of her students, to see them not as they are but as they could be. She was not afraid to point out people's failures. 'I believe our great trouble is that we won't stir up the courage to look at failure.'[174] She taught the students to grow through adversity, to 'feed on difficulty.' She had great patience also, finding inspiration and example in the life of St Francis. 'Such a hotch-potch of people he had, pious ones, quarrelsome ones, stupid ones, and he delighted in them all. He was so large and gentle and terribly wise.'[175]

Training for Florence Allshorn was understood to be a reciprocal process. She certainly did not see herself as the fount of all wisdom, imparting her insight and blessing to those around. She had a remarkable capacity for learning from others, even when they were much younger and more immature than herself. She once said that, 'no student had passed through her hands that had not taught her something.'[176]

She made a point of making friends with the students and showed that she was genuinely interested in them and in their future. She entered fully into the more light-hearted moments of college life, 'trundling hoops round Clissold Park for a dare or sleeping out with the students in the summer garden.'[177]

Florence Allshorn appreciated everything that was beautiful and wanted to instil similar appreciation in those who lived with her. She developed the cultural side of life at college. She added more books about art and poetry in the library. She took the students to art galleries and fostered their enjoyment of music. She made her own home as beautiful as possible and tried to dress attractively. This may not have been conventional 'missionary' behaviour in that day, but to Florence Allshorn it was an expression of real Christianity.

2.5.2 Edmund R. Morgan

E. R. Morgan was Warden of the College of the Ascension at Selly Oak and represented the anglo-catholic tradition within the Church of England. In 1928, he edited a volume of seventeen essays, entitled *Essays catholic and missionary*, in which he contributed two chapters.

In the second of these, entitled *Missionary vocation and training*, he considers the meaning of vocation in the life of a missionary, a priest or a 'religious'. Drawing from the example of the disciples, Simon and Andrew,[178] he points out that the initiative for vocation lay with Jesus, not with the brothers, and that their vocation was primarily to follow Jesus not to undertake a task. The call is 'to a person, and not primarily to a task or a church.'[179] Morgan also reminds us that the two apostles cannot possible have had any idea of what would be involved and that Jesus always calls those who follow him to unquestioning obedience. In this there is nothing special about a vocation to the priesthood or to missionary work, since to *every*

174. J.H. Oldham, *Florence Allshorn: and the story of St Julian's* (1951), p. 51.
175. *Ibid.*
176. J.H. Oldham, *Florence Allsthorn* (1951), p. 53.
177. *Ibid.*, p. 49.
178. Mark 1:14.
179. E.R. Morgan, 'Missionary vocation and training', in: *Essays catholic and missionary* (1928), p. 239.

Christian, Christ says, 'He that does not take up his cross daily and follow after me is not worthy of me.'[180] There is no such thing as special sacrifice in Christianity and, as Morgan says, 'strictly speaking it is erroneous and misleading to speak of missionary work as involving a 'call to special sacrifice.''[181]

Morgan also stresses the need to test the genuineness of the call, since it is all too easy for an individual to make a mistake or be self-deluded. Missionary work affords 'obvious compensations against inferiority, a certain position and importance and publicity, and . . . a manner of escape from temptation and the difficulties which lie near home, which not merely covers our defeat but wins approbation from religious people.'[182] To safeguard against presumption or mistake, the prospective missionary needs confirmation of the authenticity of their call, which may come through human society, circumstances, the church, the training college or the missionary society. Those who are not finally accepted for work overseas should see in that the means whereby God guides them to a different but not inferior form of service.

Finally, Morgan turns to the question of missionary training. He identifies the basic problem of missionary education as 'an acute form of the problem of all modern education; the problem of the adjustment of an enormous and ever-enlarging field of 'subjects' to the training of character.'[183] He argues that there are a hundred subjects you could include in a missionary training curriculum with the result that the missionary might become a 'walking encyclopaedia in these ever-widening realms of knowledge.'[184] A balance must be maintained between the acquisition of relevant knowledge and the development of the inner life. On the one hand, so many facts could be pumped into the individual that may result in 'a distracted and dissipated life, busy on its circumference but impoverished at its centre.'[185] On the other hand, if the whole time and energy of training is given to the building and discipline of the interior life, that may induce a forced and narrow intensity which is divorced from the real world.

Morgan suggests four key components in an effective training programme. First, the training of a missionary should correspond with the steps in the development of vocation. The one must constantly interact with the other. 'Vocation determines training, and training fosters vocation.'[186] Secondly, training must develop subtle cultural sensitivity. He warns against the dangers of that 'heinous presumption' when missionaries preach to people of another race without any attempt to understand their culture or spiritual aspirations. Thirdly, missionaries need to be trained to relate their biblical, theological and historical understanding to the task of mission. Morgan believed that the traditional disciplines of the theological curriculum should be taught from a missiological perspective. Thus church history should be studied as the story of the *Gesta Christi per orbem,*[187] or the story of the growth of

180. Matthew 10:37.
181. *Ibid.*, p. 241.
182. *Ibid.*, p. 243.
183. *Ibid.*, p. 245.
184. *Ibid.*
185. *Ibid.*
186. *Ibid.*, p. 246.
187. The acts of Christ throughout the world.

the universal church. Fourthly, Morgan maintains that missionaries must be trained with the capacity to receive.[188] They will face the strain of the unfamiliar, and often a climate, that will try their patience, their temper and their energy. They may endure constant disappointment, criticism and failure. At the same time, they may lack many of the familiar supports that were the mainstay of their spiritual life at home. Missionary training can provide the opportunity in which the individual may learn to find in God alone those resources which will keep him in their ministry. In this respect, 'the essential inward purpose of missionary training will be identical to that of a retreat.'[189] The missionary must learn 'to be alone with the living God,' 'to hearken to what he will say concerning us.'[190] At the centre of missionary training, therefore, must be the religious life of the training community. 'Missionary training is centred in the college chapel, in eucharistic worship and oblation, the Divine Office, the daily exercise of prayer and meditation and self-examination.'[191]

2.5.3 Gwenyth Hubble

Gwenyth Hubble was principal of Carey Hall, Selly Oak, from 1945 to 1960. She also served in the Working Committee of the Department of Mission Studies of the World Council of Churches. In an article entitled 'Reasons for missionary training,' that was published in the *International Review of Missions* in 1963,[192] she seeks to answer the question that she had often been asked by parents whose daughters studied at her college: 'Why does she need further training?'[193] Given that a young man or woman is already well trained and experienced in their own profession, and may even be an ordained minister, is it really necessary for them to undergo yet more preparation? Hubble's answer is an unequivocal 'Yes'. She admits that some outstanding missionaries do a good job even though they have no specialised training. She also acknowledges that some 'average' missionaries survive without training, but she is convinced that they would have been saved from making many mistakes, and spared a great deal of heartache, if they had been thoroughly prepared before they went.

Specialist training is necessary, in Hubble's view, because missionary candidates have a great deal to learn, 'for there is much they do not know when they become missionary candidates.'[194] First, 'the average candidate does not know enough about the world of today, and about that part of the world in which he is to serve.'[195] Hubble does not blame them for their ignorance. She understands that they may have had few opportunities to meet people of other races and cultures, and

188. E.R. Morgan, 'Missionary vocation and training', in: *Essays catholic and missionary* (1928), p. 249.
189. *Ibid.*
190. *Ibid.*
191. *Ibid.*, p. 250.
192. G. Hubble, 'Reasons for missionary training', in: *IRM* 52 (1963), pp. 257-265. The article was first given as an address at Buck Hill Falls on November 24th, 1962, at the Assembly of the Division of Foreign Missions of the National Council of the Churches of Christ in the USA.
193. G. Hubble, 'Reasons for missionary training', in: *IRM* 52 (1963), p. 257.
194. *Ibid.*, p. 258.
195. *Ibid.*, p. 259.

had little incentive to read about the history, politics or economies of other countries. During their period of training, they will have the opportunity to start filling in some of these crucial gaps in their knowledge. They may encounter 'an African who is not only a Christian but is also a keen nationalist, and learn to understand his attitude to the West and ... his political and social aspirations.'[196] They may be faced with the stark realities of poverty, injustice and the population explosion, with all their implications for mission. They may also have time to reflect on their own culture, and its underlying beliefs and values. An Indian lecturer at Selly Oak said he had a real problem in teaching missionary candidates about Indian culture because 'they don't understand their own.'[197]

Secondly, the missionary candidate needs greater knowledge 'of the gospel of which he is a messenger and the God of whom he is going to speak.'[198] Hubble quotes from a pamphlet on missionary training, which states with reference to non-theologically trained candidates, 'No one who has dealt with modern missionary candidates would question their sincerity or their Christian character, but they know surprisingly little about the Bible.'[199] But, Hubble continues, head knowledge of the scriptures and Christian doctrine is of little value if it is not accompanied by a personal knowledge of Jesus Christ. 'Some missionary candidates have the head knowledge and can discourse in high-sounding language about Christian Dogmatics, yet they have not, as D. T. Niles says, 'met Him."[200]

The third area where Hubble contends that the candidate needs knowledge is in the understanding of themselves. Many missionary candidates have an exalted picture of themselves and what they are going to achieve. They have quite unrealistic ideas about themselves and their characters. They have some important lessons to learn. They have to realise 'that they will not be the inestimable and highly important asset and gift to the church to which they go that they and their congregation had fondly imagined.'[201] They need to follow the Pauline injunction not to think of themselves more highly than they ought. They need to see themselves from God's perspective rather than from their own. That may be the difference between 'the image of a successful, highly qualified activist and that of a sinful man saved by, and utterly dependent on, the mercy and grace of God.[202]

A period of training will often reveal the weaknesses in a candidate's character. His or her strengths may have been evident for some time. The loving context of a community provides the opportunity not only for candidates to recognise their own limitations and faults but also, by the grace of God and with the support of those around, to seek to correct wrong attitudes and bring their lives more in line with the standard and example of the Christ, whom they profess to follow.

---

196. *Ibid.*
197. *Ibid.*, p. 260.
198. *Ibid.*
199. *Ibid.*, p. 260, quoting from the pamphlet produced by the Division of Foreign Missions, *New trends in missionary training in the United States* (1957).
200. *Ibid.*, p. 261.
201. *Ibid.*, p. 263.
202. *Ibid.*

2.5.4 Conclusion

Allshorn, Morgan and Hubble wrote as principals of missionary training institutions. They were not speaking theoretically, but from their own experience in training. They came from differing Christian traditions, but were all broadly in sympathy with the ecumenical movement. They were aware of the breadth of subjects that might be included in a training programme, and were clearly influenced by the recommendations that came out of the various meetings of the IMC. Their greatest concern was for the more personal aspects of missionary training, though the way they expressed that concern different according to the traditions from which they came.

First, they were concerned about the spiritual development of the candidates. Hubble stressed the importance of having a personal knowledge of Jesus Christ. Morgan wanted students to be able to nurture their inner spiritual life so that they could constantly hear God's voice and feed on his truth. As an anglo-catholic, he laid emphasis on the eucharistic and the corporate spiritual life of the training community.

Secondly, these trainers shared a common conviction about the need for reality in the lives of the candidates. Allshorn wanted them to be real and unpretentious about their faith. Morgan told them to examine the genuineness of their vocation. Hubble encouraged them to be realistic about their own abilities.

Thirdly, these three principals encouraged their students to appreciate the world around them, though again they differed in their emphasis. Allshorn taught them to appreciate the beauty of art and nature. Hubble stressed the importance of appreciating the culture of other peoples. Morgan urged them to be aware of world events and to understand their significance.

All three of them spoke of the pastoral care of the students, but Allshorn's observations about the emotional needs of candidates are particularly noteworthy. She had witnessed too many emotional casualties in her own time of service in Africa. Within the limitations of a relatively short training course, she was determined to do what she could to prevent a recurrence of such tragedies.

2.6 CONCLUSION

Edinburgh 1910 drew attention to the appalling standard of training that was given to the majority of missionary candidates. It called for the situation to be remedied and made suggestions regarding both the nature and the content of that training.

The subsequent conferences of the IMC and CWME emphasised the importance of developing the character of missionary candidates. Those who were sent out, it was affirmed, must go with the right motivation and with a willingness to serve under national leadership. They must also demonstrate qualities of humility, sensitivity and adaptability.

In the period after the Second World War, it was also recognised that candidates must be made aware of the breadth of the missionary task and the changes that were taking place in non-western countries. They must realise the difference between being a missionary pioneer in the days of empire, and being a partner or servant of the church in an age of post-colonialism. They must be prepared for social and political involvement in a rapidly changing and sometimes dangerous world.

Edinburgh had made it clear that a divided church could only give an imperfect witness to the non-Christian world. The search for a visible expression of the unity of the body of Christ was pursued with increasing urgency as the century proceeded. Those who were engaged in overseas mission were encouraged to work alongside Christians of other traditions in a spirit of true ecumenicity.

The Conference of British Missionary Societies, through the various activities of the Board of Study for the Preparation of Missionaries, went some way to providing academic and practical preparation for missionary candidates, but failed to establish a central college of missionary studies. It was left to individual denominations and institutions to fill the vacuum.

A number of missionary training colleges were already in existence in 1910, and other new institutions were founded in the next few decades. Some of these only served one mission agency, or one denomination. Of those that have been examined in this chapter, St Colm's and MTC emphasised the value of training within a residential community. They gave great importance to the development of character and the spiritual life of candidates. Tyndale Hall and Dalton House were examples of colleges whose initial emphasis on missionary training declined as the needs of the home ministry became more dominant. The Selly Oak Colleges stand as an excellent example of ecumenical co-operation. They provided the highest level of academic training and were most actively involved in the conciliar movement.

Three of the colleges demonstrate the strategic role played by the principal in directing a training institution. Miss Small at St Colm's, Florence Allshorn at Foxbury, and Godfrey Buxton at the MTC, all stamped their personality on their schools. To a large degree the success of those programmes depended on their vision and personality.

The reflections of those who had been engaged in the training of missionaries in Britain reveal similar priorities in training to those found in the training colleges: the fostering of the spiritual life; the formation of Christian character; the nurturing of the right attitudes; and the development of good relational skills. While the academic content in missionary training was never ignored, it would seem that personal formation was regarded as the most essential component in an integrated training programme.

In conclusion, it is possible to draw a number of principles about the nature and content of missionary training which had received general approbation during this period. The first was affirmed repeatedly, that missionary candidates needed specialised missionary training. Secondly, it had been recognised that this training must integrate spiritual, moral, pastoral, academic and practical preparation. Thirdly, although this ideal had not always been realised, it seems to have been agreed that the best context in which to provide such integrated training was that of a residential community. Fourthly, it had been acknowledged that candidates must be made aware both of the breadth of human need in the world, and of the church's responsibility to meet that need, Fifthly, it had been shown that missionary candidates must be prepared to be engaged in mission in a spirit of ecumenical and international co-operation.

This survey and these findings will provide the background against which we can proceed to examine and evaluate the training programme of the three colleges that would eventually be united as All Nations Christian College.

3. Mount Hermon Missionary Training College (1911[1]-1971)

3.1 INTRODUCTION

Mount Hermon had the longest history of the three colleges that were to merge as All Nations Christian College in 1971. Unlike All Nations Bible College, which was founded by an established missionary organisation with the support of a considerable circle of friends and well-wishers, Mount Hermon came into being as the result of the vision and initiative of a single remarkable individual, Miss Emily B. B. Whitfield (1874-1927).

This chapter considers the history of Mount Hermon from its foundation in 1911 to its incorporation into All Nations Christian College in 1971 (3.2). It examines the doctrinal basis and distinctive characteristics of the college (3.3), the nature of the programme that it provided (3.4), the composition of the student body, their selection and their fields of service (3.5). The chapter concludes with an evaluation of Mount Hermon as a missionary training centre (3.6).

3.2 FOUNDATION AND HISTORY

During the sixty years that Mount Hermon was an independent college, there were four principals. The first was the founder, Miss Emily Whitfield (1911-1927). The second, Miss Irene Crocker (1927-1960), remained as principal for thirty three years. Her successor, Mrs Roxie Fraser (1960-1964), usually known as Mrs J. O. Fraser, stayed for less than five. The final principal, Miss Meg Foote (1965-1971), introduced significant changes into the ethos and curriculum of the college, preparing it for the merger with All Nations.

3.2.1 Miss Emily Whitfield (1911-1927)

Emily Banks Butler Whitfield (1874-1927) was born on July 12th, the elder daughter of the Rev. Frederick Whitfield. Her father served as the vicar of St Mary-in-the-Castle, Hastings, from 1875 to 1899. Her mother died when she was just nine years old.

She exhibited an interest in spiritual matters at an early age. On one occasion, she spent so much time reading the Bible that it was taken away from her so that she would not over-study.[2] At the age of twelve, she wrote a hymn which included the verses:

---

1. For a discussion on whether MHMTC was founded in 1911 or 1912, see section 3.2.1.
2. Mrs Keith-Steele, 'The later Miss Emily B.B. Whitfield', in: *MRANs* 95 (December 1928), p. 69.

Simply believing in Jesus,
Simply trusting his care,
Will make my burden easier,
And make it lighter to bear.

Bringing a soul to the Saviour,
Or showing another the way,
Is doing some work for Jesus,
And pleasing him every day.[3]

As she grew up, she began to work in her father's parish. She became secretary of the local branch of the Children's Scripture Union, taught in Sunday School and spoke at the Band of Hope and Temperance meetings. When her father retired to South Norwood, Emily initially moved to live with him, but after a while she left home to work in the parish of All Saints, Peckham. For the next ten years, she was involved in various kinds of Christian work in several London parishes. At this stage in her life, she tended towards anglo-catholic views and was remembered in one church as one of the few people in the congregation who made the sign of the cross in the recital of the creed.[4] At the same time, her spiritual life had been profoundly affected by the teaching of the Keswick convention, which she attended for the first time in 1896, and then on many subsequent occasions.

Although she greatly enjoyed parochial ministry, she longed to be a missionary. She applied to three missionary societies, and was rejected by all of them on the grounds of poor health. While she was undergoing a period of convalescence, she became convinced that God wanted her to train others to go. Although she could not become a missionary herself, she could go in spirit into all the world through those whom she prepared.

There is some confusion over the date when she founded Mount Hermon Missionary Training College. October 1912 is the date given by her sister, Mrs Keith-Steele, in a brief biography which appeared in the *Missionary Review*: 'In October 1912, she (Miss Whitfield) started taking young women for training for the mission field at her own house, Victoria Park.'[5] The same date is given by Mrs Geoffrey Thomas, wife of the honorary secretary and warden of All Nations Bible College.[6] However, the Silver Jubilee of the college was celebrated in 1936, and a statement in the *Missionary Review* in 1938 asserts: 'The college was founded in January 1911, and was opened at Victoria Park by the late Miss E. B. B. Whitfield, who was both founder and principal.'[7]

---

3. *Ibid.*
4. Mrs Keith-Steele, 'The late Miss Emily B.B. Whitfield', in: *MRANs* 96 (March 1929), p. 85.
5. Mrs Keith-Steele, 'The late Miss Emily B.B. Whitfield: founder of Mount Hermon Bible College', in *MRANs* 96 (March 1929), p. 98. This brief biography of Miss Whitfield was published in a series of articles in: *MRAN* from December 1928 to March 1930.
6. Mrs G. Thomas, 'Brief notes on the early days', in *MRANs* 105 (January 1931), p. 36.
7. *MRANs* 141 (February 1938), p. 10. This article also claims that the college was reopened in 1920, whereas the official brochure of MHBC states: 'The college, situated on North Side, Clapham Common, was (re)opened by the late Miss Emily B. B. Whitfield in September 1921,' *ANBC & MHBC Brochure* (1932), p. 15.

Miss Whitfield herself wrote in July 1922 that the college had been founded nearly eleven years before.[8] She also states that the first course began in January.[9] That would make January 1912 the most probable date for the founding of the college, with preparations being made in 1911 and the two first students being accepted into residence before the beginning of the new year.

Miss Whitfield's uncle, the member of Parliament for Hammersmith, left her a house in Victoria Park, in the East End of London. It was situated close to the boroughs of Poplar and Bethnal Green, providing excellent opportunity for the students to gain practical experience in working among the poor and disadvantaged.[10]

Although Miss Whitfield began with only two students, others came in the following months. By the end of the year, the house was filled to capacity. After four years, a second house was given to the college, and that too was soon filled. During the First World War, one of the houses was hit in an air raid. No-one was injured, but the incident led to the temporary closure of the college. Although this was inevitably a disappointment, Miss Whitfield was convinced that God allowed Mount Hermon to be closed because it had fulfilled its purpose, at least for the time being.[11] By the time of its closure in 1918, more than seventy girls had received training at the college.

The college remained closed for more than eighteen months. Miss Whitfield was unsure whether to open the college again. One fateful Sunday afternoon in July 1920, when she was listening to a sermon at the Keswick convention, she was struck by the words, 'Hew thee two tables of stone like unto the first, and I will write upon these two tables the words which were upon the first tables' (Ex. 34:1).[12] She was convinced that God was asking her to reopen the college, but she was fearful of the continuing responsibility of running such an institution. In her uncertainty she asked God for a specific sign. She asked for four students and their fees. She promised that if God would grant this, she would take it as his guidance and go forward at once.[13] The next morning she received a letter from a friend, from whom she had not heard for a long time. The letter began with the words, 'I am compelled to write to you this afternoon, under the constraint of the Spirit, to ask if you will take four girls into your Home and train them for me for abroad. I do not know if your Training Home is in existence, but whether or no, can you take them. . . ? The fees for all will be paid.'[14] She thanked God for this clear guidance, and set about plans to start again.

In December 1920, she reopened the college in a house in Lewin Road, Streatham,[15] but it soon became inadequate for the needs of the college. When

8. E.B.B. Whitfield, 'Mount Hermon Missionary Training College (for ladies)', in: *MRAN* 63 (July 1922), p. 12.
9. Quoted by Mrs Keith-Steele, 'The late Miss Emily B. B. Whitfield: founder of Mount Hermon Bible College', in: *MRANs* 97 (May 1929), p. 99.
10. 'The fruit of a woman's indomitable faith', in: *Life of Faith* February 23, 1938, p. 167.
11. Mrs Keith-Steele, 'The late Miss Emily B.B. Whitfield', in: *MRANs* 97 (May 1929), p. 99.
12. The sermon on this text was being preached by the Dr. Stuart Holden, who later spoke at the dedication of the college after the war.
13. Mrs Keith-Steele, 'The late Miss Emily B.B. Whitfield', in: *MRANs* 97 (May 1929), p. 99.
14. *Ibid.*
15. 'The fruit of a woman's indomitable faith', in: *Life of Faith* February 23 1938, p. 167.

she began to look for a new site, a former student suggested a house on the north side of Streatham Common. 'On the Common!' said Miss Whitfield, 'I'm afraid that will not do for us. Don't you know the Common is only for aristocrats?'[16] Even so, she agreed to look around the house and recognised how suitable it would be for the college. After much discussion and prayer, Miss Whitfield became assured that God wanted the college to have this property. She made an offer well below the asking price, which the owner initially refused. Two weeks later he offered her the property at fifty pounds less than she had offered, and agreed to include all the fittings. Miss Whitfield immediately put the whole matter in the hands of her solicitor, asking him to go forward with the purchase. When she left his office, she suddenly felt overwhelmed by her decision. 'What have I done? Given my word to take a house costing over £2,000 when we have not one penny.'[17]

She need not have worried. The next morning she received a cheque for £20, which was to be the first of many donations received towards the cost of the new home. Half an hour before the financial transaction was to be signed, a friend of the college phoned to offer a loan of £2,000. In time, that loan was fully repaid, the last £500 coming from a legacy given to Mount Hermon.

As more missionary candidates applied to come to Mount Hermon, it became apparent that even this house was inadequate for their needs. An adjacent property, 18 North Side, was procured through the loan of a friend. By 1922, the college could take thirty students and every place was filled. Numbers continued to rise, and by December 1926, there were eighty four students![18] At that point, Miss Whitfield believed they had reached saturation point. In the autumn of 1926, she wrote, 'We can take no more unless God expands us, which up to the present we do not think he will. 'The Lord can count' (Psalm 100), and he knows just the right number, and when we have had extra students he has always provided the extra room! How good it is to have a God who is willing to take the responsibility for bedrooms.'[19]

On September 30 1927, Miss Whitfield died at the age of fifty three. She had been greatly loved and respected. Many were deeply saddened by the news of her death. More than 350 students had come under her 'able tuition and godly influence.'[20] Many wrote to express their appreciation for all that she had done for them and meant to them. 'She was a real mother to me, right to the end of her life,' wrote one student.[21] An editorial in *Missions Review* spoke of her 'unique personality which developed in originality and strength as the years went by, making her interesting and attractive in an unusual degree to a wide circle of friends and acquaintances that came into contact with her.'[22] Some years later, on the occasion of the silver jubilee of the college, reference was made to 'her wonderful confidence in

16. Mrs Keith-Steele, 'The late Miss Emily B.B. Whitfield', in: *MRANs* 98 (July 1929), p. 110.
17. *Ibid.*
18. *MRANs* 85 (December 1926), p. 153.
19. Mrs Keith-Steele, 'The late Miss E.B.B. Whitfield', in: *MRANs* 101 (March 1930), p. 152.
20. The opinion of the trustees, quoted in 'The fruit of a woman's indomitable faith', in: *Life of Faith* February 23 1938, p. 167.
21. Anna Mishkova in: *MRANs* 91 March 1928), p. 11.
22. *MRANs* 96 (March 1929), p. 84.

God, her marvellous grasp and knowledge of the Scriptures, her practical outlook and her steadfast life of faith.'[23]

3.2.2 Miss Irene Crocker (1927-1960)

It had always been Miss Whitfield's desire to foster close co-operation between Mount Hermon and All Nations Bible College, which was established nearby. On several occasions she discussed the possibility of linking the two colleges together. Two weeks before her death in 1927, she asked if All Nations could take over the work of Mount Hermon. The trustees of Mount Hermon discussed the matter and confirmed her wish that the college should be transferred to the council of All Nations. In consequence, from the autumn of 1927, the two institutions shared the same governing body and trustees. One of the first decisions of the All Nations Council was that Mount Hermon should continue on the same interdenominational and faith lines and in the same buildings.[24] They also changed the name of the college to the 'Emily Whitfield Bible College' out of their high regard for the founder and first principal and in recognition of all that she had accomplished.[25]

The council appointed Miss Irene Crocker (1900-1971) as the new principal. She had been trained at Carfax in Bristol, and had spent eight years working with the London Jews' Society in the East End of London.

Miss Crocker was just 27. It was not easy for her to follow Miss Whitfield, who had founded the college and had been so much older and more experienced. She encountered antagonism from other members of staff and opposition towards the modest changes she wished to introduce to the programme. By and large, she continued to run the college along much the same lines as her predecessor. She maintained the same emphasis on biblical studies, the same insistence on the authority of Scripture and the same rejection of biblical criticism. In 1958, one member of staff was asked to leave because she was not in sympathy with the conservative position of the college.[26]

After the declaration of war in 1939, Mount Hermon had to be evacuated to a rectory in Lytchett Matravers, Dorset. That was their temporary home until 1943, when the Rev A. Phillips, who had invited them to share his home, was called to work in another parish. The property at Streatham had been requisitioned by the borough council and was no longer available. Once again a new home for the college had to be found.

Eventually a suitable property was discovered by the Rev Llewellyn Roberts at 39 Mount Avenue, Ealing. The disused garage was converted into an acceptable

23. *MRANs* 134 (September 1936), p. 56.
24. G. Thomas, 'The future of Mount Hermon Missionary Training College', in: *MRANs* 90 (November 1927), pp. 145-6.
25. Ibid. After a year, however, the council decided to change the name to 'Mount Hermon Bible College (founded by the late Miss Emily B.B. Whitfield).' In 1943, the council decided to change the name of the college yet again (according to the minutes of the meeting of October 6 1943). After the necessary legal requirements had been carried out, the college reverted to its orginal title 'Mount Hermon Missionary Training College' on July 2 1945.
26. Minutes of the Management Committee, November 13 1958.

lecture hall.[27] In 1959, a new three-storey building was erected next to the original property.[28]

In the following year, Miss Crocker retired from her role as principal. She had served in that position for thirty three years and her departure left an enormous gap in the life of the college. A series of tributes appeared in *Outgoings*, which give some indication of how much she was appreciated and how great was her influence. Alan Redpath's comments were typical of many: 'I, among thousands of others, have come to hold Miss Crocker in high esteem, not only for her abilities and efficiency as Principal of the college, but as a gracious Christian lady with a testimony which the Lord has been able to use so richly in blessing countless numbers of lives.'[29] Dr. Marjory Foyle, who had been a student from 1947-1949, wrote appreciatively of her discernment, her ability as a teacher, her gifts of leadership and her loving concern for each individual.[30] Miss Ruth Giesner, a student from 1954-1956 and later a tutor at All Nations Christian College, described Miss Crocker as 'a principal who mattered to us because we loved her.' She continued: 'Miss Crocker taught me to live one day at a time. She gave herself entirely to the immediate present, whether gardening or interviewing, and although at first it surprised me that she never seemed concerned over future events, yet now I value that example.'[31] Miss Meg Foote, who served as principal from 1965 to 1971, and who knew Miss Crocker well, described here as 'a very shrewd and perceptive person, and a real pastor.'[32]

Before we leave the principalship of Miss Crocker, something must be said about some of her colleagues. Miss Dorothy Bee joined the staff of the college in 1925, two years before Miss Crocker became principal. She eventually retired in 1955, after thirty years of devoted and faithful service, as secretary, accountant and lecturer. When she left, appreciation was expressed for her efficiency, her understanding, her sympathy and her wise counsel.

There were others who were not full-time members of staff, but who exerted a profound influence on the lives of those they taught. Dr. Jesse Sayer, who joined Mount Hermon in 1923, taught for fourteen years without pay. He was described in his obituary as 'a man with a great love of scripture, who aimed to make faith easy and unbelief difficult; one whose judgement was always sound, generous and conciliatory.'[33] Dr. F.W. Willway lectured at Mount Hermon from 1928 to 1938 on first aid, home nursing and hygiene. He had originally intended to be a medical missionary to Mongolia, but while he was waiting to leave he worked with the Mission to Deep Sea Fishermen, which so captivated him that he stayed in that ministry for forty three years. On his death, the chairman of the council of Mount Hermon wrote:

27. On April 23 1948, the new lecture hall was dedicated to the memory of the late Henry Oakley, who had served for many years as chairman of the Board.
28. This provided six double bedrooms for students, three rooms for staff and a number of guest rooms and extra bathrooms, and was dedicated by the Rev A.T. Houghton.
29. Alan Redpath, 'Greetings for Miss Crocker's farewell', in: *Outgoings* 11:3 (1960), p. 4.
30. M. Foyle, 'Greetings for Miss Crocker's farewell' in: O*utgoings* 11:3 (1960), p. 7.
31. R. Giesner, 'Greetings for Miss Crocker's farewell', in: *Outgoings* 11:1 (1960), p. 10.
32. Miss Meg Foote, personal interview, July 14 1999.
33. 'Dr Jess Sayer', in: *MRANs* 137 (April 1937), p. 96.

'The students greatly appreciated his lectures, his deep interest in their welfare and the happy merriment his presence encouraged.'[34] Another favourite of the students was Dr. C.K. Mowll, who served as Honorary Secretary of Mount Hermon. He also lectured on first aid and often expounded scripture. He was described by a fellow member of the council, as 'a most loveable man and his very presence seemed to bring an infection of happiness and goodwill. There are few men to whom it has been given, in addition to the gifts of teaching and leading which he possessed to an extraordinary degree, to be able to enter with real sympathy and insight into the sorrows and perplexities of other lives.'[35]

The success of a missionary training programme depends not only on the life, the gifts and the vision of a principal, but also on the quality and dedication of the other members of staff. Miss Crocker was fortunate to have the support of a loyal and hard working assistant such as Miss Bee, and the services of gifted and godly visiting lecturers.

3.2.3 Mrs. J. O. (Roxie) Fraser (1960-1964)

When Miss Crocker was about to retire, the management committee of MHMTC considered the appointment of a married couple to college, the husband to serve as principal, the wife as matron.[36] This appeared to reflect an evangelical tendency to appoint men to positions of leadership even where the appointment of a woman seemed more appropriate, and where the previous principals and founder had also been women.[37] In the event, the committee appointed a widow, who had considerable experience both in leadership and in ministry. What is also significant is that the committee chose to appoint someone who had herself been a missionary. This was the first time that Mount Hermon had a principal who had served overseas.

Mrs Roxie Maud Fraser, better known as Mrs J.O. Fraser (1906-1972), was born in China, where her father, Frank Dymond, served as a missionary with the United Methodist Mission. She was educated in England, and graduated in history from Bristol University. She went out to China as a single missionary in 1929, but soon caught the eye of James O. Fraser, who was nearly twenty years her senior and had served for many years with the China Inland Mission among the Lisu people of south-west China. After marriage, Mrs Fraser worked among the Lisu alongside her husband. He encouraged her in her own ministry, and regarded her as a better preacher than himself. As their daughter, Eileen Crossman, wrote many years later, 'His own idea of married life was of an equal yoke, both partners in the work together. He wanted Roxie to travel with him and preach with him. He would happily go down to the river and wash the clothes or carry the baby. It was a companion and co-worker he had always longed for, not a housekeeper.'[38]

34. H. Oakley, 'Dr Frederick W. Willway', in: *MRANs* 144 (September 1938), p. 53.
35. G.J. Byrnell, 'Christopher K. Mowll', in: *Outgoings* 1:3 (1940), p. 2.
36. The minutes of the Management Committee, March 20 1959.
37. K. Fiedler, *The story of faith missions* (1994), points out how often within the faith missions movement, even if a woman was successful in pioneering some new work, a man was often appointed as her successor, p. 301.
38. Eileen Crossman, *Mountain Rain* (1982), p. 162.

After the death of her husband in 1938, Mrs Fraser continued to work with the China Inland Mission. She experienced internment under the Japanese and, after her return to England, she served as candidates' secretary of the China Inland Mission and principal of their Training Home.

The first few months at MHMTC proved extremely difficult for Mrs Fraser. At the end of her first term in office, she handed in her resignation on the grounds that 'it was impossible to continue with the unsympathetic attitude and entire lack of co-operation of the staff.'[39] The central issue concerned Mrs Fraser's style of leadership. She was convinced that the regime under Miss Crocker had been too strict and authoritarian, and sought to relax some of the rules which she deemed unnecessary. The staff, who had served under the former principal, disagreed with this new approach and deplored the lack of discipline in the college. In the event, the Committee asked the two staff members in question to resign, and asked Mrs Fraser to withdraw her resignation. The Committee also expressed 'dissatisfaction at the rigidity of the past regime, particularly the unequal proportion of academic and practical subjects taken in the college diploma.'[40]

Mrs Fraser wanted to raise the academic standards of the college and encouraged students to enter for the Certificate of Religious Knowledge (CRK). Among the first batch of students, twelve passed, and distinctions were obtained in six papers.

From her own experience in China and her internment in a prisoner-of-war camp, Mrs Fraser was aware of the harsh realities of missionary work and the dangers it could bring. She was anxious to continue in the tradition of her two predecessors in providing the kind of preparation which would equip them for the challenges and rigours they would face.

She was concerned that the students learned to maintain the right priorities in their ministry. Firstly, she wanted them to know how to develop and maintain their own prayer lives, for she recognised that 'prayer is the source of power and the place where we so often fail.'[41] Secondly, she constantly reminded her students of the primacy of evangelism. In her view, the primary objective of missionary work was to share the good news of the love of God. She was well aware of how easily missionaries were distracted from this task. 'How easy it is to get absorbed with things and lose the prime motive of our work. A Chinese in North China once said something I shall never forget. "Missionaries are doing excellently at everything but the thing they came out to do." '[42]

The college continued to prosper under Mrs Fraser's leadership. Miss Elizabeth Sutherland joined the staff in 1959 as resident tutor and supervisor of practical ministry. Miss Doris Houchin, a student from 1944-45 who had worked in the Congo, served as bursar from 1961-1963. Some attempts were made to modernise the training programme and upgrade the facilities. A new lecture hall was built, and the old one was converted into a library.

39. Minutes of the Management Committee, December 19 1960.
40. Ibid.
41. Mrs J.O. Fraser, 'From the Principal', in: *Outgoings* 13:1 (1961), p. 2.
42. Mrs J.O. Fraser, 'From the Principal', in: *Outgoings* 12:2 (1961), p. 3.

While Mrs Fraser was principal, the college celebrated its Silver Jubilee. In fifty years, more than one thousand women had studied at Mount Hermon. The college was still in touch with 750, and 100 of those had studied under Miss Whitfield. It is strong testimony to the affection in which the college was held that the students took the trouble to maintain their links. It is also an indication of the importance which the staff gave to providing ongoing support for their alumnae.

When Mrs Fraser accepted the position of Principal, she anticipated she would stay for five years. 'After many years in China and in the China Inland Mission Training Home, I did not expect to be here longer than that.'[43] However, towards the end of that time she suffered ill-health and was only able to stay in office for four and a half years. After her retirement in December 1965, she moved to California.

3.2.4 Miss Meg Foote (1965-1971)

The fourth and, as it turned out, final principal of Mount Hermon was Miss Meg Foote (b. 1911), a graduate of London University and a qualified teacher. Miss Foote came to Mount Hermon with eighteen years' experience in student work in the United Kingdom and Europe: first, as a travelling secretary with the Inter-Varsity Fellowship; and, later, as the Women's Secretary. She served for many years on the Executive Committee of the International Fellowship of Evangelical Students and exercised leadership in many camps, houseparties and missions. She was also involved in the Christian Education Fellowship and the Social Workers' Christian Fellowship.[44] Having had the responsibility for initiating women staff workers into student work and running courses for student leaders, Miss Foote was familiar with the student world and with contemporary models of training.

Before assuming her role as Principal, Meg Foote had the opportunity to spend several months in India and south-east Asia. She had strong family connections in India, where her father had been in charge of a rifle factory, and other relatives had served in the Gurkhas.[45] She was able to visit many friends, made during her student work, and many Mount Hermon graduates. She was also able to familiarise herself with the problems, pressures and opportunities of many forms of missionary activity. It was an ideal preparation for her future work. She wrote: 'What a privilege it has been to see something of the work of such a variety of missionary societies in different cultures in both primitive and civilised settings, to have the opportunity of discussing problems of missionary work and of training leaders on the field, as well as here at home, and with missionaries of every age group and stage of experience.'[46]

When Miss Foote arrived at Mount Hermon, she encountered antagonism and an antipathy to change, just as her predecessor had done. One member of staff, who

43. Mrs J.O. Fraser, 'From the Principal', in: *Outgoings* 15:2 (1964), p. 1.
44. Editorial, *Outgoings* 16:2 (1965), p. 10.
45. Interview with Miss Foote, May 24 1996. Her grandfather headed up a geological survey from Madras.
46. Miss Foote, 'From the Principal', in: *Outgoings* 16:2 (1965), p. 9.

had hoped to be appointed as principal, objected to almost every proposal Miss Foote made and was hardly willing to speak to her at all. Within two years of her arrival at the college, all the previous staff had left and Miss Foote was able to build up her own team. She approached Miss Margaret Jones, a science graduate from Trinity College, Dublin, who had served for five years as a travelling secretary for the Inter-School Christian Fellowship,[47] and Miss Anne Long, an English graduate, who had taught at Gipsy Hill College of Education. Both had just completed theological degrees at London Bible College.

This team was further strengthened by the coming of another graduate, as bursar and tutor, Miss Muriel Cockrem, who had been a missionary teacher in Lahore (pre-partition) throughout World War Two, and then for many years the personnel secretary of the Bible and Medical Missionary Fellowship (now InterServe). She relieved Miss Foote of all the administrative work, and later served as the secretary to the Formation Committee, which planned the merger of the three colleges.[48]

Miss Foote was appreciative of Mount Hermon's achievements in the past, but realised that some traditions, which had developed and been continued for fifty years, were due for a change. The style of leadership at the college was hierarchical. The principal was not expected to do any menial tasks, but to have servants, or groups of students, who performed these tasks for her. Miss Foote felt that this style of leadership provided the wrong example for those who were going to serve in a post-colonial era. She wanted Mount Hermon students to learn to be the servants of the people, to whom they were called. She insisted on cleaning her own room, and would often share with the students in doing some of the dirtiest jobs around the college. If she, as their principal, was willing to get her hands dirty and perform some of the lowliest jobs, she trusted that they would do likewise when they went overseas.[49] She recommended that the students should destroy the 'neglected duties book', which involved such heinous crimes as failure to feed the cook's cat. She encouraged them to apologise in person if they had let someone down.

The students at MHMTC had little experience of Christians outside their own denomination, or beyond the evangelical tradition. Miss Foote wanted them to learn to appreciate other Christian perspectives. She encouraged students to attend churches of other denominations, and to discuss among themselves those issues of doctrine on which denominations disagreed. On one occasion, she initiated a long discussion among Baptist and Scandinavian Lutheran students on the issue of baptismal regeneration. While neither side agreed with the other, they did learn to respect each another's opinion, and to recognise the validity of their arguments.

Miss Foote arranged for students to visit the Benedictine Home for the Elderly that was situated nearby, so that they could meet Roman Catholic Christians. She invited speakers to present evangelical and ecumenical perspectives on the state of the church in different continents. She also encouraged discussion on issues relat-

47. When she was invited to join the staff of Mount Hermon, Margaret Jones replied, 'Meg, you can have no idea what I think of women's Bible colleges.' To which Miss Foote retorted, 'Actually, it's because I do, that I want you to come.'
48. From a letter from Miss Foote, dated January 31 1997.
49. Miss Foote, personal interview, May 24 1996.

ing to church unity. These were all significant innovations and would not have been countenanced at the college a few years before. With the help of her new staff, who were well qualified both theologically and educationally, Miss Foote was able to improve the academic standard of the college. She encouraged students who wanted an externally accredited qualification to sit for the University of London Diploma of Theology, a higher award than the CRK. She expanded the library to include works by liberal and critical scholars. She insisted that students should understand other views and encouraged open discussion during lecture classes. She decided to broaden the curriculum and extend the length of the college course from two to three years. The extension of the course made possible 'not only a more adequate study of the scriptures and Christian doctrine, but greater opportunity to learn how to study them for oneself and acquire tools for life-long use.'[50]

Miss Foote wanted the students to get more experience in ministry and the college to have a greater impact on the neighbourhood. Termly, evangelistic meetings were planned by the students to reach out to the local community. Special meetings were organised for local children, and seminars were conducted for Sunday School teachers in the surrounding churches. A new feature of the college programme was 'a time of consecutive practical experience in a local church over a period of months to learn at first hand the opportunities, problems and pressures of Christian ministry, followed by a period back in college for evaluation of the experience gained, and for the study and discussion of some subjects such as church unity, ethical problems etc., which will be far more meaningful in the light of such experience.'[51] All third years students were expected to spend seven months out of college in their final year, working in a parish so that they could gain 'more insight in the administration and life of the local church from the inside, to learn more of the day to day spiritual warfare with its discouragements and disappointments as well as its privileges and joys in the fellowship of an experienced team.'[52]

Miss Foote regularly consulted with mission leaders, who had knowledge of the contemporary missionary enterprise, and, in the light of what they shared, she reviewed the kind of missionary training that was needed in the contemporary world. She encouraged students to develop an appreciation of different cultures by interacting with ethnic minority communities in West London. She made them aware of the new patterns of missionary work in a rapidly changing world. She warned them not to expect to be in positions of power or control, and to recognise that national Christians should now be setting the agenda. In 1968, she wrote, 'Closing doors to traditional patterns of missionary work in some areas can be God's challenge to discover his contemporary pattern to cross new and different frontiers, to open our eyes to unbounded opportunity in partnership with younger churches.'[53]

From the very beginning, Miss Foote also made it clear to the Management Committee that she was not willing to perpetuate a women's college, but also wished

---

50. Ibid.
51. Miss Foote, 'The Principal's Letter', in: *Outgoings* 17:1 (1965) p. 7.
52. Miss Foote, 'Principal's letter' in: *Outgoings* 17:2 (1966), p. 3.
53. Miss Foote, 'Principal's letter', in: *Outgoings* (1968), p. 3.

to train men and married couples.[54] Within three weeks of assuming the leadership of Mount Hermon, Miss Foote had a long conversation with David Morris, principal of All Nations, about the possibility of a merger between their respective institutions.[55] Discussions continued for the next few years until it became clear that three colleges, Mount Hermon, All Nations and Ridgelands, were ready to be integrated into one institution. When the news of this proposal became public, Miss Foote explained why she was convinced that this was the right step forward: 'It has become increasingly evident that a small college with limited staff, facilities and finance cannot provide adequately the variety and types of courses needed to meet the very flexible modern missionary situation. Provision must be made for the growing number of married students, where both husband and wife need training, and there is a growing conviction that to perpetuate the segregation of the sexes in training is unrealistic. Such segregation was in line with the educational pattern of the days when the colleges were founded and was obviously right in subsequent years. In many parts of the mission field today, however, it is important that men, women and married couples have learnt to live and work together, recognising, appreciating and being able to harmonise their distinctive contributions before they reach the field.'[56]

Miss Crocker, Miss Bee and Mrs Fraser gave their unreserved, enthusiastic, and prayerful support and encouragement to the coming changes and merger of the colleges.[57] In 1971, the merger became a reality. On June 28th, a service of thanksgiving[58] was held to give thanks to God for the work of Mount Hermon Missionary Training College over the previous sixty years, and in September the college became part of the new All Nations Christian College.

3.2.5 Conclusion

The four principals, who led Mount Hermon from its foundation to the merger of 1971, made distinctive contributions to its development. Miss Whitfield was a visionary, who recognised the need for a missionary training centre for women. It was her initiative and indomitable faith which led to the founding of the college and its reconstitution in 1920.

Miss Crocker consolidated what Miss Whitfield had begun. She faithfully adhered to the vision of its founder and steered the college through the dark years of the Second World War and the traumas of relocation. Her long period of tenure provided stability and continuity for the college. On the other hand, when she retired, the college had inevitably become set in its ways and inured to change. Yet change was necessary, for a training programme which had emerged in the days of the British Empire was ill-suited to prepare women for ministry in the post-colonial world.

54. Miss Foote, personal interview, May 24th, 1996.
55. Ibid.
56. Miss Foote, 'Principal's letter', in: *Outgoings* (1969), p. 3f.
57. From a letter from Miss Foote, dated January 31 1997.
58. A number of the members of the council took part in the service, including Canon A. T. Houghton, E.W. Oliver and J.A. Baldock. Canon A.S. Neech gave the address.

Mrs Fraser brought to the college a wealth of experience, both in mission and missionary preparation. She recognised the need for some changes to be made to the training programme at Mount Hermon, but was to some extent inhibited by the traditions of the past as well as by her own failing health. In the words of her successor, 'she had the vision for change, but neither the energy nor the staff to effect it.'[59]

When Miss Foote accepted the position of principal, she was fully aware of the need for a radically new approach to missionary training. Her clearsightedness, decisive leadership and gracious perseverance effected a marked change in the college, preparing the way for the future merger.

All four principals shared a deep personal faith, dedication to mission, high regard for the authority of Scripture and a commitment to holistic missionary training, but the world for which they were training their students was rapidly changing. Miss Whitfield pioneered missionary training for women before the outbreak of the First World War and continued with the same pattern when she re-established the college in 1920. Miss Crocker faithfully followed the example of the founder during her long tenure of office. When she retired in 1960, Mrs Fraser inherited a college that had been run on similar lines for nearly fifty years. She understood that change was necessary and began to implement some innovations, but it was left to Miss Foote to undertake the radical overhaul in the training programme that was demanded in an ever changing world.

The changes that Miss Foote introduced can be seen in her teaching and her style of leadership. She encouraged students to have a more positive and discerning attitude both to liberal scholarship and to the ecumenical movement. She moved away from the pattern of education where only one view was presented and lecturers simply dictated verbatim notes to the students. She rejected the authoritarian and hierarchical leadership structure adopted by her predecessors, as she felt this was unsuitable in contemporary society and a wrong model to give students for their future ministry. She chose to adopt a model of servant-leadership, which she hoped would be the pattern which students would follow as they went out to serve in partnership with national Christians in newly independent nations.

3.3 Doctrinal basis and character

The doctrinal basis and character of MHMTC are reflected in the early reports and brochures of the college and in the short biography of Miss Whitfield that was published soon after her death. They may be summarised as follows: first, the teaching at the college closely resembled that which was presented each year at the Keswick Convention (3.3.1); secondly, there was a clear commitment to the inspiration, authority and trustworthiness of the Bible (3.3.2); thirdly, with regards to its financial affairs, the college adopted the policy of 'faith missions,' which were attracting an increasing number of recruits who required training (3.3.3); and fourthly, the col-

59. Miss Foote, personal interview, July 14 1999.

lege was an interdenominational college, welcoming all Christians, while retaining its own independence. It would not be beholden to any single denomination or missionary society but would serve as 'a handmaid for all' (3.3.4).

3.3.1 The influence of the Keswick Convention

From its inception MHMTC was profoundly influenced by the Keswick Convention. This is evident both in Miss Whitfield's personal life and in the frequent references to Keswick in the college literature. Every year a large party of staff and students attended the convention, and Keswick speakers regularly lectured at the college.

The influence of Keswick can be seen in those aspects of spirituality and doctrine that were emphasised at Mount Hermon: the need for individual conversion, the call for deeper consecration to Christ, the authority of the Scriptures, the centrality of the cross, and the second coming of Christ. Little emphasis was given to the doctrine of the church. More importance was laid on the fellowship individual believers could already enjoy with one another than on the desirability for the structural unity of the visible church.

Both at Keswick and at MHMTC there was a strong emphasis on mission. For many, missionary service was viewed as the highest expression of the consecrated life. Mission was understood almost exclusively to mean evangelism, soul-winning, bringing individuals to personal faith in Jesus Christ. Little emphasis was given to social action, and though many of the students were teachers or nurses, who would be involved in educational or medical work, they were constantly reminded of the primacy of evangelism.

To this extent the staff at the college were in sympathy with the vision propounded at the Edinburgh conference. They too were concerned with the evangelisation of the world and the sole focus of the college was to prepare women for that task. However, they differed from the view expressed at Edinburgh and at subsequent conferences of the IMC, that the church was the main vehicle for the propagation for the gospel. Rather they saw the missionary societies as the primary agencies through whom the task of world evangelisation would be accomplished.

3.3.2 The commitment to biblical authority

One of the characteristics of the Keswick movement was its commitment to the authority of Scripture and its rejection of those trends in contemporary scholarship which appeared to undermine the Bible's credibility or trustworthiness. From the start Miss Whitfield made it clear that the aim of MHMTC was to uphold the authority of Scripture and to provide students with a thorough grounding in its contents. She was adamant that, 'the college must stand for and preach the whole Bible, the Word of God, from cover to cover.'[60]

60. Mrs Keith-Steele, 'The late Miss Emily B.B. Whitfield', in: *MRANs* 97 (May 1929), p. 98.

Students were encouraged to have a constructive, rather than a destructive, approach to biblical criticism. Every year, lectures were given on the origin, transmission and inspiration of the Bible, and on archaeological discoveries that supported the trustworthiness of the biblical narrative.[61]

Although no doctrinal statement survives from 1911, an early brochure stated: 'The college gives sound teaching in the whole Word of God. Modern views of the Bible are neither taught nor tolerated in the college.'[62] In 1927, the college adopted the doctrinal statement of ANBC, which affirmed the inspiration, historical trustworthiness and final authority of both Old and New Testaments.[63] This was permanently exhibited in the entrance hall of the college and was read out every year at the Annual General Meeting.[64] The principal and tutors were required to sign a copy of this statement, and visiting lecturers were requested to give verbal assent. The statement of faith remained the same until 1971.

The attitude of the college reflected that of many evangelicals during this period. Unable to cope with the attacks made on the reliability of the Scriptures, they tended to retreat from academic scholarship into personal pietism. They accepted the trustworthiness of the Word of God as an item of faith and sought to live under its authority. It was only after the Second World War that things began to change. Evangelical scholars, such as F.F. Bruce, W.J. Martin and R.V.G. Tasker, were appointed to posts in the theology departments of universities. The Inter-varsity Fellowship encouraged the publication of scholarly publications, such as the *New Bible Commentary* and the *Tyndale Commentaries.* This led to greater confidence among evangelicals, and a willingness to engage in academic debate. The influence of this change of attitude among evangelicals can be seen at Mount Hermon during the principalship of Meg Foote. The college remained firmly committed to the authority of Scripture but there was a new openness and readiness to learn from more liberal scholarship.

3.3.3 The adoption of 'faith mission' principles[65]

Miss Whitfield founded MHMTC on the same principles that had been followed by faith missions. She insisted that the college would be run in complete dependence

61. Miss I. Crocker, 'Principal's letter', in: *MRANs* (1930), p. 150.
62. College brochure nd, p. 4., sic.
63. *Articles of Association of Mount Hermon Missionary Training College*, March 28 1930. See appendix 1.
64. 'Report of the Annual General Meeting', in: *MRANs* 101 (March 1935), p. 329.
65. Hudson Taylor, who founded the China Inland Mission in 1865, is usually regarded as the father of faith missions according to K. Fiedler in *The story of faith missions* (1994), p. 32 and J. Herbert Kane in *A Concise History of the Christian World Mission* (1978), p. 96. Kane offers the following comment on faith missions: 'The term *faith mission* has been applied to a number of interdenominational agencies which, because they have no 'captive constituency,' must to an unusual degree look to the Lord for the supply of their needs. They themselves, however, would be the last to claim that they have a monopoly on faith. Their missionaries have no guaranteed income, though they do have a support scale which they try to maintain. They do not go into debt, nor do they solicit funds. They prefer to make their needs known to the Christian public and look to the Lord to move in the hearts of His people.' (Ibid., p. 101).

on God.[66] She believed that God would supply all their needs, just as he had done in the case of the children of Israel. She often quoted Scriptures where God promised to take care of the physical needs of his children.[67] Whenever there was a particular financial need, the whole Mount Hermon family, students, staff and friends of the college, were encouraged to make it a special item for prayer. They often witnessed remarkable answers to those prayers . Money was received at the eleventh hour to meet a crisis or pay an urgent bill.

Miss Whitfield never allowed appeals for money, although she was prepared to make the needs of the college known. When £1000 was required for the construction of a new hostel, this was mentioned in the *Missionary Review*.[68] But as Miss Whitfield had said on a previous occasion when she spoke of the cost of the new building, 'We state the sum, merely as an amount to lay before the Lord, not as an appeal.'[69]

The fees of Mount Hermon were kept as low as possible. Miss Whitfield was determined that no suitable candidate, who was called of God, should be denied admission through lack of funds.[70]

Through careful budgeting and use of resources the staff at Mount Hermon were able to train their students at less than half the cost it took to train the men at All Nations.[71] The accounts for the financial year ending 31st March, 1935, showed the total expenditure for training 40 students that year was £1,923, a cost of less than £50 for each student. The expenditure at All Nations for 26 students, was £3,140, or £120 per student.[72]

One reason for the extra cost at All Nations were the amounts paid to visiting professors and technical instructors. These totalled nearly £700 in 1935. By contrast, Mount Hermon only paid out £32 as fees for 'special classes.'

Costs were also kept low, because of the large number of gifts that were sent to the college by well-wishers. These included fruit, medicine, a chest of tea,[73] books, a sofa,[74]a case of dried fruit, eggs, maps,[75] rhubarb,[76] a case of onions,[77] herrings and a piano stool.[78]

Over the years, the college adhered to the 'faith' policy of the founder. In 1959, when the college undertook an extensive building programme, no appeal was made

66. Mrs G. Thomas, 'Brief notes about early days,' in: *MRANs* 106 (January 1931), p. 36.
67. 'Bring all the tithes into the storehouse...' and 'The barrel of meal shall not fail...', cited by Mrs Keith-Steele, 'the late Miss Emily B.B. Whitfield', in: *MRANs* 97 (May 1929), p. 98.
68. Miss E.B.B. Whitfield, 'Mount Hermon Missionary Training College', in: *MRAN* 74 (September 1924), p. 277.
69. *Ibid.*, p. 261.
70. Mrs Keith-Steele, 'The late Mrs Emily B.B. Whitfield', in: *MRANs* 97 (May 1929), p. 98.
71. 'Mount Hermon Bible College: Accounts for the year ending 31st March, 1935', in: *MRANs* 129 (August 1935), p. 336.
72. 'All Nations Bible College: Accounts for the year ending 31st March, 1935', in: *MRANs* 129 (August 1935), p. 333.
73. *MRANs* 119 (October 1933), p. 206.
74. *MRANs* 121 (February 1934), p. 230.
75. *MRANs* 122 (April 1934), p. 246.
76. *MRANs* 123 (June 1934), p. 260.
77. *MRANs* 125 (November 1934), p. 288.
78. *MRANs* 135 (November 1936), p. 72.

for funds. However, on the insistence of past students and interested friends, information about special needs was made available to those who asked.[79]

3.3.4 Interdenominational character

A further similarity between MHMTC and the faith missions can be seen in its acceptance of students from a wide variety of denominations. The first principle of the China Inland Mission read: 'The mission is interdenominational. Missionaries from all Protestant Churches can become members if they agree to the statement of faith.'[80]

The growth of the faith mission movement and the demand for the training of their recruits was one of the compelling reasons behind the opening of such institutions. As faith missions provided the vehicle through which evangelicals from many denominations could serve together on the mission field, so colleges like MHMTC provided the context in which they could train together.

Within any interdenominational college or mission a degree of doctrinal disagreement had to be tolerated. Staff and students were united by their common commitment to the Bible and a common experience of conversion to Christ. Differences of opinion over secondary issues could be set aside because of general agreement on the major doctrines of the faith.

The interdenominational character of MHMTC was reflected in its governing body. Following its reopening in 1921, Mount Hermon had a council of twenty three members,[81] including Anglicans, Baptists, Congregationalists, Brethren, and members of the Free Evangelical Churches. Seven of the council were Anglican clergy, six were ordained ministers in other denominations. The council also included four women. Six members served as trustees of the college and as an advisory council to the principal.

Forty years later the council, now called the management committee, maintained a strong interdenominational character, though approximately half of its fifteen members were Anglicans. Five were women. The management committee included representatives of both denominational and interdenominational missionary societies.[82]

3.3.5 Conclusion

The teaching that was given at MHMTC bore a close resemblance to what was presented each year at the Keswick Convention. There was a strong emphasis on personal salvation and personal piety. This teaching produced among the students deep devotion to Christ and consecration to his service. They developed a strong inner spiritual life which stood them in good stead to cope with the pressures and challenges they would face overseas.

---

79. 'Editorial' in: *Outgoings* 11:1 (1959), p. 3.
80. Quoted in K. Fiedler, *The story of faith missions* (1994), p. 33.
81. *Two year's course of MHMTC* (nd), p. 4.
82. 'The Management Committee', in: *Outgoing* 12:3 (1961), pp. 15-17.

The weakness of the teaching was in its excessive individualism. The students appeared to have little understanding of, or commitment to, the universal church. The mission on which the students embarked was one of proclaiming personal salvation through faith in Christ. It was ecclesiologically weak and only represented one dimension of biblical teaching regarding salvation and the kingdom of God.

Like the Keswick Convention, the college had a high view of the inspiration of the Bible. It based all its teachings on Scripture and sought as one of its primary objectives to give their students a solid grounding in the whole of the Bible. Staff and students worked from an agreed basis of faith and a common and understanding of mission. Mount Hermon students knew what they believed and went out with confidence to share the good news of what God had done in Christ. At the same time, there was a phobia over any form of critical scholarship, and an innate suspicion of other Christian traditions. This continued until the 1960s when the growth of evangelical scholarship made it easier for colleges like MHMTC to consider alternative views of Scripture without being dubbed as heretical.

The college was also influenced by the principles and practices of the growing number of faith missions. No appeals were made for funds. When the college faced a financial crisis, the whole community was encouraged to pray, and 'expect that God will supply their every need through the hands of his children.'[83] The records of the college show how on several occasions, urgently needed funds were provided, sometimes in quite unexpected ways, after a prolonged time of prayer. The college did seek to live 'by faith', even though the cynic might say there is a fine distinction between making an appeal for funds and making financial needs known.

Like the faith missions, MHMTC was an interdenominational institution, welcoming students from many different churches, whose doctrines over issues, such as baptism, Holy Communion or church order, varied considerably. To a degree, then, the college exhibited a limited ecumenicity, providing a focus for unity and fellowship which the students sometimes lacked within their own denominations. At the same time there was an ambivalence towards the wider ecumenical movement. Some of the board members, staff and students came from independent evangelical churches which were highly critical of those who belonged to other traditions. Many belonged to main-line denominations but felt themselves to be a despised minority within them. They often developed a ghetto mentality and found their true fellowship among like-minded evangelicals from other denominations. As a consequence the students at MHMTC trained for mission largely in isolation from the rest of the Christian world.

3.4 THE PROGRAMME

The primary purpose of the institution was to prepare women for the mission field. An early college brochure states: 'The Home was founded fourteen years ago at Victoria Park East, for the training of young ladies, called of God, to mission work

83. 'The principles of the CIM,' quoted in K. Fiedler, *The story of faith missions* (1994), p. 33.

at home or abroad.'[84] The original name of the institution was 'The Mount Hermon Missionary Training College,' and the missionary emphasis was retained throughout the sixty years. On her retirement, the second principal, Miss Crocker, reflected on the years she had led the college: 'Missionary is the third word in our title, and though in keeping with Bible colleges we own the absolute authority of the Bible and have given it the central place in our studies, yet the missionary emphasis has been maintained.'[85]

In their desire to provide adequate training for future missionaries, the staff at Mount Hermon were as much concerned with spiritual growth, character formation, and practical training, as they were with academic study. At the 1931 anniversary meeting, Miss Crocker considered the educational philosophy of her predecessor and the kind of training Mount Hermon aimed to provide. She concluded that the basic structure of any missionary training programme must be:

1. to provide a thorough knowledge of the Scriptures;
2. to develop the character of the candidates;
3. to give them practical experience of Christian work; and
4. to foster their spiritual growth.[86]

The next principal, Mrs Fraser, was chosen because of her missionary experience in China. Her successor, Miss Foote, conscious of the missionary emphasis of the college, spent several months visiting mission stations in Asia before assuming her responsibilities as principal.

Miss Crocker was often asked why two years[87] was necessary for the preparation of missionaries. She replied that it was necessary because of the magnitude of the message, the weakness of the messengers, and the sacrifices that would be encountered.[88] She believed that a thorough grounding in Scripture, a life transformed by the Holy Spirit, and an attitude of mind which gladly accepts whatever difficulties might come, were essential qualities for every prospective missionary. This view of missionary training was reflected in the programme offered at Mount Hermon.

3.4.1 Spiritual training

The academic year began in September with a Quiet Day. The whole day was given to prayer and waiting upon God. Services were held at 3.00 p.m. and 6.30 p.m.[89] Every Sunday a prayer meeting was held at 8.00 am, before the students went to their respective churches. Each morning, half an hour was set aside for private prayer.[90]

---

84. 'Objects', in: *Mount Hermon Missionary Training College* (London, MHMTC, nd), p. 1.
85. 'Principal's letter', in: *Outgoings* 9:3 (1958), p. 1.
86. I. Crocker, *MRANs* 106 (March 1931), p. 51.
87. The usual length of the course at Mount Hermon was two years, but students were also accepted for one year or even less, according to College brochures published in 1925 and 1965.
88. *MRANs* 117 (April 1933), p. 179.
89. *MRANs* 94 (September 1928), p. 45.
90. *MRANs* 101 (March 1930), p. 150.

As Miss Crocker wrote in 1934: 'Time is given in training when the student can truly meditate upon God and not feel that some more practical duty is calling.'[91] As Principal, she longed to see more of Christ in each student as the term progressed. She spoke of the inspiration she felt as she observed an added dignity, a greater winsomeness, charm and serenity in those who were under her care.[92]

The Keswick Convention had a strong influence on the college and its teaching. Miss Whitfield received her 'call' to restart the college while she was attending a Keswick meeting, and in subsequent years she organised a large houseparty at the convention for students and friends of the college. This tradition was maintained by her successor, Miss Crocker, who often made reference to the convention in her principal's letters. In August 1931 she wrote: 'Some of you who read this letter will no doubt have enjoyed this year's 'Keswick' with the wonderful realisation of the presence of the Lord in our midst. Speakers were lost sight of and charged with God's message which was given in the power of the Holy Spirit. It was a time when all who allowed the Holy Spirit to have full sway were blessed.'[93]

The students at Mount Hermon were regularly reminded of the importance of the 'Spirit-filled life.' G.F. Byrnell, the honorary treasurer of the college, addressing the anniversary meeting in 1934, said: 'If there is one thing the missionary needs above all others, it is to know the filling of the Holy Spirit. If they have never experienced the filling of the Holy Spirit, they had better stay at home.'[94] The following spring, when a number of visiting lecturers spoke about some Chinese Christians and British missionaries whose lives had been transformed by the Holy Spirit, many students entered into a similar experience. This had a considerable impact on the life of the community, bringing greater unity, more mutual consideration, and a passionate concern for those who did not know Christ. Miss Crocker wrote, 'Spring term 1935 will be a term that will not be forgotten by any who were in the college at the time, for more than three quarters of the college were blessed, and it was inspiring to hear day after day how the Lord touched first one and then another.'[95]

Mrs Fraser sought to inspire the students of her day through the lives of men like George Muller 'with his deep humility and single eye for Jesus Christ.'[96] Miss Foote exhorted them to prove 'the unchanging faithfulness of the Lord in the midst of change, His unalterable mercy in face of our faithlessness and infidelity.'[97] At the same time, she did not allow her students to become complacent, or uncritical, of their evangelical faith. She encouraged them to 'learn from other theological traditions and to have a positive approach to biblical criticism.'[98] She also wanted them to rethink the application of biblical faith to the contemporary world. She urged them to face the challenge of their generation,

91. *MRANs* 121 (February 1934), p. 255.
92. *Ibid.*
93. Miss I. Crocker, 'Principal's letter', in: *MRANs* 108 (April 1931), p. 74.
94. G.F. Byrnell, 'Address at the 23rd anniversary meeting', in: *MRANs* 122 (April 1934), p. 243.
95. Miss I. Crocker, 'Principal's letter', in: *MRANs* 127 (April 1935), p. 308.
96. 'From the Principal', in: *Outgoings* 14:1 (1962), p. 3.
97. 'Principal's letter', in: *Outgoings* 17:2 (1966), p. 2.
98. From a letter from Miss Foote, dated January 31 1997.

and not to recoil 'from the transforming power of obedience to the true implications of discipleship'.[99]

3.4.2 Character formation

'What we are is more important than what we say or do, and what we say or do is determined by what we are.' This favourite saying of Miss Whitfield was quoted by Dr Graham Scroggie at the Silver Jubilee Meeting.[100] It was one thing for the students to develop their own personal pietism. It was quite another for them to evidence the reality of that inner life in their relationships with others.

Miss Crocker was aware of the faults and weaknesses in her students. She knew only too well that some students loved singing hymns or leading in prayer, but were a pain to live with. Speaking of a hypothetical student, she wrote, 'See how Mary enjoys her religion, but nobody else does!'[101] She was also aware that some students were lazy and rarely did their fair share of duties while others were always ready to go the extra mile. The latter were 'born missionaries', who were willing for any sacrifice God might ask them to make. 'Everything they touch and do will be done for the master.'[102]

Mount Hermon also aimed at teaching the students stewardship of time, and the importance of tidiness and punctuality. They were encouraged to use every moment of the day to advantage, and to perform even the most humdrum duties to Christ's glory. As Miss Crocker wrote in her principal's letter, 'A careless worker in the ordinary things of life will be slipshod concerning the spiritual life.'[103]

Inevitably there were a number of frustrations which arose from living within a community – the frustration of trying to light a fire, the pressure of finishing the preparation of a sermon, the struggle of eating food you didn't enjoy, the disappointment of being laid aside with an illness. All these difficulties were viewed by the staff as opportunities through which the student's character could develop and mature.

Miss Crocker, aware of the harsh realities of the field, was concerned to prepare her students for the future. She welcomed former students back to the college, asking them to share what missionary work was actually like. In this way, those preparing learned from those in places, so remote that they only received post once a year. They met those on leave from tropical countries and saw for themselves 'the havoc wrought on the fresh colour of their youth.'[104] They heard about the realities of spiritual warfare, the heartbreak of those who turned away from Christ after an initial profession of faith, the strain and worry of allowances coming late, or not at all. There was no attempt to shelter the students from the truth of what they were about to encounter. They needed to face up to the future and, before they left their

99. *Ibid.*
100. *MRANs* 135 (November 1936), p. 67.
101. *MRANs* 109 (October 1931), p. 85.
102. *MRANs* 117 (April 1933), p. 179.
103. *MRANs* 122 (April 1934), p. 241.
104. *MRANs* 137 (April 1937), p. 95.

own native shore, they needed to begin to develop the grit and determination that alone would enable them to remain true to their calling.

An additional part of the character training was the official college uniform. 'During training students are expected to wear navy blue dresses, with cuffs, collar, coat and Deaconess bonnet.'[105] A modified uniform was still required in 1953. 'A plain tailored coat and navy dress with which can be worn a pale blue collar or scarf will still be the official wear for all outside meetings, but navy or grey skirts and white blouses can now be worn during lectures and studies.'[106] The wearing of an official uniform had its advantages. It offered 'protection when working in urban priority areas and mitigated differences of wealth and background among the students.'[107]

3.4.3 Practical training

Practical ministry was a major component of the training programme. Every week students were expected to be engaged in some form of Christian ministry. Some took Sunday School classes in the rougher districts of inner city London: Bermondsey, Walworth, Stockwell and Brixton. The students learned, often through bitter experience, that it was far from easy to teach a group of unruly and undisciplined children, many of whom had little desire to hear the gospel.[108] Others worked among factory girls, who were far from home and lonely in the evenings and at weekends. They would seek to befriend them, inviting them to the college to have a cup of tea, to sing some hymns and to listen to students tell their life stories.[109]

Twice a month, a small group of students would visit local lodging houses. The sordid conditions, in which people lived and the tragic reasons that had brought them there made a deep impression on the students, most of whom had grown up in a fairly protected environment. For many it was their first encounter with abject poverty and degradation, and a good preparation for situations they would face in their missionary work. In the Easter and summer vacations students were expected to take part in mission treks or other evangelistic activities. In June 1923, three separate groups of students cycled around villages in Hertfordshire, Surrey and Kent, visiting houses, distributing tracts and holding open-air meetings. The students took little with them, and were never sure where they were going to stay or how they would eat. Mostly they received a warm welcome, but on one occasion they had to sleep on the table that had been left out for a prayer meeting. On another occasion, a group found that they had nothing left to eat except a piece of cheese, so they held an emergency prayer meeting. Half a mile further on, they found a new loaf of bread lying in the middle of the road.[110]

Some observers expressed criticism of this itinerant evangelistic work. They felt that it was inappropriate for young ladies to go wandering around the countryside.

105. *Mount Hermon Missionary Training College* (1925), p. 2.
106. Dorothy Bee, 'Transformations', in: *Outgoings* 7:4 (1953), p. 5.
107. From a letter from Miss Foote, dated January 31 1997.
108. *MRANs* 136 (February 1937), p. 81.
109. *Ibid.*, p. 97.
110. *MRAN* 67 (June 1923), p. 130.

It was regarded as risky and unbecoming, and they wrote to the principal, stating that 'it ought not to be allowed.'[111] Miss Whitfield, however, saw this practical experience as an indispensable part of missionary training. It provided 'invaluable lessons of prayer, trust and launching out in faith,' she wrote. 'Surely the finest training for the mission field any student can get.'[112] Most missionary societies agreed. 'We think this is the finest bit of training our candidates are getting,' wrote one. 'Please let our girls take part in the evangelistic treks,' requested another. 'We want them to get this experience before they go to the mission field.'[113] By 1926 the college was sending out no fewer than ten separate evangelistic teams, who spent several weeks in the summer cycling, or walking, around the counties of Sussex, Somerset, Dorset, Kent, Essex, Suffolk, Surrey, Oxford and Cambridge.[114]

This pattern of weekly ministry during term time and involvement in missions, camps and evangelistic treks in the holidays, continued in the years preceding and following the war. The move of the college to Ealing brought new opportunities for ministry within the local community. As the number of Asian immigrants grew in that part of London, the students at Mount Hermon were able to become acquainted with the religions and cultures that they would encounter overseas.[115]

The most significant development in the area of practical ministerial training was the introduction by Miss Foote of block placements. Third year students were sent out for a period of several months to gain more in-depth experience in Christian ministry. They were usually attached to an Anglican parish, or a church of another denomination, rather than to a parachurch organisation. While this kind of in-service training was common in Bible colleges in America at this time, Mount Hermon was one of the first colleges to introduce it in Britain.

3.4.4 Academic study

The detailed description of a typical week, described in the January 1930 issue of *Missions Review,* gives an overall picture of the content and balance of subjects in the curriculum.[116]

Much time was devoted to biblical and theological studies. These were recognised as providing the essential foundation for missionary work. The students had to know what they believed, and to be familiar with the biblical text. There was a strong emphasis on the inspiration and authority of Scripture. The course on archaeology and the Bible emphasised the reliability of the biblical text.[117]

Church history and the history of missions were also taught. Students were expected to know the main events in the developments of the Christian Church and the reasons which had led to its many divisions. They were encouraged to learn from the successes and failures of the generations of missionaries who had

111. *MRAN* 77 (April 1925), p. 25.
112. *Ibid.*
113. *Ibid.*
114. *MRAN* 88(June 1927), p. 201.
115. Sally Stringer, 'Southall India group activities', in: *Outgoings* 13:2 (1962), p. 16.
116. A summary of that curriculum is given in appendix 3.
117. J. Sayer, *Constructive criticism* (lecture notes, 1934).

preceded them. In addition they were given a course on comparative religion to enable them to understand the worldview of those among whom they would work. The second principal, Miss Crocker, was concerned that her students should 'understand the Eastern mind.'[118] Over the years, more time was given to the study of different worldviews and the major religions of Hinduism, Islam and Buddhism. In the aftermath of the Second World War, the students also studied Communism, Nazism and Fascism.[119] Miss Foote was particularly anxious to expand the horizons of the students. 'Ethics, apologetics, other religions and anthropology may sound academic to the uninitiated, but are indispensable if we are to communicate the gospel intelligibly to those whose thought and culture patterns are so foreign to our own.'[120]

The importance of effective communication was acknowledged, so lectures were given on how to preach and teach. Students were required to give a sermon or talk to their peers, and then their presentation was constructively criticised.[121] In 1958, a course on journalism was introduced.[122] Lectures were also given on first aid, nursing, hygiene, motor mechanics,[123] cookery, book-keeping, dress-making and typewriting.[124]

Surprisingly, the curriculum contained a series of lectures on English literature. It is uncertain whether this was included to improve the students' general overall education or to equip them with knowledge which they could pass on to their converts. If it was the latter, it would seem that the students were being encouraged to pass on their culture as well as their faith.

3.4.5 Conclusion

It is not possible to do justice in a few pages to a programme that spanned sixty years and inevitably went through a number of changes and developments. But while the details of the programme changed, as subjects were added or discarded, the holistic emphasis of the training was maintained.

First, the development of the spiritual life was given priority. This was reflected in the timetable, and was emphasised in worship, in lectures and in official publications.

Secondly, the transformation of the character was set before the students as a sine qua non of effective service. This was communicated to the students as much through the lives of the staff as through their words. It was their personal integrity, their genuine love for people, the sincerity and reality of their Christian faith, as much as their instruction, which impacted the lives of those who knew them and studied under them. It was their lives that were remembered long after their lessons

118. Miss I. Crocker, 'Principal's Report', in: *MRANs* 105 (January 1931), p. 34.
119. B.J. Fraser, 'The Christian answer to Communism, Nazism and Fascism', in: *Outgoings* 5:3 (1945), p. 3.
120. Miss Foote, 'Principals' letter', in: *Outgoings* (1968), p. 4.
121. Miss I. Crocker, 'Principal's Report', in: *MRANs* 136 (February 1937), p. 80.
122. Dorothy Moreton, 'Journalism', in: *Outgoings* 9:3 (1958), p. 6-8.
123. *Outgoings* 7:15 (1956), p. 6.
124. *Outgoings* 8:4 (1957), p. 2.

were forgotten. It was their example rather than their erudition that left the most permanent impression.

Thirdly, the students were given opportunities to gain experience in Christian ministry and develop their gifts of communication, through work among the poor in inner city London, through weekly ministry in local churches, or through evangelistic treks and camps held during the vacations. Miss Foote felt that this training was inadequate and introduced block placements, so that students could gain a more realistic picture of the challenges of regular ministry.

Fourthly, a considerable proportion of the training programme was devoted to academic study. Students were required to attend two or three lectures each morning. Initially, a relatively narrow range of subjects were covered and many of the missiological issues raised in international missionary conferences were not addressed. The strong doctrinal position taken by the college tended to discourage a thorough examination of alternative views. The horizons of the students were not always sufficiently stretched and their presuppositions were not adequately challenged.

Miss Foote was not happy with the inadequacies and limitations of the academic course. She introduced a range of new subjects into the curriculum which she saw as essential components of a contemporary and relevant missionary training programme. She reacted strongly against the traditional approach of the college, which presented only one point of view, feeling that it was important for students to hear a number of perspectives. She encouraged discussion, and challenged students to think through issues for themselves.

One of the accusations levelled against Bible colleges at the Edinburgh Conference was that the academic standards were low.[125] This could be said of Mount Hermon in its early years. The residential staff did not have theological qualifications, though many of the visiting lecturers were well qualified in their fields. By the time of the merger in 1971, standards had risen considerably. The academic qualifications of tutorial staff had increased, and a number of students were being prepared for external academic awards.

3.5 The students

Most of those who studied at Mount Hermon in the years before the Second World War came from the United Kingdom or continental Europe, though a few came from further afield. In April 1925, when there were 74 students[126] at the college, Miss Whitfield wrote they came from 'Sweden, Denmark, Belgium, France, Switzerland, Germany, Russia, Canada, Ireland, Scotland, Wales and England.'[127] In subsequent years, students also came from as far afield as China, Estonia and Norway,[128] Latvia, Poland and British Honduras.[129]

125. World Missionary Conference, *Report of Commission V* (1910), p. 89.
126. The normal age for admission to the college was between the ages of 18 and 28, according to the 1925 college brochure, p. 3.
127. Miss E. Whitefield, 'Principal's report', in: *MRANs* 80 (November 1925), p. 78.
128. Miss I. Crocker, 'Principal's letter', in: *MRANs* 129 (August 1935), p. 334.
129. 'The fruit of a woman's indomitable courage', in: *Life of Faith*, February 23, 1938, p. 168.

When they had completed their training, most students proceeded to their country of service immediately, or in a short space of time. With reference to the eighteen students who left in September 1924, Miss Whitfield wrote that 'fourteen expect to be on the field by the end of the year, two are going into home ministry and two will complete further medical training before they proceed overseas.'[130]

According to statistics presented by Miss Crocker at the annual rally held in the Central Hall, Westminster, in 1930, 64% of the 277 students who had trained at Mount Hermon were serving 'overseas on the mission field.'[131] One hundred were involved in Christian work in the United Kingdom.

There was enormous diversity in the countries of service, which included Mongolia, China, Japan, India, Burma, Tibet, Palestine, Egypt, Sudan, Morocco, Belgian Congo, Nigeria, Germany, Spain, Eastern Europe, Argentina, Peru, Colombia, Bolivia and Canada.

In the post-war years, most Mount Hermon students continued to go overseas as missionaries, but there were significant shifts in their countries of service, as is shown by figure 1. In the years 1948 to 1950, most students went to Africa or South Asia (particularly India), whereas twenty years later Europe and the Far East had become popular places of service.

	1948-1950 Students	1968-1970 Students
Africa	16	9
South Asia	16	6
Far East	2	10
Latin America	3	2
Europe	1	9

Figure 1 *Fields of service of Mount Hermon Students*

The students also served with a wide variety of mission organisations. These included denominational societies, like the Church Missionary Society, Bible Churchmen's Missionary Society, the South American Missionary Society, the Strict Baptist Mission etc., and interdenominational societies like the China Inland Mission, Africa Inland Mission, Sudan Interior Mission, Qua Iboe Mission, Japan Evangelistic Band, North Africa Mission, Heart of Africa Mission, Regions Beyond Missionary Union, Irish Church Missions, Unevangelised Fields Mission, etc. In the years before the merger, it is evident that the vast majority went out with interdenominational societies.

While many of those who trained at Mount Hermon were sent out to do general missionary work, a considerable number were trained as nurses or midwives. In one year, 1935, nearly a third of the students were nurses, and in the same year Miss Crocker could write, 'At present we have 26 girls either for General or Maternity training in various hospitals in London and the provinces.'[132]

130. 'Principal's report', in: *MRANs* 80 (November 1925), p. 74.
131. Miss I. Crocker, 'Report to the Annual Rally', in: *MRANs* 102 (May 1930), p. 168.
132. 'Principal's report', in: *MRANs* 126 (January 1935), p. 295.

The students at Mount Hermon were predominantly Caucasian, and exclusively evangelical. In the early years, they came from the United Kingdom and other European countries, though subsequently some were received from Africa, Asia and Latin America. They belonged to a variety of denominations but, by choosing this particular college, identified themselves with an evangelical expression of the Christian faith. When they left Mount Hermon, almost all of them chose to go overseas with a missionary society that held a similar doctrinal position.

The choice of mission agency revealed the close connection between the college and the faith missions movement. While a number of students went out with denominational (notably Anglican) societies, the majority chose to serve with interdenominational missions, most of which would be categorised as faith missions. Students chose these societies because they identified with their doctrinal position and their emphasis on evangelism. They were content with the level of Christian unity which they represented, a unity which was a spiritual bond between fellow believers. They often felt more at home within the limited ecumenicity of a faith mission than within their own denomination. As D. W. Bebbington expressed it: 'The various faith missions provided an outlet for separatist tendencies without disturbing the peace of the existing denominations.'[133]

The choice of fields of service indicated the changes that were taking place with the ending of the colonial era and the beginning of the post-colonial period. In the days of the British Empire a large number of students from colleges like MHMTC had found opportunities for missionary service within its colonies and dominions. Even as late as 1950, almost 80% of Mount Hermon alumnae went to countries in Africa (Egypt, Sudan, Nigeria etc.,) or South Asia (India and Burma), which had been under British rule. Twenty years later, less than 50% were sent to Africa or South Asia. The former colonies were not always well disposed towards missionaries, whose nationality identified them with a former colonial power. Western agencies had to seek for new opportunities for missionary service, and in many cases they found them in the Far East and in Europe.

3.6 Conclusion

Mount Hermon was founded only a year after the Edinburgh Conference. Yet it is remarkable that in all the college archives and journals, there is not a single reference to the Edinburgh Conference, the International Missionary Council or the International Review of Missions. This is all the more surprising since the conferences of the IMC were considering precisely those issues being addressed at colleges like Mount Hermon. Even in the earliest days of the IMC, it appears that the kind of evangelicals who were involved in Mount Hermon were intrinsically suspicious or ignorant of the ecumenical movement. Yet many of the members of their Board belonged to denominations that were fully involved in that incipient movement,

---

133. D.W. Bebbington, *Evangelicalism in modern Britain: a history from the 1730s to the 1980s* (1989), p. 225.

and many of the Mount Hermon students went out with missions that were members of the Conference of British Missionary Societies, a division of the British Council of Churches.

The influence of the faith missions movement is seen not only in the financial policy adopted by the college but also in this antipathy towards the ecumenical movement. Like the faith missions, the college paid little attention to the doctrine of the church or the desirability of visible unity. The Keswick Convention gave opportunities for Christians from different denominations to worship God together and faith missions provided them with an avenue for service together, so they saw little need for any further expressions of unity, especially not with those whom seemed to be moving away from the basic tenets of the Christian faith.

This antagonism towards the ecumenical movement, and towards Christians of other traditions was not shared by all the staff of the college or all the members of the management committee. Miss Foote, in particular, was at pains to encourage students to work alongside Christians from different denominations, and to appreciate the strengths of different traditions. One of the chairmen of the management committee, Canon Alan Neech, general secretary of an evangelical Anglican missionary society, also served for three years as Chairman of the Conference of British Missionary Societies.

Mount Hermon inevitably reflected the culture of British society at the beginning of the twentieth century. In its rules and regulations it bore a striking resemblance to private boarding schools. Britain still claimed an Empire that spread around the globe. The style of leadership and the attitudes towards people of other races resembled those of the colonial era.

There was a tendency to confuse British civilisation with the Christian faith, and to assume that the British way of doing things was the right way. Insufficient attention was paid in the college curriculum to the importance of understanding and appreciating the culture and worldview of other peoples. In the early years of the college's life, the only course that dealt with this aspect of missionary preparation was a course on world religions, but even here the emphasis seemed to be on showing what was defective in the other belief system rather than on trying to understand and appreciate its strengths. This was a serious defect in the college programme and one that could have been corrected if the staff had been more conversant with the deliberations of the IMC and the CWME, where issues of cultural sensitivity were frequently discussed.

When Mrs Fraser was appointed as principal, she had the advantage of many years experience as a missionary in China. She was aware of the rapidly changing situation in the world, as the process of decolonization gathered momentum. She was also aware of the changes that were necessary in the college programme to prepare students to face new challenges, but her ability to effect change was hindered by the antagonism of the staff and her own failing health.

Miss Foote had an equal appreciation of the changes that were needed in a post-colonial era and was able to build her own staff team to implement them. She addressed issues of attitude and of curriculum content. She realised that students must be sent out, not with an air of racial or cultural superiority, but with a willingness to be servants of the national church. In that respect Miss Foote was in step with the thinking expressed at Tambaram (38), Willingen (52) and Ghana (57/58). She increased the number of courses dealing with world religions and culture, and widened the students' horizons with courses on ethics, apologetics and world affairs. Like Gwenyth Hubble, she recognised that most missionary candidates did not know enough about the world in general let alone that part of the world in which they hoped to serve.

One of the major criticisms levelled against Bible Colleges at the Edinburgh Conference of 1910 was that the training they offered was often weak academically and far below the standard of a university education. During much of its history, the same criticism could be made of Mount Hermon. The academic standards was low and the students were not sufficiently challenged to think through wider contemporary missiological issues.

There was not always agreement about the balance that should be maintained between the practical and the academic side of the training. By 1960, the Management Committee felt that the academic side received too little attention, and that was gradually corrected by Mrs Fraser and Miss Foote.

Those who taught at the college exhibited both faith and dedication. They were committed to an evangelical understanding of biblical truth and exhibited a strong faith in God who had called them into this ministry. They believed in the power of prayer, making it the focal point of college life. They taught the students by example that the only way Christian ministry could be carried out effectively was through dependence on God, who is totally trustworthy.

The staff at Mount Hermon aimed to provide holistic and practical missionary training. Their emphasis on the building of character and the development of the spiritual life provided a good preparation for the rigours and pressures of missionary life. It can be said that those who leaving Mount Hermon were much better equipped for their missionary task than those who had not had the benefit of such training.

The record of the college is adequate testimony to its effectiveness. More than 1200 young women were trained at Mount Hermon and sent out into every corner of the world to serve in the name of Christ. Only a small percentage of the graduates remained in their home country after completing their training. Many who went out from Mount Hermon achieved distinction in their field of service. Many worked as missionaries for more than forty years. Several died as martyrs for their faith. Miss Whitfield may not have been able to go out as a missionary herself, but as a result of her initiative, many others were enabled and equipped to go in her place.

4. Ridgelands Bible College (1919-1971)

4.1 Introduction

Mount Hermon Missionary Training College and Ridgelands Bible College were both founded in the second decade of the present century, the former just before the beginning of the first World War, the latter just after its conclusion. Both were established in South London as evangelical interdenominational colleges to prepare women, primarily from the United Kingdom, for mission service at home and abroad. There were, inevitably, similarities in their ethos and programme. At the same time, there were significant differences in the emphases of the training given and the social and educational background from which their students came.

The purpose of this chapter is to examine the distinctives of Ridgelands Bible College (RBC), through an examination of its history from its foundation in 1919 to its amalgamation with MHMTC and ANBC in 1971 (4.2), its doctrinal position and character (4.3), the components of its training programme (4.4) and the constitution of its student body (4.5).

4.2 Foundation and history

The name of Mrs Howard Hooker is synonymous with that of Ridgelands Bible College. It was as a result of her vision and drive that the college came into being. Together with her husband, she served as co-principal from 1919 to 1923, and after his untimely death she continued as principal for a further 38 years. She retired in 1961, and for the next ten years the college was led first by Mrs Molly MacKenzie and then by Miss Daphne Johnson.

4.2.1 Mrs Mary Howard Hooker (1919-1961)[1]

Mary Reader Harris (1881-1965) was the eldest daughter of an eminent Christian lawyer. After leaving school, she attended the Royal Academy of Music to study the organ and elocution. Influenced by her parents' Christian commitment, she became involved in a variety of mission and evangelistic activities. She led open-air services in Battersea, London, and helped in religious conventions in many parts of the country. In 1905, she married an able young solicitor, James Ayerst Howard Hooker, who was a parliamentary agent and junior partner in the firm of Wyatt and Co.[2] He identified with his wife's concerns and encouraged her in the development of her ministry. They had two children: Kenneth, who was subsequently ordained into

1. Although her own name, after marriage, was Mary Hooker, she is always known as Mrs Howard Hooker.
2. Christine I. Tinling, *Ridgelands calling!*, (1933), p. 16.

the Anglican ministry, and gave the address at the final garden party of RBC in 1971; and Joan, who married the renowned Bible teacher, Dr Graham Scroggie.

Initially, Mrs Hooker had no thoughts of starting a ladies' training college, but a number of factors led her in that direction. First, she desired to share the gospel with those around her and to see others trained to do the same. Secondly, she was a gifted teacher and, at a relatively young age, she taught at the Bible College at Clapham Common, which was led by the Rev. Oswald Chambers. In 1911, she began lecturing on one book of the Bible each week and making blackboard outlines for the help of the students.[3] Thirdly, she was interested in the world mission of the church and served on the Candidates' Committee of the Zenana Bible and Medical Mission (ZBMM)[4]. Along with other members of that committee, she soon became aware of the inadequate preparation provided for educated young women going to the mission field.

In response to a request from the committee, she began to look for suitable courses of biblical studies for their candidates. When she was unable to find anything suitable, she wondered whether 'she ought to do something to provide it.'[5] So, in October 1917, she opened the Church Workers' Training School at Tothill Street, Westminster.

By the end of the first term, students were asking to be taken into residence. Initially two students, Miss J. Leak and Miss E. Page, came to stay in Mr and Mrs Hooker's home in Wimbledon. After their period of training, they went to India as missionaries.

When the house opposite their own home in Wimbledon became vacant, it was rented as a hostel to meet the growing need for student accommodation. The furniture and funds were provided by Christian friends.[6] Within a year the house was full, but by that time a larger need had become apparent.

Members of the ZBMM and other missions still felt that more thorough training was needed. They were looking for 'a more organised training course to meet the requirements of their candidates'[7], and they believed that this kind of training could only be provided in a larger residential college.

Mr and Mrs Hooker began to wonder if God was calling them to establish such an institution, 'to give up the privacy of their home and live with the students under the same roof.'[8] It was a difficult decision to make, as it was for all those who pursued the ideal of residential missionary training. C. Tinling, who wrote the story of the early years of the college, commented: 'The thought of institutional life was not congenial to them, and one can well understand that it was positively repellent to the busy lawyer who prized the sacredness and quietness of his home.'[9] Another factor for consideration was what effect such a step might have on their children, when they discovered that they were expected to share their parents with others.

3. *Ibid.*
4. Now InterServe.
5. Tinling, p. 17.
6. Mrs Howard Hooker, 'The quarry', in: *RCR* 2 (1925), p. 4.
7. *Ibid.*
8. Tinling, p. 18.
9. *Ibid.*

At about this time, a close friend, who had provided the finances for the opening of the hostel, announced that he had found an ideal house for a permanent college. On his recommendation, Mr and Mrs Hooker went to view the property and discovered that it was, as he had said, exactly suited to their needs. The same friend then offered to provide the rent for the first three years. On the basis of this promise and with the encouragement of several praying friends, the Hookers invited a select number to join a small college council and Ridgelands Bible College was formed. The first group of fifteen students entered the college in September 1919.[10]

The house had been taken on a three years' agreement with the option of purchase within twelve months at a price of £10,000.[11] Soon after the college was opened, a day of prayer was held when staff and students focused on the financial needs of the college. 'Within 24 hours, the sum of three thousand pounds had poured in.'[12] Many others gave generously and it became clear 'that they were being guided towards the purchase of the freehold.'[13] Ten days before the final payment was due, the college received an interest free loan of £2,000 which provided them with the requisite total.

After these initial encouragements in the early days of Ridgelands, it came as an enormous shock to the college and its supporters when Mr Hooker died suddenly in 1923. Although he had a full-time job as a solicitor in the city, he had served as the honorary secretary of the college and provided able legal advice. Every morning before departing for his office, he would lead family prayers for the college community. He also gave generously to the work of the college. His death was a personal tragedy for Mrs Hooker, depriving her of her closest supporter and adviser. 'Not only to his own family, but to the College, it was a crushing blow and at first it looked as though everything must cease and the work, so happily begun, must be given up. To Mrs Hooker it was like building a wonderful castle and having it knocked down again. Yet out of that trouble there came a stronger building and a deeper knowledge of God and his divine supplies.'[14]

The newly established college faced other crises. The general depression which affected the British economy in the late 1920s and early 1930s caused a decrease both in financial support and in the number of applicants. The possibility of closing the college was considered and a potential buyer came to view the house. News of the impending sale was shared at a reunion of former students and urgent prayer was offered that Ridgelands might remain open. The crisis passed. The prospective purchaser wrote to say that she was no longer interested in the property and the number of applications increased gradually until the house was full again.

The threat of war in 1938 again raised the question of the future of the college. Mrs Hooker wrote, 'At the end of September, when the war crisis suddenly appeared, it seemed as though the college had finished its work. Present students rang

10. Mrs H. Hooker, 'Ridges and furrows', in: *RCR* 2 (1926), p. 1.
11. Tinling, p. 20.
12. *Ibid.*, p. 22.
13. *Ibid.*
14. *Ibid.*, p. 25.

up to say that they felt they must join national emergency units of various kinds, and we were asked if Ridgelands could be mobilised as a hospital.'[15]

The following year Ridgelands did close, but only for four years. In 1943, it reopened on a new site in Bexley, Kent. For the next eighteen years, Mrs Hooker remained as principal with Miss Burton as vice-principal. Mrs Hooker was 80 when she eventually retired in 1961. Even then, neither she nor Miss Burton were convinced that the time had come for them to leave. Miss Burton wrote to the council, saying that 'she and Mrs Hooker were retiring only because it was the wish of the council and not because they had God's guidance to do so.'[16] A few months later, partly because of a bout of ill-health, Mrs Hooker had evidently changed her mind. She wrote to the council, expressing her conviction that 'from recent events, the present condition of her health and the doctor's advice, she and Mrs Burton felt sure they were in the will of God in tending their resignation.'[17]

After Mrs Hooker left, the college could never be quite the same. She had founded Ridgelands and served as principal over a period of forty two years. She dedicated her whole life to the training of young women for Christian service. As Mildred Cable, the pioneer missionary to China and Turkestan and President of RBC, wrote: 'Mrs Howard Hooker and her staff have brought all the experience of the years and their personal love and devotion to Christ, and placed them at the disposal of younger women.'[18]

Mrs Hooker was deeply committed to providing the best possible all-round training for her students. She was quick to offer encouragement, but 'never let us get away with second best.'[19] She was a gifted expositor of the Scriptures, and lived out in her personal life what she taught in the classroom. 'She was a very gracious and godly lady,' said one of her former students, 'who led by example.'[20] At the same time she was a strong leader, authoritarian in her style of leadership, and somewhat regal in her manner. She inspired both awe and respect among her students.

During her principalship, Mrs Hooker was ably supported by Miss Dorothy Burton. Miss Burton, a former student of RBC, served on the staff as a lecturer from 1921 and as vice-principal from 1943. Trained as a Froebel teacher, she was an able communicator, whose lectures combined systematic analysis of the biblical text with practical contemporary application. She maintained good contact with a class, and would often catch someone's eye to check that they were still listening. She was approachable, and 'always had time for people, inviting them round for tea, even though she was very busy.'[21]

The words of one former student reflect the feelings of many: 'She was the heart of the college. She was a brilliant lecturer and a woman who listened to God. I

15. Mrs H. Hooker, 'The Principal's letter', in: *RCR* 13 (1938), p. 3.
16. Minutes of the Executive Committee of RBC, June 23 1960.
17. Minutes of the Executive Committee of RBC, October 28 1960.
18. A. Mildred Cable, in the foreword to Christine Tinling's, *Ridgelands calling!* (1933), p. 5.
19. Josephine Mary Haslam Jones (née Stancliffe), student 1950-1, in college survey, March 1997.
20. Rosemary Corfe, student 1961-3, in college survey, March 1997.
21. Margaret Wynne (née Ellis), in college survey, March 1997.

immensely admired her love and loyalty to Mrs Hooker and her humility in accepting some things that would have been different if she had been in charge. She had the immense gift of playing second fiddle excellently.'[22] Mrs Daphne Harman[23] was particularly impressed with 'her prayer life and the resultant power in her unfolding of each book of the Bible.' It was also said of Miss Burton that 'she was such an attractive Christian.'[24]

4.2.2 Mrs Molly MacKenzie (1961-1966)

Molly Hill was born in Kenya in 1909. At the age of one and a half she was sent back to England, where she grew up on her grandfather's estate in Shropshire. She was educated at home by a governess and then spent one year at Malvern Ladies College. At the age of 18, she returned to Kenya, where her father was serving as Minister of Agriculture.[25]

Her family were wealthy and influential. Molly had everything she could wish for in material terms, but spiritually she had very little to encourage her.[26] The social round of parties, shows and big-game safaris soon lost their attraction. She used to go to her room at night and cry out, 'there must be more to life than this.'[27]

On September 19th 1931, she was invited by a friend to attend the Nairobi Keswick Convention. Until this point, Molly had had scant regard for missionaries. 'She had been brought up to regard all missionaries as a nuisance, people who were a disturbing factor in African life.'[28] But on that providential evening, she felt God speaking to her directly. 'She knew she was filled with the love of Jesus. For hours that night she praised God with hands upraised.'[29] On the next evening, she felt God calling her to be a missionary. Alfred Buxton invited her to join a pioneer group to open up the Northern Frontier Province of Kenya. The Rev. Barclay Buxton offered her training at Dalton House, the college for women that had been founded by the Bible Churchmen's Missionary Society's (BCMS)[30]. In 1934, she went to Ethiopia with BCMS. In 1935, she married another BCMS missionary, Colin MacKenzie. She remained in Ethiopia until 1952, serving under the leadership of Alfred Buxton, the son-in-law of C. T. Studd and brother of Captain Godfrey Buxton, who founded the Missionary Training Colony.

Mrs MacKenzie returned to the United Kingdom for her son to complete his adult education. At the same time, Mildred Cable invited her to join the Bible Society as area Secretary for the six West Midlands counties. In 1961, she was invited to succeed Mrs Hooker as principal of RBC. She was to remain in this position until 1966.

---

22. Rachel Jackson, (née Salmon), student 1955-7, in college survey March 1997.
23. Mrs Daphne Harman (née Johnson) was a student at RBC from 1952-4 and principal from 1966-71.
24. Mrs Daphne Harman (née Johnson), correspondence, October 15th, 1997.
25. From personal correspondence, October 15th, 1997.
26. Peter Hocken, 'The unquenched spirit in Molly MacKenzie', in: *Renewal* (June, 1994), p. 12.
27. Interview with Mrs Molly MacKenzie, August 9th, 1997.
28. Peter Hocken, 'The unquenched spirit in Molly MacKenzie', in: *Renewal* (June, 1994), p. 12.
29. *Ibid.*
30. Now Crosslinks.

Mrs MacKenzie had a magnetic personality, attracting an increasing number of students to the college 'from all strata of society including some from Africa.'[31] Under her energetic leadership, Ridgelands began to take on a new lease of life. As the number of students began to increase, the lecture hall had to be extended. The academic level of the teaching was raised and more students were encouraged to sit for the Certificate of Religious Knowledge (CRK), awarded by Cambridge University.

She was a gifted Bible teacher with a strong ministry of encouragement, and a deep concern that each student might reach her greatest potential.[32] She was also determined that those who trained at the college should be prepared for the rigours and difficulties of missionary life, with which she herself was so familiar. She wanted to prepare people who were 'tough', who could stand when others might be tempted to give up. 'Better to lose people here than on the mission field.'[33]

Mrs MacKenzie impressed the students with 'her devotion to the Lord and her burning concern for evangelism.'[34] This enthusiasm for evangelism, together with her concern for world mission, made a deep effect on many students, and an increasing number of students decided to become missionaries and work overseas. 'She was a dynamic, inspirational leader and, as an evangelist herself, she taught us a lot about personal evangelism and practical missionary training.'[35]

In 1964, six students were sent to an Anglican church in Farnborough to take part in a Sunday School teachers' week-end. In this particular parish, 'some 75 people had been baptised in the Spirit.'[36]. The effect of this weekend on the six students from Ridgelands was quite dramatic. They experienced a radical spiritual renewal and returned to the college in a state of great excitement and spiritual enthusiasm. Many years later, Mrs MacKenzie could still recall the amazing transformation that was evident in them: 'They came back completely alive; it was a wonderful thing to see them completely changed.'[37] Mrs MacKenzie's own experience at the time of her conversion, some forty years earlier, enabled her to appreciate the importance and reality of what had taken place in her students.

The council were concerned at this whole episode, because the experience of these students appeared to contradict the traditional teaching of the college on the work of the Holy Spirit. Council members were also aware that a number of splits had occurred in churches up and down the country as a direct result of this charismatic teaching. They also felt that Mrs MacKenzie was too sympathetic towards this new movement and had not dealt with the issue as forcefully as the situation required.

At about the same time, the chairman of the executive council had received reports of serious complaints concerning the administration of the college. Together with a small group of council members, he held a meeting with the staff, who ex-

31. Shirley Crook, student 1962-4, correspondence, October 16th, 1997.
32. Shirley Crook, student 1962-4, in college survey, March 1997.
33. Interview with Mrs Molly MacKenzie, August 9 1997.
34. Victoria Schian (née Lampert), student 1961-3, in college survey, March 1997.
35. Catherine Ranger (née Mathers), student 62-64, in college survey, March 1997.
36. Peter Hocken, 'The unquenched spirit in Molly MacKenzie', in: *Renewal* (June, 1994), p. 13.
37. *Ibid.*

pressed a number of concerns. They felt that the principal was a perfectionist, who expected impossibly high standards and criticised those who did not achieve them. They also felt that she did not delegate responsibility to others, and assumed pastoral care for all the students herself. When the chairman spoke privately to the principal, she 'immediately confessed to having kept all the responsibility in her own hands and tried to maintain the highest standards at the college in her own strength.'[38]

Having listened to both sides, the members of council reached the conclusion that the principal was a perfectionist who had an authoritarian style of leadership and found it difficult to tolerate the slightest imperfection. They also recognised that she was suffering from extreme exhaustion. They recommended that Mrs MacKenzie 'should be immediately released from all responsibilities of the college in order to take a prolonged leave-of-absence till the end of the academic year when the matter of the Principalship would be reviewed again.'[39].

Mrs Mackenzie left RBC in February 1966. She still hoped that she might be able to return to her position as principal of the college, but the council felt that that would be unwise. They expressed their appreciation for all that she had done for the college during her period of leadership.

4.2.3 Miss Daphne Johnson (1966-1971)

After the departure of Mrs MacKenzie, Edith Owers, a former missionary and RBC student, took over the temporary leadership of the college. She ran RBC for a few months with the assistance of Elizabeth Horsford, until Miss Daphne Johnson (b. 1927) was appointed as the new principal.

After completing her teacher training, Miss Johnson had taught for three years, before going to Ridgelands for a period of missionary training. She had not been called for interview prior to her acceptance at the college, and on her arrival at Ridgelands, she fell in love with the place: 'It exuded a sense of order, quietness and ease, and confirmed to me that this was God's place for me.'[40] Over the next two years, she particularly appreciated the way in which the whole of Monday morning was devoted to worship and meditation.

When she completed her training in 1952, she expected to serve as a missionary with the South Africa General Mission (SAGM). Instead, she was asked to work in the British headquarters of that society. Seven years as Youth Secretary were followed by seven years as Prayer Secretary. During that time she was able to spend six months visiting all the SAGM fields.

Before her appointment as the new principal of RBC, Miss Johnson expressed her views about the ethos of RBC and the nature of its training. The minutes of the Council record: 'She felt that the only preparation necessary for Christian service was devotional. She was not at all keen on CRK, much less on the Diploma of Theology, as she felt that these could be taken at other colleges.'[41]

38. Minutes of the Executive Council, January 30 1966.
39. *Ibid.*
40. Interview with Mrs Daphne Harman, June 11 1996.
41. Minutes of the Executive Council, June 5 1966.

Significantly, the executive council endorsed her view both of the college and the nature of its training. It was stated in the minutes that 'Ridgelands' emphasis had always been on the study of the Bible, and the devotional life. It was not a missionary training college, although many of the students went to the mission field after their training. It was felt that CRK should be subsidiary rather than primary on the syllabus.'[42]

Miss Johnson was a very different personality from her predecessor. She showed a quiet enthusiasm and gentle godliness. She liked things to be done in an orderly manner and wanted to restore a sense of peace and order in the college. She felt that the atmosphere of the college had become rather intense, and wanted to help the students to learn to relax.[43]

She was thirty nine at the time of her appointment. In the words of one former student, 'she commanded respect in spite of her youthfulness and was approachable. She encouraged one by her own example to desire a deeper relationship with Jesus.'[44] She was a capable leader who 'would speak privately in a firm but understanding manner on issues of discipline.'[45]

She served as principal for five years during which time a number of students continued to work overseas to serve as missionaries. From 1967 to 1970, Miss Johnson had the help of a vice-principal, Miss Margaret Manton, who had served for five years on the faculty of the London Bible College. Miss Manton was 'a great gift to college life with her academic expertise, outstanding gift of teaching, plus a sense of humour.'[46]

When the possibility of a merger of several Bible colleges was first raised, Daphne Johnson did not feel that it was right for RBC to become involved. She expressed her opinion very forcibly to the Council. She pointed out that RBC had a unique aim and therefore justified its existence in its present form. She argued that it provided a basic biblical training for those who had no specific calling overseas. She also believed that there was a place for a single sex college,[47] and that some women would value the opportunity to study and prepare for Christian service without having to cope with the distraction of male students. She was also particularly concerned for the number of women who married clergymen or missionaries 'without having any preparation to enable them to share in their husband's ministry or cope with the pressure they would inevitably face.'[48] She was not opposed to the merger of other colleges, but did not feel it was the right way forward for Ridgelands.

On January 29th 1969, the Council met to make a final decision on whether or not RBC should participate in the proposed federation of Bible Colleges. The chairman, Mr Leslie Lyall, commented that nearly all denominational and interdenomi-

42. *Ibid.*
43. Telephone conversation with Mrs Daphne Harman, August 10 1997.
44. Muriel Trayner (née Gooding), student 67-69, in college survey, March 1997.
45. *Ibid.*
46. Mrs Daphne Harman (née Johnson), correspondence, October 16 1997.
47. The college did rent outside accomodation for a few married couples – Mrs Molly MacKenzie, correspondence, October 16 1997.
48. Interview with Mrs Daphne Harman, June 11 1996.

national training colleges in the British Isles were now co-educational. He pointed out that as educational standards in Britain and overseas were continually rising, the demand for higher academic standards and more comprehensive training became increasingly apparent.[49] He also read out a letter from Mr. Godfrey Buxton, founder of the Missionary Training Colony and brother-in-law of Mrs Hooker, who warmly recommended the present proposals for the federation. Miss Johnson repeated her opposition to the scheme and expressed the view that the ever increasing size of training colleges and the growing extent of co-education pointed to the greater need for a small all-women's college. However, the majority of the council felt otherwise and passed the resolution 'that we agree in principle to join the proposed federation of Bible colleges.'[50]

On July 3rd 1971, the final Garden Party and Gift Day was held. The closing speaker was the Rev. Kenneth Hooker, son of the founder and first Principal. On July 31, Ridgelands Bible College in Bexley closed and became part of All Nations Christian College.

4.2.4 Conclusion

For all but ten of its fifty-two year history, Ridgelands was led by one remarkable woman, Mrs Howard Hooker. The story of the college is her story. It sprang out of her recognition of a need, it survived the tragedy of her husband's death, it thrived in the pre-war years and declined with her failing health. The fortunes of the college were temporarily revived with the coming of Mrs MacKenzie and Miss Johnson. Towards the end of the sixties it became increasingly apparent that the future of the college lay not in maintaining its separate identity, but in pooling its resources with other colleges to create a larger, more viable institution.

The three principals of RBC differed considerably in their personalities and their styles of leadership. Mrs Hooker was authoritarian in her teaching, gracious in her personal conduct. An impressive and awe-inspiring lady, she provided a model of how a Christian lady should conduct herself. Mrs MacKenzie attracted people through her own personal charisma and zeal for evangelism. She was a perfectionist, whose demands for the highest standards for herself and her staff resulted ultimately in her own exhaustion and their criticism of her leadership. Miss Johnson was less authoritarian in her style of leadership. She led by example rather than by dictat, creating a sense of order and harmony in the community.

The principals differed also in their perception of the college's role. Mrs Hooker was initially inspired to establish the college to provide training for missionaries going overseas, yet from the start the college prepared candidates for Christian service both at home and abroad. Whatever their future field of service, Mrs Hooker made sure that all her students had a vision for the needs of the whole world. When Mrs MacKenzie became principal, she laid greater stress on the needs of the overseas mission field and, during her time, a higher proportion of RBC alumnae went

49. Minutes of the Executive Council, January 29 1969.
50. *Ibid.*

overseas. Miss Johnson did not see the college primarily as a missionary training institution, though she recognised that a number of students did become missionaries. She was particularly concerned with the preparation of the future wives of ministers and (Anglican) clergy, seeing that as one of the unique roles that the college could perform.

There was a further difference of opinion in the importance that each principal attached to academic study. Mrs Hooker advocated a devotional approach to Scripture. She wanted her students to know the text of the Bible and to apply its truth to their own lives and their relationship with God. Mrs MacKenzie had discovered from her time as a missionary in Africa that a more academic approach to the Bible was necessary, especially for those planning to work among university students. She consequently encouraged students to sit for the CRK exam. Her successor, Miss Johnson, disagreed. She felt that RBC should concentrate on the devotional approach, and that students, wanting an academic qualification could find it through other Bible colleges.

4.3 Doctrinal basis and character

Ridgelands was founded to provide 'clear teaching of the Bible from the standpoint that the Scriptures *are* the inspired record of the revelation of God to man, not merely that they contain such.'[51] It was strongly influenced by the Keswick Convention particularly with regard to its teaching on sanctification. The college sought to train women for Christian service at home and overseas[52] and to equip them with 'practical instruction in the work of soul-winning, public speaking, personal work, open-air meetings, visiting etc.'[53]

4.3.1 Doctrinal basis

The theological stance of the college was set out in the Declaration of Faith (1919), read out by the chairman of the Board on the annual Commemoration Day, and signed by every Trustee and member of the Executive Council had on a yearly basis. The opening paragraph of this declaration read:

> We believe in the Scriptures of the Old and New Testaments as fully inspired of God and verbally inerrant in the original writings, and that they are of supreme and final authority in faith and life.[54]

This commitment to a conservative view of the Bible was maintained throughout the history of the college. When Mrs MacKenzie became principal in 1961, the college brochure asserted that the basis of the teaching at Ridgelands remained

51. Mrs H Hooker, 'The quarry', in: *RCR* 1 (1924), p. 3.
52. Christine Tinling, *Ridgelands Calling* (1933), p. 16.
53. *Ibid.*, p. 4.
54. 'Commemoration Day' in: *RCR* 1 (1924), p. 12.

'one of belief in the full inspiration of the Old and New Testaments as the supreme authority in faith and life.'[55]

The college aimed to provide clear systematic biblical teaching, and to nurture in every student a deep love for the Bible[56] and a confidence in its message. The students learned relatively little about other views. Although a course was offered on biblical criticism, the aim seemed more to alert students to the errors of contemporary scholarship than to suggest any new insights they might gain from the perspectives of others. This antipathy towards liberal scholarship, characteristic of evangelicals during the first half of the twentieth century, must be understood in the light of the extreme views that dominated the wider theological world at that time. As H. H. Rowley commented on the state of Old Testament scholarship in the first half of this century: 'Towards the text of the Old Testament, there was a rooted suspicion, and commentators vied with one another in the ingenuity with which it was emended. Any guess was to be preferred to a text which was assumed to be untrustworthy.'[57]

Ridgelands was founded as an interdenominational institution, but in its early years it developed close associations with the Church of England. The majority of the board, a large proportion of the supporters and, in Mrs Hooker's day at least, the majority of the students were members of the established church. As one student wrote, 'The ethos was Anglican. Connections with the Brethren were discouraged.'[58] Among the courses taught at the college was one on the Book of Common Prayer.

In later years, a broader denominational representation was achieved at RBC. Students had the opportunity to understand different perspectives and appreciate alternative styles of worship. As one student expressed it, 'living with students from different traditions helped to knock some corners off our view that our denomination was right.'[59]

4.3.2 The second blessing

Like Mount Hermon, RBC was strongly influenced by the Keswick Convention. One aspect of Keswick teaching that was emphasised at the college was that of the 'second blessing.' The second blessing was thought of as a crisis experience through which Christians needed to go if they were to reach a higher level of sanctification.

This crisis experience involved three steps. First Christians must surrender their whole lives to Christ in an act of total consecration. They must be willing for Christ to be Lord of every area of their lives. Secondly, they must be filled with the Holy Spirit. They should not rely on their feelings but should simply trust that their prayer for the Spirit had been answered. Thirdly, they would then receive power for effective and victorious Christian living.

55. *College Brochure* (1961), p. 3.
56. Christine Tinling, *Ridgelands calling* (1933), p. 39.
57. H.H. Rowley, *The Old Testament and modern study* (1951), p. xv.
58. Elizabeth Curry, student 1957-9, in college survey, March 1997.
59. Josephine Mary Haslam Jones (née Stancliffe), student 1950-1, in college survey, March 1997.

This 'second blessing' was understood as a decisive crisis in the Christian life. It meant the start of life on a new spiritual plain, where complete victory over sin was achievable. This teaching sounded to many like a form of perfectionism. As M. Rowlandson commented: 'Some of Keswick's speakers came perilously close to teaching sinless perfection, but the majority followed the dictum of the French theological Theodore Monod (who spoke at Keswick): 'We ought not to sin, and we need not sin, but as a matter of fact we do sin''[60]

This teaching was promoted at RBC and all students were encouraged to seek the 'second blessing.' Many discovered a new depth in their spiritual lives through this experience, but others found it unhelpful and reacted against the dogmatic position the college held. When Meg Foote was approached about the possibility of becoming principal of RBC (before she had become principal of MHMTC), she declined on the grounds that she could not endorse this aspect of the college's teaching.[61]

4.3.3 A single sex college

Mrs Hooker recognised the need for gifted and well-educated women to be trained for Christian service and to be prepared for positions of leadership and responsibility both at home and overseas. She was aware of the spiritual needs in Britain and started her Church Workers' Training School in Tothill partly to train Bible teachers and church workers for the home country. At the same time, she was aware of the fact that many 'who had graduated as medical doctors, nurses or teachers were liable to be sent forth (as overseas missionaries) without any specific missionary training.'[62] Her association with the ZBMM Committee convinced her that those who were going to be sent overseas to face the rigours of Christian service must receive adequate preparation. Students were usually accepted between the ages of 21 and 30, though some exceptions were made to this rule. Most were well educated and had spent some years in professional work. They tended to come from wealthier families.

The purpose in providing training only for women was to spare them from the distraction of male fellow-students. For some who studied at RBC, this was seen as a distinct advantage. At least one student chose RBC 'to avoid hassle with boy friends.'[63] Others, however, felt that this was a weakness in the programme. 'Being a single sex college, it did not prepare you for working with male colleagues.'[64]

The question as to whether RBC should remain as a college for women was hotly debated when the possibility of a merger with ANBC was raised. Miss Johnson wanted the college to stay as a single sex institution. The council disagreed and the merger went ahead.

---

60. M. Rowlandson, *Life at the Keswick Convention: a personal recollection* (1997), p. 22.
61. Personal interview, July 14 1999.
62. Christine Tinling, *Ridgelands calling* (1933), p. 16.
63. Rosemary Corfe, student 1961-3, in college survey, March 1997.
64. Muriel Trayner (née Gooding), student 1967-69, in college survey, March 1997.

4.3.4 The art of soul-winning

The college prepared women for Christian service at home and overseas. A number went out with faith missions. D. W. Bebbington, commenting on the growth of these missions in his book *Evangelicalism in modern Britain,* writes that 'undenominational missionary colleges, such as All Nations and Ridgelands, sprang up to serve them (the faith missions).'[65] But whether students were preparing to remain in Britain or work abroad, it was Mrs Hookers' intention that the training they received should be practical. She was not interested in sending out those who had only a theoretical knowledge of Christian truth or who lacked the ability to communicate what they themselves believed. Consequently she placed great emphasis on practical training in every aspect of Christian ministry.

> People who do not win souls at home are not likely to be more successful abroad. No man or woman becomes automatically changed during a voyage to another land. We must give our candidates time to learn the wonderful art of soul-winning.[66]

The college brochure explained that training in evangelism and pastoral work was gained through such activities as campaigns, camps, missions, hospital visiting, house to house visitation and Sunday School teaching.[67]

4.3.5 Conclusion

Like Mount Hermon (MHMTC) and All Nations Bible College (ANBC), Ridgelands was committed to the inspiration and trustworthiness of the Bible. In reaction to the liberal theology that was prevalent in most universities and many denominational colleges, it was the intention of the founder and the board to provide teaching that accepted Scripture as the reliable and final authority for Christians in all matters of belief and conduct.

Like the other two colleges, RBC was heavily influenced by the teaching of the Keswick Convention. Where it differed from MHMTC and ANBC was in its strong advocacy of the doctrine of the 'second blessing.'

The expressed purpose of the college was to train 'educated' women for Christian service. In 1970, it was one of the few Bible colleges in the country that only accepted women. Opinion was divided as to the advantages and disadvantages of having a female college. In the end, contrary to the wishes of the last principal, the Council decided to abandon this aspect of the college ethos and to become part of a larger co-educational institution.

The strong emphasis on the art of soul-winning reflected an individualistic approach to mission that was characteristic of faith missions during this period. Mis-

65. D.W. Bebbington, *Evangelicalism in modern Britain* (1989), p. 225.
66. Mrs H. Hooker, in a paper read to the United Missionary Fellowship at the Mildmay Conference centre, quoted in *Ridgelands calling!* (1933), p. 27.
67. 'The aims and basis', in: *RBC Brochure* (1957), p. 2.

sion was understood almost exclusively in terms of personal evangelism, of one individual bringing another to personal faith in Christ. This could be described as an individual theology of mission.[68] Those who adopted this approach had little understanding of the role of the church or the place of social action in mission, other than as a preparation for evangelism.

4.4 The programme

The fullest account of the training provided at the college, at least in its early years, is given in three chapters of Christine Tinling's *Ridgelands calling!* (1933) and in an address given by Mrs Howard Hooker at a missionary convention.[69] The order in which the various aspects of college life are described in Tinling's book probably reflects the priority they were accorded. The deepening of the spiritual life and the development of character are considered first. This is followed by a discussion of the academic courses and the practical work in which students were involved.

4.4.1 The deepening of the spiritual life

The development of a strong devotional life was regarded as the most important component of the training at Ridgelands. 'The people who know their God shall be strong and do exploits,'[70] was the undergirding principle of the college.

Many former students expressed their appreciation of this dimension of the college's life. 'We had plenty of encouragement to develop our relationship with God.'[71] 'Our spiritual life was encouraged because there might be no spiritual props on the field.'[72] 'Mrs Hooker encouraged us to discover a deeper experience of the Holy Spirit without bringing any pressure to bear.'[73] 'There was a strong emphasis on personal and corporate devotion.'[74] 'The spiritual life was paramount and we were taught deep things beyond our experience, but later grew into them.'[75]

Every morning from 7.15 to 8.15 a.m. and every evening from 9.30 to 10.00 p.m., a period of silence was observed for personal devotions. The staff did not dictate to the students how they were to use this time, but they gave them 'the opportunity for quiet and a chance of forming the habit of prayer. For therein lies the chief secret of an effective life.'[76] For some, it was a new and strange experience to be confronted with long periods of silence. 'I was unused to these long

68. See J.A.B. Jongeneel, *Philosophy, science and theology of mission in the 19th and 20th centuries: Part 1* (1995), p. 162.
69. Christine Tinling, *Ridgelands calling!* (1933), pp. 27-32 and 39-51.
70. Daniel 11:32.
71. Margaret Butler, student 1960-2, in college survey, March 1997.
72. Shirley Crook, student 1962-4, in college survey, March, 1997.
73. Rachel Jackson (née Salmon), student 1955-7, in college survey, March 1997.
74. Valerie Collett, student 1956-8, in college survey, March 1997.
75. Mrs G.M. Forrest-Hall (née Martin-Harvey), student 1935-7, in college survey, March 1997.
76. Mrs H. Hooker, in: Christine Tinling's *Ridgelands calling!* (1933), p. 30.

times for prayer, and it was something of a shock to my system. I learned to get used to it, however.'[77]

The whole of Monday morning was set aside for corporate prayer, singing and Bible study. Tinling expresses her amazement that although this time of worship lasted a solid two hours and attendance was not obligatory, 'nobody wants to miss it, so the drawing room is packed.'[78]

The spiritual tone of the college was set not just by the structure of the day, the exposition of Scripture or the times of worship. It was the personal example of the staff, whose lives demonstrated devotion and commitment to God. 'I felt the staff were real people whose spirituality was caught as they shared in morning prayer.'[79] As one student said of Daphne Johnson, 'She encouraged me by her own example to desire a deeper relationship with Jesus.'[80]

4.4.2 Character training

Mrs Hooker was convinced that difficulties on the mission field were largely connected with the relationship between missionaries. Although the premature return of missionaries to their home country was officially attributed to a breakdown in health, she believed that 'it was often caused by friction and failure to live victoriously.'[81] Furthermore she argued:

> There is a great need for character training, but this is largely unrecognised. The candidate herself probably desires training, but not transformation. Unenlightened parents do not see what is lacking in their children and so fail to grasp the need for preparation.[82]

Mrs Hooker was also concerned at the unwillingness of missionary societies to invest adequate funds in the training of missionaries, and the undue haste with which they despatched new recruits to the field. She believed that such a policy was short-sighted, and its consequences potentially disastrous. She contended:

> Those who take the long view usually become convinced that preparation is worthwhile. Every candidate, whatever be her qualifications, needs to be tested out in community life. Character cannot be diagnosed in a hurry: sufficient time must be given, too, for the growing of new characteristics and this growth must be natural and not forced.[83]

Mrs Hooker suggested a number of questions that could be used as a guide in the evaluation of a student's character and personal development:

---

77. Anon, in college survey, March 1997.
78. *Ridgelands calling!* (1933), p. 32.
79. Hester Dain (née Quirk), student 1951-2, in college survey, March 1997.
80. Muriel Trayner (née Gooding), student 1967-9, in college survey, March 1997.
81. Mrs H. Hooker, quoted in C. Tinling's *Ridgelands calling!* (1933), p. 27.
82. *Ibid.*
83. *Ibid.*, p. 28.

> Is she loyal to recognised authority?
> Is she reliable or forgetful concerning allotted duties?
> What is her influence on her fellows: is it good, undesirable or negligible?
> Is she likely to develop gifts of leadership?
> Can she act wisely in the matter of blending official and personal relationships?
> Does she grumble or is she consistently cheerful when circumstances aretrying?
> Does she make friends easily or not? Can she pull together with those whose temperament is different from her own?

A number of steps were taken in the daily routine of the college to encourage the development of character and to assess each individual's personal growth. Every term three students were elected to the student committee. Each had the responsibility to serve as the senior student for three weeks. At the end of their period of office they stepped, thus learning both to exercise and to vacate a position of authority. At the end of each term, the three committee members reported to the principal on the conduct of each student within the community.

Every morning after breakfast, each student was required to be involved in domestic duties for one hour. The bedrooms were cleaned first, then the corridors and the bathrooms. The whole building was kept meticulously clean.

Punctuality and thoroughness were strongly encouraged. Twice a day articles, left lying around were cleared away and listed in the 'Scran'[84] Book. The 'Late' Book recorded those who failed to arrive on time, and the 'Slack' Book contained the names of those who failed to complete a duty for which they were responsible.

Former students remember how they were required to keep the college spic and span, and how they were taught that 'thoroughness is unsupervised excellence.'[85] Some appreciated that the enforced discipline was a good preparation for coping with the pressures of their future ministry. Others found the perfectionist standards demanded, even at the kitchen sink, to be rather irksome. 'I remember having to wash the soap container in the sink after each meal and laying Mrs Hooker's breakfast tray 'just so' or else!'[86] Another recalled, 'we were only allowed to dry one plate at a time, and there was no singing allowed during housework.'[87]Some felt that they were treated like children who were subject to 'rules that determined when we went out and what time we had to return.'[88] This was particularly difficult for those who had come from responsible positions in their secular work.[89]

Most recognised the value of learning to live, work and share responsibility with other people, especially those of a different temperament or from a different

---

84. A term derived from officers' training ships in the navy, where things left lying about by cadets were thrown into a 'scran' bag.
85. Wendy Moynagh (née Martin-Harvey), student 1937-9, in college survey, March 1997.
86. Angela Wheeler (née Gerard), student 1957-9, in college survey, March 1997.
87. Mrs Jenny Yohannes (née Bennett), student 1964-6, in college survey, March 1997.
88. Margaret Green (née Russell), student 1958-9, in college survey, March 1997.
89. Kathleen Carswell, student 1966-8, in college survey, March 1997.

cultural background. Because they were sent out as teams for their weekly involvement in Christian ministry, they learned to grow more considerate of others and to develop ways of 'working alongside awkward people.'[90]

The importance which was attached to character training at RBC is reflected in the criteria used for the final assessment and grading of students. According to a statement made in the *Ridgelands College Record,*[91] the awarding of the college diploma was based on:

1. Examination marks:	weekly, intermediate, final
2. Efficiency in practical work:	teaching, visiting, speaking
3. Discipline in character:	punctuality, reliability, tidiness, unselfish consideration of others, influence shown in the community.
4. Loyalty to authorities	

These criteria reflect the disciplinarian and authoritarian ethos of the college. Some students found it difficult to accept and felt that there was 'too much emphasis on submission to those in authority.'[92] At the same time, they recognised that Mrs Hooker and her successors were deeply concerned that they should grow to spiritual maturity, and be thoroughly equipped for the harsh realities of life and the challenges of Christian ministry.

4.4.3 Practical training

The Church Workers' Bible School at Tothill Street was founded to provide clear biblical teaching and practical instruction in Christian ministry. When Mrs Hooker opened Ridgelands two years later, her objectives remained the same. She wanted students to understand the Scriptures and be able to communicate effectively to others.

All students were required to attend speaker's classes, where they were given instruction in articulation, voice production, breathing and posture. They were taught about the preparation of material, the organisation of thought for logical presentation, and the adaptation of that material to varying audiences. As part of their training, they were expected to give a ten minutes talk to the class, which would then be critiqued by their peers and the staff. The first year students were allowed to read from a full script, while the second year students only had recourse to notes.[93]

As Miss Burton had been on the staff of the Froebel College, she was able to give classes on the psychology of children and principles of pedagogy. She encouraged the students to develop their artistic talents and to make effective use of visual aids. In 1934, choral training was introduced under Mr Jacques Hopkins, who in-

90. Margaret Green (née Russell), student 1958-9, in college survey, March 1997.
91. 'College News', in: *RCR* 13 (1938), p. 7.
92. Margaret Butler, student 1960-2, in college survey, March 1997.
93. Tinling, p. 42.

volved virtually the whole community in the choir. During Mrs MacKenzie's time, Bryan Gilbert, a well-known Christian musician, was invited to give guitar lessons.

Students going to remote and primitive areas were given further specialised training. This might include instruction in soil conservation and cultivation, or how to run a basic clinic. Practical experience in Christian ministry was gained in local churches, clubs and missions. Students took meetings for out-patients at the Bermondsey Medical Mission and the Wardley Street Medical Mission. They took a dinner hour service at the Anglo-American Laundry in Summerstown, and ran a Bible class at the Day Servants' Hostel. They organised open-air meetings every Wednesday during the summer term, and led a Girl's club at St Matthew's, Fulham, on Thursday evenings. They spoke at meetings for mothers and children, led Sunday School classes and, in any one year, visited around three thousand homes.

During the vacations, students were engaged in running holiday clubs for children, beach missions and evangelistic campaigns. One such campaign took place from May 26th to 31st 1929, in the parish of St Matthew's, Fulham.[94] The campaign was led by the Rev. Bryan Green of the Children's Special Service Mission, and a large number of RBC came to assist him, conveyed to Fulham in a coach. Every home in the parish was visited prior to the mission, and leaflets were distributed outside factories, the local cinema, the engineering works, the laundry, and even inside a public-house. Although a General Election took place during the same week and it was thought that the lighter evenings of early summer might discourage attendance, many adults came to the meetings and some 'were won for the Lord who had been the objects of much prayer for a long time past.'[95] But it was in the earlier meetings for children that the greatest response was seen. Although Mr Green anticipated only about fifty children, they came in hundreds. Every evening about twenty stayed behind for an after-meeting, where Mr Green explained how they could receive Christ as their Saviour. One little girl who attended, on being asked when she received Christ, said: 'In the spare time you gave us.'[96]

The emphasis on practical training remained after the war and under subsequent principals. Mrs MacKenzie 'sent the students to Trafalgar Square to gain experience in evangelism and learn how to relate the gospel across social and cultural barriers.'[97] As the college sought to keep pace with social change, new strategies of evangelism were attempted. 'Coffee-bar evangelism was undertaken in a very rough housing estate in Dartford: others had fine talks with young people playing 10-pin bowling; some students are helping at a girls' remand home in Gravesend.'[98]

When George Verwer, the founder of Operation Mobilisation (OM), came to Britain, Mrs MacKenzie invited him to come to RBC to talk about his work. As a result, 'several teams of students went from RBC to Europe and gained valuable experience in evangelism.'[99] Subsequently, several students joined OM and went overseas.

94. 'The Fulham Campaign', in: *RCR* 5 (1929), p. 11-12.
95. *Ibid.*
96. *Ibid.*, p. 12.
97. Interview with Mrs M. MacKenzie, August 9th, 1997.
98. Daphne Johnson, 'Principal's letter,' *RBC Newsletter* (April, 1969), p. 3.
99. Mrs MacKenzie, correspondence, October 16th, 1997.

4.4.4 Academic studies

The Authorised Version of the Bible was the primary textbook at RBC.[100] Every week, an outline was given of one book of the Bible. Lectures were also given on the Life of Christ, the Book of Acts and the Letter to the Romans. A course entitled 'How we got our Bible' included an examination of contemporary criticism of the biblical text. Some felt this was inadequately dealt with and there was no opportunity for discussion. One student recalled that she was forbidden to discuss liberal views about the Bible, although it was something which concerned her deeply. The memorisation of Scripture was emphasised, and this was required to be absolutely accurate, down to the correct punctuation. Students got a mark for every verse that was recalled with complete accuracy, and no mark at all for a verse which had a single mistake.[101]

In the post-war years the curriculum was expanded to include more comprehensive studies of the Old and New Testaments, doctrine, church history, missionary principles and methods, comparative religion, social anthropology, modern heresies and contemporary issues.[102]

The lectures provided students with a good biblical foundation. Devotional application of the text was encouraged rather than prolonged discussion of its literary pedigree. There was noone on the staff with adequate theological training though many of the visiting lecturers were well qualified academically. Some students would have liked a course on apologetics and more opportunity to discuss controversial issues.[103]

Some students were encouraged to take the Certificate of Proficiency in Religious Knowledge (the CRK Certificate), and during Mrs Mackenzie's time the proportion of students doing this increased considerably. During her work as a missionary in East Africa, she had encountered university students, but felt ill-prepared to answer their questions. She was determined that RBC students should be academically well-qualified as well as being spiritually prepared.

During the latter years, increasing attention was devoted to pastoral studies. Mrs Helen Lee was an expert on pastoralia and was much appreciated. Dr Marion Ashton lectured on the pressures and challenges to be faced in Christian ministry. One series of talks was entitled 'The way of peace in the midst of tension.' These and similar lectures were eventually published in a series of booklets.

4.4.5 Conclusion

Ridgelands was committed to fostering the spiritual lives of its students, just as the Edinburgh Conference of 1910 had recommended. The commitment to spiritual development was reflected in the structure of the curriculum and in the personal lives of the faculty members. The particular understanding of the doctrine of sanc-

---

100. After 1961, the Revised Standard Version was used.
101. Tinling, p. 42.
102. *College brochure* (1961), p. 3.
103. Valerie Collett, student 1956-8, in college survey, March 1997.

tification was a help to many but represented a narrow approach to spiritual development.

The college also recognised the importance of character formation and saw the intimacy of a small community as an ideal context in which to foster personal transformation. It is debatable whether the disciplinarian approach to training adopted at the college did develop character, or whether it simply forced students to conform during their period of training. Anne Small, at the Edinburgh Missionary College (see chapter two), believed that the imposition of rules simply produced a certain pattern of behaviour and did not encourage the development of self-discipline or prepare students to organise their own lives or make their own decisions.

One of the points of controversy in the college was over the approach to Scripture. All staff and students regarded the Bible as reliable and authoritative, but the basic approach taken by the college was devotional. Priority was given to learning and memorising the text and applying it to one's own personal life. Matters of literary criticism were barely considered. Controversial issues arising from the text were ignored. This was frustrating to many students and inadequate in the view of one principal, Mrs MacKenzie. She believed it was important for students to be given a more academic approach to the Scriptures, if they were going to minister effectively in the modern world.

A second and related issue which surfaced in the life of the college was the educational style. The standard approach was the formal lecture where students wrote notes or even a word for word copy, of what was said. This led to a degree of frustration among the students, many of whom were university graduates and had held responsible positions in the secular world. There was no course on apologetics and no stimulus to grasp thorny and difficult issues. One position would be put forward by the lecturer and students would be expected to accept that position without question. One visiting lecturer, asked to lead a discussion on Arminianism and Calvinism, remarked that ' at the end of the discussion, Mrs Hooker told the students what to believe.' [104]

4.5 Students

Ridgelands opened in 1919 with fifteen students. By 1926, numbers had risen to thirty five, but they fell during the recession. In 1938, there were twenty seven students at the college. During the rest of Mrs Hooker's principalship, numbers remained around thirty, though they dropped somewhat in her closing years. Under Mrs MacKenzie, there was an average of forty students every year, and under Mrs Johnson an average of thirty.

In 1938, Mrs Hooker wrote to her former students: 'There are now four hundred and twenty-two of you, who have lived together with us in College during your training days, and are now all over the world.'[105] By 1971, more than a thousand

104. Meg Foote, personal interview, July 14 1999.
105. Mrs H. Hooker, 'The Principal's letter', in: *RCR* 13 (1938), p. 1.

had been trained at the college. RBC usually accepted students between the ages of twenty-one and thirty, though some exceptions were made. The average age of those who studied there was twenty-eight.

4.5.1 Social and academic background

Ridgelands students tended to come from well-educated backgrounds. The first issue of *Ridgelands College Record* (RCR) remarks: 'It may not be uninteresting to note that students have come to us from the following Colleges: 'Newnham, Girton, Westfield, Bedford, Holloway, London School of Medicine, Trinity College (Dublin), Queen's University (Belfast), and Froebel College.'[106]

4.5.2 National and denominational background

The majority of students came from Britain. Some came from continental Europe and occasionally students were accepted from further afied. In 1938, there were students from Norway, Switzerland, Canada and India. In 1964, the student body included two Africans, one German, one Belgian and one Dutch student. In 1970, students came from Switzerland, the Netherlands, Finland, Sri Lanka (previously Ceylon) and South Africa.

In the early days of the college, it appears that the majority of students were Anglicans. Over the years an increasing proportion of students came from other denominations, but incomplete records make it impossible to know the exact percentage of denominational representation.[107] However, it is interesting to observe that in 1964 five students were engaged to Anglican ordinands.

4.5.3 Areas of service

Between 1919 and 1961, approximately thirty three per cent of those who left RBC went overseas as missionaries.[108] When Mrs Mackenzie became principal, the percentage of those becoming missionaries rose to nearly fifty per cent.

India was the commonest destination for missionary service in the early days of the college, a natural consequence of Mrs Hooker's association with the ZMMF. By 1929, there were more than thirty former students working in the subcontinent. Nine years later, that number had risen to fifty six, which represented forty percent of all the students who became missionaries.[109]

The remaining sixty percent of RBC missionary alumnae were scattered in different parts of the world: thirteen were serving in other parts of Asia, with four in

106. 'College News', in: *RCR* 1 (1924), p. 14.
107. Of the 62 students who filled in the March 1997 survey, two-thirds of the students said they were Anglicans when they went to RBC, and seventeen percent were Baptists.
108. By 1925, 43 out of 120 alumni were serving abroad. By 1934, 100 students were overseas, out of a total of three hundred.
109. 10% went to the rest of Asia, 20% to Africa, 13% to Continental Europe, 7% to the Middle East and the remainder to the Americas according to lists given in the article 'Ridgelands Students Working Abroad', in: *RCR* 13 (1938), p. 29-31. The post-war statistics are not available.

Papua under the New Guinea Evangelisation Society; ten were working in the Middle East; eight were in North America; and one in Argentina.

A number of students went to Africa. In 1938, seven were involved in medical work In Uganda with the Ruanda Medical Mission. Thirteen were working in North Africa, particularly Morocco, Algeria and Egypt. Thirteen were in South Africa, many of them with Young Women's Christian Association.

Most went out with denominational missionary societies. These were predominantly Anglican societies, such as the Church Missionary Society or the Bible Churchmen's Missionary Society. A few went out with interdenominational societies.[110]

Although the records are incomplete, the information available indicates considerable longevity of missionary service among the alumnae. It was not uncommon for former students to remain overseas for twenty, thirty or even forty years.

4.5.4 *Conclusion*

The students at Ridgelands differed in a number of respects from those that went to Mount Hermon. They tended to come from wealthier families, be more highly educated and better qualified professionally.

A smaller percentage of those from Ridgelands became missionaries than was the case at MHMTC. Those who did go overseas tended to be concentrated in fewer fields of service, but the fields of service spread all over the world as the years went by.

The students at RBC were predominantly Anglicans, whereas MHMTC had a higher proportion from other denominations. Consequently more RBC students went overseas with Anglican missionary societies.

4.6 Conclusion

Ridgelands was established to prepare qualified women of different denominations and nationalities for posts of responsibility in Christian missionary service at home and overseas. After sixty two years, more than one thousand students had received training for ministry. Although the mission focus was not as strong as that at the other two colleges which merged in 1971, between a third and a half of the alumnae became missionaries. For some RBC provided a basic course of biblical studies and spiritual preparation for home ministry, for others, it was a preparation for Christian service within the context of marriage.

The strengths of the college are obvious. First, there was the strong emphasis on personal spiritual growth, nurtured through the structure and ethos of the college and modelled in the lives of the staff. Secondly, all three principals gave great importance to the development of Christian character, and the smallness of the community was the ideal context for forging right attitudes. Thirdly, the students were

110. *Ibid.*

given a love of the Bible, a working knowledge of its content, and the skills with which to communicate its message. Fourthly, they left the college with a clear understanding of the basics of Christian doctrine. 'I understood that faith in the Triune God and not feelings is the basis and anchor of the Christian life.'[111] Many former students testify to the impact the two years at Ridgelands had on their lives. As one expressed it: 'It was two of the best years of my life.'[112]

There were weaknesses in the training also. The academic level of teaching was not high and the staff were not well qualified. A narrow perspective of biblical interpretation was presented and, at least in the early days, an intolerance exhibited towards alternative views. Debate on controversial topics was not usually encouraged, and issues, which concerned some students deeply, were not discussed. The authoritarian climate of the college, which seems to have intensified in the declining years of Mrs Hooker, proved irksome to those who had held responsible posts in the secular world. It raises the question whether an imposed pattern of discipline is the best preparation for the life of self-discipline that mission work in its very nature often demands.

Yet in spite of those weaknesses, many of which were the product of the age in which the college was established, Ridgelands did provide effective and appropriate training for several generations. As the last principal, Daphne Johnson observed of her time as a student: 'Looking back now it would seem that everything was wrong, but for me it was very right.'[113] Mrs Hooker may have been a formidable, even autocratic, principal but many are grateful that she founded Ridgelands and deeply appreciate the influence that she and others exerted on their lives.

Ridgelands owed its origin and its ethos to Mrs Hooker. Her personality, her beliefs, her understanding of personal spirituality, and her style of leadership left a deep impression on the life of the college and the minds of her students. She was born during the reign of Queen Victoria, and in her manner and authoritarian leadership she resembled a gracious aristocratic lady from that period. She grew up in the days when Britain was a great colonial power and she founded a college which would train young ladies to take the gospel into the far flung corners of the Empire and beyond. This undoubtedly coloured her view of mission and it is not clear whether the college ever seriously came to grips with the nature of mission in the post-colonial age. Most students came from wealthier and more privileged families, in contrast to those who studied at Mount Hermon. They enjoyed considerable status in their own country and belonged to that section of society from which many entered the diplomatic or colonial service. It was not always easy for those coming from such a background to rid themselves of colonial attitudes, and divest themselves of racial or social pride.

The college had strong personal connections with the established church. Mrs Hooker was a committed Anglican, as were the majority of the staff and council. Two thirds of the students who attended the college were Anglicans. The college

111. Joan Potter, student 1960-2, in college survey, March 1997.
112. Ann Bräker (née Walton), student 1963-5, in college survey, March 1997.
113. Mrs Daphne Harman (née Johnson), student 1950-2, principal 1966-71, in college survey, March 1997.

offered a course on the Anglican Prayer Book and many of the students served in local Anglican parishes. A large number of students went overseas with Anglican missionary societies. Many others married Anglican clergymen.

With these assocations with the Anglican Church, the college was potentially closer to the ecumenical movement than either of the other two colleges with which it was united in 1971. But during the first half of the twentieth century, only a few evangelical Anglicans were involved with the ecumenical movement or with Christians from non-evangelical traditions. They tended to keep to themselves and form their own evangelical ghetto within the established church. They were often more at home with nonconformist evangelicals than with their fellow Anglicans. Their concept of Christian unity was that of a fellowship of true believers. They were unsure whether the search for visible unity was attainable, or even desirable.

Doctrinally, the college was conservative and remained so throughout its history. Priority was given to the devotional application of Scripture than to the academic study of the biblical text. The main focus of the training was in the area of personal evangelism. Little attention was given to the role of the church in mission, or the responsibility of the church to be involved in social and political action. In the extant literature of the college, there is no reference to the Edinburgh Conference of 1910, the International Missionary Council, or the International Review of Missions. There was either an unwillingness to enter into serious debate about the nature of mission, or a reluctance to interact with Christians who took a different doctrinal stance. In consequence, the college's understanding of mission remained somewhat static during this period. Mission continued to be understood essentially in terms of proclamation. Students were sent out to bring the light of the gospel to those who were in darkness and ignorance. They might become involved in educational or medical work as an expression of Christian love, but they were to concentrate on the primary task of evangelism.

5. All Nations Bible College (1923-1962)

5.1 Introduction

Like Mount Hermon and Ridgelabds, All Nations Bible College owes a great deal to the Keswick Convention. It was at the convention of July 1921 that a group of Christian leaders began to discuss the possibility of founding an interdenominational Bible college to train men for missionary service. They were concerned that there was no such college in England.[1] They consulted and prayed much about the matter and 'the result was that All Nations Bible College was opened on February 13 1923.'[2] As a later principal, the Rev Henry Curr, was to observe of All Nations, 'It may truly be said to be a product of the Convention.'[3]

This chapter will trace the history and development of All Nations from 1923 to 1962 under its respective principals (5.2), consider its doctrinal basis and the purpose for which it was founded (5.3), examine the components of its programme (5.4) and study the selection, background and subsequent service of its alumni (5.5). The chapter will conclude with an evaluation of the first forty years of the college (5.6).

5.2 Foundation and history

The body that was to assume the responsibility for opening this new college was the All Nations Missionary Union. This organisation had been founded in 1892 under the name of the Missionary Pence Association. It was the vision of one man, John Jackson. His intention was not to create a missionary society in the ordinarily accepted meaning of the word, but to develop an association which 'should devote its energy and influence to helping any missionary society or individual missionary.'[4] Many joined the movement and such large sums were raised that it was felt advisable to change the name to the All Nations Missionary Union.[5] After Jackson's death, it became an incorporated body so 'its scope of work was enlarged and powers were granted for undertaking trusts for missionaries and societies.'[6]

In 1921, the president of the ANMU was Dr Frederick B. Meyer, a well-known and greatly respected evangelical leader. As soon as he heard about the proposal for an interdenominational college, he gave his full backing. He was convinced that

1. G. Thomas, 'A short account of the foundation of the ANBC', in: *MRAN* 147 (April 1939), p. 16.
2. 'The All Nations Bible College', in: *MRANs* 83 (July 1926), p. 117.
3. H.S. Curr, 'Principal's letter', in: *MRANs* 98 (July 1929), p. 102.
4. 'All Nations Missionary Union (Incorporated)', in: *MRAN* 98 (July 1929), p. 359.
5. The association produced a bi-monthly magazine that contained news and articles of almost all the British evangelical missionary societies. This publication was initially called *Missionary Pence*. Its name was later changed to the *Missionary Review of All Nations*.
6. 'All Nations Missionary Union (Incorporated)', in: *MRAN* 98 (July 1929), p. 359.

such a college was one of most urgent needs in London, both for the training of evangelists and for the preparation of missionaries.[7]

A council meeting was held on September 23rd 1921 at a house in Grange Road, Upper Norwood.[8] An adjacent property, a large mansion with extensive grounds, was available for sale for £5,000. A lady who had been at the Keswick Convention had already written to the council, pointing out the suitability of this property for such a institution. The council members surveyed the grounds of the estate,[9] which was called 'The Lawns', and after careful discussion passed a unanimous decision to establish a college for the training of men and women for missionary and other Christian service.[10]

Once the decision of the council become known,[11] it received widespread public support. The first donation for the proposed college was received on October 25th 1921. A number of eminent evangelicals gave their backing to the project. W. Graham Scroggie, pastor of Charlotte Chapel in Edinburgh and a popular conference speaker, wrote: 'The serious proposal to establish in London, or elsewhere, an institute of interdenominational character, that shall have as its object a thorough grounding of its students in the Scriptures and the preparation of them in other ways for missionary service, is long overdue.'[12]

From the start, however, there was some uncertainty as to whether the project would ever get off the ground. Many recognised the need for such a college, but lacked the confidence or the faith to implement the vision. Even when the All Nations Missionary Union began to consider setting up the college, some were unsure whether it would be possible, or whether they were the right group to undertake such a venture. By January 1922, 'no steps had been taken even to acquire a building for such a purpose.'[13] Yet, whenever the members of the council sought advice from others, they met nothing but encouragement. More significantly, William Edwards, a city merchant and the treasurer of the council, was enthusiastic about the project and convinced that there would be sufficient support forthcoming from the public. He wrote, 'I have seldom known any proposal that has been so welcomed, as the proposal of the All Nations Missionary Union to start a college for the training of men for the foreign field.'[14]

The contract for the property called 'The Lawns' was signed on April 5th 1922 and one month later a simple service of dedication of the house and grounds was

7. F.B. Meyer, 'Our plea for an interdenominational training college', in: *MRAN* 60 (October 1921), p. 158.
8. Some years later this house was itself purchased by the college and became the student hostel. Its grounds were adjacent to the property that was bought in 1923.
9. When they went to view the house and grounds, the gates were locked and no keys were available, so they assisted one another over the fence, Dr Meyer protesting that *never* had he done such a thing before. From *A brief history: 1923-1958* (1958), p. 4.
10. Minutes of the council, September 23 1921.
11. Articles about the proposed college appeared in the October issue of the *MRAN* 60 (October 1921), pp. 158-164.
12. W.G. Scroggie, in a letter published in: *MRAN* 67 (June 1923).
13. J.F. Arthur, in: *MRAN* 65 (January 1923), p. 64.
14. W. Edwards, 'Missionary college and Bible school: shall we go forward?' in: *MRAN* 61 (January 1922), p. 195.

held, with Dr Meyer presiding.[15] 'It was a solemn meeting among beautiful surroundings with the bright blue sky; opening with the hymn, 'When I survey the wondrous cross,' and followed by prayer by Dr Meyer, who in a few solemn dedicatory words offered the house and lands to the Master, that He might take it into His hands and use it according to His will, and continued by prayer and other messages.'[16] Two days later the first application was received from a candidate asking to be trained at the college for missionary service.

Originally it was hoped to open the college in October 1922, but a number of alterations needed to be made to the property, so it was not until February 13th, 1923 that the first students were received. The weekly journal, *The Christian*, carried an extensive report of the opening ceremony: 'Large numbers of Christian people gathered at the All Nations' Bible College, Beulah Hill, Upper Norwood, on Tuesday, February 13th, for fellowship in the opening ceremony of the college, which ushered in a first session of great expectations. The house itself occupies an imposing position in some twenty acres of ground, commanding an undulating landscape. Thus situated in ideal surroundings, the college hopes to equip and train a practical type of missionary-student who will be fitted to adapt himself to conditions in the foreign field, while he will be full of ardent enthusiasm.'[17]

The dedication of the college was preceded by a service at Lansdowne Hall, where a sermon was preached by Dr Graham Scroggie on the text, 'Ye shall receive power' (Acts 1:8).[18] After lunch most of the assembled crowd were ferried down to the college grounds by motor-bus or cars, while some walked. At the college there was some difficulty because none of the rooms were large enough to hold all those who had come. Consequently three simultaneous meetings were held in separate rooms, while the various speakers, including several members of the council, distributed themselves as much as was possible. Dr Meyer addressed all three meetings but he remained seated while doing so, because he had recently overstrained his heart and was undergoing a period of recuperation.

5.2.1 Frederick B. Meyer (1923-1924)

Dr Frederick Brotherton Meyer (1847-1929) was appointed as the first principal of the college. After successful ministries in Liverpool and Leicester, he came to London and was pastor successively of Regent's Park Church and Christ Church, Westminster Bridge Road. From 1904 to 1921, he served as the President of the Free Church Council. A popular speaker at Christian conventions, he wrote a number of devotional studies on biblical characters. He was a man of 'dignified appearance, compassionate heart, ceaseless industry, prolific pen and graceful style.'[19]

---

15. May 6 1922.
16. G. Thomas, 'A short account of the foundation of the ANBC', in: *MRAN* 147 (April 1939), p. 17.
17. 'New Missionary Centre', in: *The Christian* (February 22, 1923), p. 19.
18. 'Opening Day at All Nations Bible College', in: *MRAN* 66(March 1923), p. 93.
19. Arthur Clarke, 'Meyer, Frederick Brotherton (1847-1929)', in: *The new international dictionary of the Christian Church* (1978), p. 657.

Meyer was an evangelical who was 'equally at home both in evangelical non-denominationalism and in the more official structures of the church.'[20] He included bishops among his friends and received a congratulatory message from the Archbishop of Canterbury on his 80th birthday. He was conscious of the evangelical tradition of social involvement and strongly believed that Christians should be involved in society. In the words of Derek Tidball, he 'demonstrated a balance between evangelism and social concerns when talking of holiness. Personal purity and social justice stood shoulder to shoulder.'[21] In the debate on the nature and authority of Scripture, which absorbed evangelicals for so much of the time, Meyer accepted the verbal inspiration of the Bible but stopped short of accepting the term inerrant.

Although he was already elderly and in declining health, he was deeply enthusiastic about the proposed college and gladly accepted the invitation of the council to become the founding principal. However, as things turned out, he was unable to retain that position for long.

Ten weeks after the opening of the college, he set sail for a five month preaching tour of Australia and New Zealand. He had been intending to travel there for many years, but his doctors had advised against it . In the middle of April he felt that it was imperative for him to make this trip, so he met with the executive council to seek their advice. They felt they could do nothing else but wish him God speed and pray that God would bring him back reinvigorated and able to concentrate his remaining years as principal of the college.[22]

The prayer of the council that he would return safely was answered. Their prayer that he would serve long as principal was not. Less than a year after his return from Australia, he resigned from the principalship. The official statement released to the press by the council of All Nations Bible College stated, 'Dr Meyer, who was appointed as the first principal of the above college, and Mr James J. Arthur, whom he called from Australia to be his aid, feel that the time has come to lay down their respective positions of principal and vice-principal.'[23] No explanation is given as to why Dr Meyer decided to leave All Nations so soon, but his obituary which appeared five years later in the *Missionary Review* said that 'he again was led to the larger ministry among the churches in many parts.'[24] His biographer, W. Y. Fullerton, gives a different perspective on his departure. He writes: 'At the end of the year, difference of opinion as to its (the college's) management led both Mr Arthur (the vice-principal) and himself to resign.'[25]

The council were sad to lose a man of his stature and expressed their gratitude for all that he had done.[26] There is no doubt that the association of his name with the college was an enormous asset in its formative period. Dr Meyer died in 1929.

20. D.J. Tidball, *Who are the Evangelicals? Tracing the roots of today's movements* (1994), p. 174.
21. *Ibid.*, p. 213.
22. 'Journey for Mission tour in Australia and New Zealand', in: *MRAN* 67 (June 1923), p. 122.
23. G. Thomas, 'Report of progress at the ANBC', in: *MRANs* 72 (April 1924), p. XIII.
24. 'The late Dr F. B. Meyer', in: *MRANs* 97 (May 1929), p. 90.
25. W.Y. Fullerton, *F.B. Meyer: a biography* (1930), p. 127.
26. *Ibid.*

5.2.2 Walter J. Cunningham Pike (1924-1925)

In July 1924, the council appointed the Rev. Dr Walter John Cunningham Pike (1871-1925) as the second principal. Pike was a natural academic, who was reading Greek at the age of 12. He was a senior classics scholar and prizewinner at Cambridge. He went on to be a professor at Glasgow University, Scotland, and Queen's University, Canada. A popular speaker, he had often shared a platform with Dr Campbell Morgan, minister of Westminster Chapel in London.

As a scholar, Pike wanted the students to develop good habits of scholarship, even though he had a low opinion of much contemporary biblical scholarship. He insisted that all students studied both Greek and Hebrew. At the same time, he wanted his students to be able to relate to the ordinary man in the street. In his first principal's letter, he wrote of the need for missionaries to find points of contact with their audience, whether it meant talking of horses, building or road-making.[27]

Pike lacked the graciousness and warmheartedness of F. B. Meyer. He had a volatile temperament. The minutes of the Council record that 'Dr Pike made various statements that were detrimental to the Board.'[28] When the Council decided not to allow the teaching of Hebrew as a regular part of the curriculum, 'There was much heated discussion on the part of Dr. Pike, some of a very unpleasant character. Dr. Pike raised his voice very much in speaking to the chairman and banged his fist on the table.'[29]

Dr Pike only remained principal for seven months, before he was forced to retire. Dr Mountain wrote in his obituary: 'After years of overstrain, a sudden nervous breakdown terminated his brilliant scholastic career. After a few weeks of retirement, one evening while sheltering from the rain on the promenade at Penzance, he just leaned his head on the shoulder of his devoted wife, and fell asleep in Christ Jesus, his Saviour and Lord.'[30]

5.2.3 Henry S. Curr (1925-1939)

On July 31 1925, the council appointed their third principal in as many years. Professor Henry Simpson Curr (1886-1957) was a Scot who had had 'a brilliant career in the universities of Edinburgh and Oxford.'[31] After obtaining his M.A. and B.D. in Scotland, he wrote a thesis on 'The theology of Jonathan Edwards' for his B.Litt. at Oxford. Later he completed his Ph.D. at Edinburgh. After pastorates at Union Grove Baptist Church, Aberdeen, and Orangefield Baptist Church in Greenock, he spent the years of the First World War with the YMCA in France. He then served for six years as Professor of Hebrew at McMasters University, Toronto, Canada, before resigning that position to come to All Nations. Initially he was appointed acting

27. W. J. Cunningham Pike, 'Principal's letter', in: *MRANs* 74 (September 1924), p. XXIII.
28. Minutes of the Council, February 2 1925.
29. Minutes of the Council, February 23 1925.
30. Dr Mountain, 'Obituary on Dr W.J. Cunningham Pike,' quoted in: *MRANs* 79 (September 1925), p. LXX.
31. 'The appointment of The Rev Professor H.S. Curr', in: *MRANs* 78 (June 1925), p. LV.

principal, perhaps because he was still relatively young, but by February of the following year he was confirmed in his position as principal.[32] He was to remain as principal until the outbreak of war in 1939.

Prior to his appointment, the council had agreed that the new principal should be a deeply spiritual person, a well-qualified academic, and a gifted communicator. He should also be totally committed to the college's doctrinal stance. Curr fulfilled all those requirements. He was at one with the college on its view of scripture. 'It is the entrance of God's Word alone that can give light to the heart and mind. . . . The written word is the counterpart of the Living Word, both being full of Grace and Truth.'[33]

Curr believed that the first essential ingredient of an effective missionary training programme was a systematic study of the Bible. Secondly, he was convinced that it should be very practical and contain courses on such subjects as medicine, house building and agriculture. Thirdly, he considered it was not essential for someone to have completed tertiary education before they could think of becoming a missionary. The indispensable qualification for missionary service was not academic but spiritual; or, in his words, 'the true missionary is not made, he is born from above.'[34]

He also recognised that the impact of a period of training at the college could remain with the students throughout their lives even though the time they spent at All Nations was relatively short. On one occasion he quoted with obvious approval a remark from *The Times*: 'The marks of Alma Mater are indelible.' He believed that although men might forget what they learned in their lectures after a few years, the impress of their training would abide to the end of their days.[35]

Curr was very aware of his responsibility as principal to create and maintain within the institution that spirit and atmosphere which would leave the best possible impression on those who studied within it. He was conscious of the need of those who taught to set an example. 'By prayer, united and private, by precept, by example, the staff strive to keep them in the love of God, first endeavouring to do so themselves, and in that way to fit the students to be the ambassadors of Christ to the ends of the earth.'[36]

As principal, Henry Curr was aware that he had men of very different ability. His ambition was not to make them all into a clone of an All Nations ideal, but to enable each individual to 'make the most of what they have.'[37] Basing his philosophy on the parable of the talents, he sought to encourage every man to discover and use his own personal resources.

He also wanted his students to learn how to learn, to become perpetual students as they pursued their future ministry. His desire for them was that they should con-

32. List of college council, dated May 1926, designates the Rev H. S. Curr as Principal, in: *MRANs* 82 (May 1926), p. 101.
33. H.S. Curr, 'The ANBC ideal', in: *MRANs* 78 (June 1925), p. LVIII.
34. H.S. Curr, 'The ANBC curriculum', in: *MRANs* 79 (September 1925), p. LXIV.
35. H.S. Curr, 'Opening meeting of the year, 16th September 1925, in: *MRANs* 79 (September 1925), p. LXVII.
36. H.S. Curr, 'The ANBC curriculum', in: *MRANs* 79 (September 1925), p. LXV.
37. H.S. Curr, 'Principal's letter', in: *MRANs* 94 (September 1928), p. 42.

stantly be discovering new truths about Christ, and so continue to grow throughout their lives in their character, their spiritual life and their ministry.

Curr was respected both for his learning and for his personal piety. He was 'an omniverous reader and took the work of preparing his lectures as the supreme task for him. His lecturing was clear and aimed at giving the student a lucid idea of the subject in hand.'[38] His teaching style consisted in dictating notes which the students copied down word for word. He did not seek close relationships with his students, and was seldom seen except when giving lectures.

He never married, but remained a rather eccentric bachelor. He was afraid of the company of women and disappeared to the security of his study when they arrived in the college. His weekly treat was to go to London to watch the 'Changing of the Guard.'

He had a peculiar sense of humour. According to the brief history of the college written shortly after Curr's death, the students 'used to say that at prayers on the first night of term, the Principal had a strange way of choosing the hymn in which the line occurs, 'Thou art in the midst of foes,' and the freshers would look around at their companions and wonder.'[39]

After the Second World War, Curr served first as principal of the Mildmay Bible College and then as principal of the Scottish Baptist Bible College in Glasgow. He always maintained close links with All Nations, and just before his death he wrote warmly of the time he spent at college: 'I spent many happy years there. I recall with great pleasure many fine men who went out from the College to home pastorates, and to the mission field, especially those who went to Africa. Everyone was always so bright and cheerful. It made teaching a continual pleasure and means of grace.'[40]

5.2.4 Rev. Edward J. Poole-Connor (1945-1948)

During the course of the Second World War, the college remained closed. In October 1945, it reopened under the leadership of a new principal. The Rev. Edward Joshua Poole-Connor (1872-1962) had a long association with the college. He was a highly respected evangelical leader and had founded the Fellowship of Independent Evangelical Churches.

Poole-Connor was strongly opposed to the ecumenical movement. He criticised the inadequacy of its doctrinal basis. He believed that it replaced the gospel of salvation with an ethical programme of Christian behaviour. He disagreed with its objective of uniting the universal church into one body. His biographer describes how 'he sought to awaken Christian people to the dangers of modernism . . . and that form of ecumenicity that is achieved at the expense of vital truth.'[41] Poole-Connor was aware

38. 'Rev. H.S. Curr, M.A., B.D., B.Litt., D.Ph., Principal of All Nations Bible College 1925-1939', in: *NAN* (Winter 1956/7), p. 6.
39. *A brief history: 1923-1958* (1958), p. 6f.
40. 'Rev. H.S. Curr, M.A., B.D., B.Litt., D.Ph., Principal of All Nations Bible College 1925-1939', in: *NAN* (Winter 1956/7), p. 6.
41. D.G. Fountain, *E.J. Poole-Connor 1872-1962: Contender for the faith* (1966), p. 14.

that some evangelicals were actively involved in the ecumenical movement but he felt that only confused the issue, since it implied that such differences as there were between modernists and evangelicals were of little consequence. In 1952, he resigned from the Evangelical Alliance because of its 'benevolent neutrality' towards the WCC.[42] Poole-Connor was the most strident opponent of the ecumenical movement of all the principals of ANBC. Those who followed him were more tempered in their attitude and more measured in their statements, but his influence created the public image of the college which remained for at least a decade after he left.

Poole-Connor's first task was to find suitable premises for the college. During the war years, the buildings at Beulah Hill had been requisitioned by the Government. They were later sold to the Croydon Corporation, who converted the grounds into a public park.[43] While a permanent new home was sought, temporary accommodation for All Nations was found in the Kensit Memorial College, in North London. In November 1946, the college moved into freehold premises, known as Taplow Hill House in Buckinghamshire, which had been purchased for it by the All Nations Missionary Union.

Taplow was to be the home of All Nations for the next eighteen years. Set in the Buckinghamshire countryside, Taplow was described by Robert Hay, the Bishop of Buckingham, as 'one of the oldest, richest and most beautiful villages in England,'[44] Taplow Hill House was situated near the river Thames and had originally been built as a family mansion. At the outbreak of the Second World War in 1939, it was sold to the Royal Netherlands Government, and considerably enlarged and refitted at the cost of some thousands of pounds as a hospital for Dutch sailors.[45] It contained forty rooms, four of which on the top floor were used as dormitories. As is stated by Williams, 'The rooms were large and well-lit, with hot water pipes running through them.'[46]

In a relatively short space of time, the Rev. Poole-Connor was able to re-establish the college and attract a good number of students. Twenty-one students entered All Nations in 1946 and nineteen the following year.[47] When he retired in 1948 to return to a wider public speaking ministry, the college council expressed their appreciation for his 'wise and spiritual leadership.' He was appointed as Principal-Emeritus and subsequently continued to visit the college once a week to lecture in Old Testament and Church History.[48]

5.2.5 The Rev. Henry Brash Bonsall (1948-1952)

The Rev. Henry Brash Bonsall (1905-1990) was born in Lancashire, in the north-east of England, but he lived for twenty two years in Canada. He received his B.A.

42. *Ibid.*, p. 182.
43. They were still being used as a public park in June 1999.
44. The Rt Rev Robert M. Hay, 'New premises formally opened', in: *ANMR*ns 2 (Winter 1947/8), p. 4.
45. E.J. Poole-Connor, 'The All Nations Bible College: 1921-1947', in: *ANMR*ns 1 (Summer 1947), p. 8.
46. D.G.V. Williams, 'From the warden's office', in: *ANMR*ns 1 (Summer 1947), p. 8.
47. *Register of students 1923-1955: All Nations Bible College*
48. 'Rev E.J. Poole-Connor becomes Principal-Emeritus', in: *ANMR*ns 5 (Winter 1948), p. 8.

and M.A. at the University of British Columbia in 1926 and 1928, and graduated in theology at Knox College in the University of Toronto in 1930. He held pastorates in several Canadian Presbyterian churches before he returning to England in 1935.[49] Early in 1938, he joined the staff of All Nations. When the college was closed during the war, he served first as vice-principal of the Word of Life Training Home at Kelvedon in Essex, and then as minister of the Stockwell Congregational Church in Colchester. After ANBC reopened in 1945, he was appointed as a part-time lecturer by the Rev. E. J. Poole-Connor. In 1947, he was nominated by the council as principal-designate, and he assumed that office the following year.

The new principal proved to be energetic and far-sighted. 'He was a man who operated on a combination of prayer and faith, with a great heart for his students and a far-reaching vision. His aim was to train ordinary men to become leaders and to prepare for the revival God had promised. Having experienced the deadening effects of liberal and modernistic trends in Canada, he was an ardent upholder of the authority of the biblical text.'[50]

He had already introduced a new three year curriculum which combined missionary, theological and specialised courses.[51] This was soon expanded, while a streamlined two-year course was inaugurated for older men, who had been demobbed from military service. He was convinced that missionaries needed as much theological training as ministers, since their responsibilities would included planting churches and training pastors. At the same time, he insisted that they needed to be equipped practically and technically: practically, so that they would be proficient preachers, teachers and evangelists; technically, so that they could turn their hand to any task that was required of them, whether it be building a house, mending shoes or taking a photograph.

The years immediately following the Second World War brought their own problems. Many of the students had come straight from the forces; some were refugees from the continent; rationing was still in force and commodities in short supply.[52] Brash Bonsall was concerned about the financial position of the college, and although there was no question of the college going into debt, he inaugurated a number of measures to improve the situation. Student fees, which only covered half of the costs, were almost doubled in the space of two years from £25 to £45 per term.[53] Students were required to give eight hours voluntary work around the college each week to avoid the necessity of employing a maintenance man.[54] An expansionist policy was adopted to raise the number of students. As Brash Bonsall noted himself, 'Lectures can be given as easily to a class of one hundred as to one of thirty.'[55] He also introduced the bursary fund to assist those students who found

49. In Lloydminster (Alberta) and Vancouver (British Columbia), according to information provided by his daughter, Mrs Ruth McGavin, who is hoping to publish a biography of her father.
50. From the unpublished biography by Mrs Ruth McGavin.
51. The Rev. H. Brash Bonsall, 'The significance of the new curriculum', in: *ANMR*ns 1 (1947), p. 9.
52. *A brief history 1923-1958* (1958), p. 10.
53 'The Principal's message', in: *ANMR*ns 6 (1949), p. 13 and 'The treasurer speaks', in: *ANMR*ns 12 (1951), p. 11.
54 'The Principal's message', in: *ANMR*ns 6 (1949), p. 13
55 *Ibid.*

that they were unable to pay all the fees. The council did not always agree with Bonsall's ideas, and was at times reluctant to concur with his suggestions.

Bonsall was a visionary rather than an administrator. He made a number of autocratic and impulsive decisions, which led to frustration among staff and students. This included deciding by himself which students should be awarded the college diploma. In January 1952, the warden and two tutors resigned. Two months later Bonsall suspended a number of students, who had broken into his study to discover who had been awarded diplomas and on what basis. The council investigated the matter, questioning seven representatives of the student body. They explained what had happened and told them that 'the events leading to the resignation of the three staff members had their origins in the principal.'[56] The principal was subsequently asked to resign.

Three years later, the college council discussed how their relationship with Bonsall might be restored. They considered the possibility of inviting him to join the council, but several council members expressed disquiet. The minutes record: 'It was generally felt that a reconciliation with Mr Bonsall would be welcomed but that any move to invite him to become an active participant in the work, in any capacity, should be the subject of serious consideration and that no hurried action should be taken.'[57]

5.2.6 The Rev. Leslie S. M'Caw (1952-1962)

The Rev. Leslie S. M'Caw (b. 1907) was first invited to give occasional lectures at All Nations early in 1952. In June, he was asked by the council if he would be willing to serve as acting principal, following the dismissal of Bonsall, and in 1953 he was appointed to the principalship on a permanent basis.

M'Caw went to Manchester University, where he was involved in the beginning of the Christian Union, associated with the Inter-Varsity Fellowship. After a postgraduate course for the Diploma in Education, he joined the staff of Manchester Tutorial College. In 1937, he was invited to join Dr. Campbell Morgan at Westminster Chapel as superintendent of the young people's institute and teacher training classes. During the war, he served as a pastor: first at a Congregational Church in Olney, and subsequently at a Baptist Church in Dunstable. He conducted weekly lecture courses at the newly formed London Bible College and wrote the chapter on the Book of Psalms for the New Bible Commentary (1953).[58]

During his varied ministry he had been worked with and come to appreciate a wide spectrum of Christian traditions: Presbyterian, Anglican, Holiness, Baptist, and Congregational. Reflecting on his own spiritual pilgrimage, he wrote: 'An earlier memorable year of 'living by faith' had taught my wife and me that an inner joy and an astonishing Fatherly care can run parallel with very difficult circumstances and the bewilderment of Christian friends. After the sudden death of my wife one Sunday morning after Easter 1950 there began a second and more 'advanced course'

56. Minutes of the council, March 11 1952.
57. Minutes of the council, January 2 1955.
58. 'The Psalms', in: *New Bible Commentary* (1953).

of walking by faith, wherein much was learnt and unlearned that could not be known otherwise.'[59]

When M'Caw took over the leadership of the college, he was very conscious of the tradition and ethos which he was inheriting. He wrote: 'All Nations stands for Keswick principles applied to the training of young men for Christian service, especially those going overseas.'[60] He often thought of the constant stream of young men who had come to the college 'through a common loyalty to Christ and because of a call to train for service in the kingdom of God.'[61] As each new academic year began, he was aware of the powerful influence that the community could exert for good or ill on those who entered it. The characters, attitudes, and even the faith, of those who lived and studied at All Nations would be as much shaped by the student body and the communal atmosphere as they would by any devotional exhortation or inspired lecture. In his editorials, M'Caw often asked for prayer for that 'unanimity of heart, assurance of purpose and humility of walk which need to be the framework of spiritual training.'[62]

From 1952-1959, Mr M'Caw was assisted by the Rev. Laurie L. Binder, who served as resident tutor. An infantry officer during the war, Binder had later become president of the Oxford Inter-Collegiate Christian Union and, subsequently, chairman of the Inter-Varsity Fellowship executive committee. After a pastorate in a Baptist church in Berkshire, he responded with enthusiasm to the invitation by Mr M'Caw to join the staff of an interdenominational college.

During the immediate post-war years, the college had grown quite rapidly. There were a large number of men who were looking for training and a worthwhile career. In the six years from 1946 to 1951, 122 new students came to All Nations. In the next six years (1952 to 1957), only seventy new students came. Inevitably the college became smaller, and by 1958 the student body was just over thirty.

M'Caw had a great many gifts. Morris, who served under him as tutor and succeeded him as principal, described him as 'the most skilled teacher I have ever met and one who was capable in many different areas.'[63] He was reserved and formal in manner and did not establish close personal relationships. Morris records that 'over the course of three years we only prayed together on about three occasions.'[64] Missionaries arriving to speak at the college would knock at his door and be told to wait in the college hall until the meeting. This personal coldness began to discourage some mission leaders from sending their candidates to the college for training.

As numbers declined, concern began to be expressed about the apparent lack of public confidence in the college. Some felt that the publicity of the college was poor. Others said that there was insufficient communication between the college and the former students, who were in the best position to make the college known. The council was also aware of a growing financial crisis and decided to review the

59. 'Brief biographies – The Principal: Rev Leslie S. M'Caw, M.A.', in: *NAN* (Winter 1956/7), p. 6.
60. L.S. M'Caw, 'Editorial', in: *NAN* (Summer 1955), p. 3.
61. *Ibid.*
62. L.S. M'Caw, 'Editorial', in *NAN* (Autumn 1955), p. 3.
63. D. Morris, personal correspondence, April 11 1998.
64. Ibid.

raison d'être of the college: 'It was felt there was a need for more time and concentration on the purpose for which the college existed. It was suggested that a special request should be made to every member to set down in writing what they considered to be the scope and aim of the college and the type of student desired.'[65]

Every institution goes through difficult times: they are painful for all those concerned. The next year was one of the most difficult in the life of ANBC, and in 1962 M'Caw was asked to resign. He was a gifted Bible expositor, who was appreciated by those who sat under his teaching and were trained under his leadership. With his leaving a whole chapter in the life of All Nations came to an end. A very different chapter was about to begin.

5.2.7 Conclusion

Between 1923 and 1962, there were six different principals of ANBC. Four (Meyer, Pike, Bonsall and M'Caw) had disagreements with the board which led to their departure or dismissal. Two (Meyer and Poole-Connor) were already in their seventies when they were appointed and, perhaps inevitably, only stayed in office for a short while. Only two principals (Curr and M'Caw) stayed for more than four years.

F. B. Meyer was a well-known evangelical figure. His association with the college as founder and first principal guaranteed a level of public recognition in its early years. He was already elderly when he assumed office, and because of his brief period of leadership did not have a large impact.

Dr Cunningham Pike lacked Meyer's public reputation and personal compassion. He was more concerned for his students to learn biblical languages than to be prepared practically for the mission field. His fiery temperament, exacerbated by his declining health, brought him into constant conflict with the council.

It was left to Henry Curr to provide a sustained period of leadership and to establish the college along the lines envisaged by the founders. Like Pike, he was a scholar,but he enjoyed better health and better relations with the college council than his predecessor. He was thorough and conscientious in the preparation and delivery of his lectures, but by insisting to teach by rote he failed to encourage students to think for themselves. He undoubtedly cared for his students but had little close contact with them. He was convinced, however, both of the necessity of the thorough preparation for missionaries, and of the impact that a period of residential training could have on the rest of the students' lives.

As Meyer provided the initial leadership at the start of the college, Poole-Connor played a similar role in its rebirth after the war. He too was a well-known evangelical figure, like Meyer before him, and his reputation and his enthusiasm for the college quickly attracted a good number of students. He was more conservative theologically than Meyer, and was highly critical of all modernism and the ecumenical movement.

Under the leadership of Brash Bonsall, the college experienced considerable development and expansion. Whereas Pike and Curr had been primarily interested

65. Minute 633, dated February 14 1961.

in the academic dimension of the college's curriculum, Bonsall was equally concerned that students should be prepared practically and technically for their future missionary work. He was a visionary but his modus operandi led to conflict with students, staff and council.

Leslie M'Caw brought to ANBC academic scholarship, pastoral experience and an appreciation of a wide spectrum of Christian traditions. He sought to maintain the traditions and ethos set by his predecessors. He was a gifted lecturer, but lacked Bonsall's personal warmth or charisma. He was not successful at promoting the college's public image, and several missionary societies stopped sending their candidates to the college for training. During his ten years as principal, ANBC began to experience numerical decline and financial difficulty. The number of students going overseas also dropped, and the rationale of the college was called into question. Clearly the college needed a new vision if it was to avoid closure.

The most serious problem that faced the council during this period was that of providing continuity of leadership for the college. Again and again, the members of the council found themselves at variance with those they had appointed. Sometimes this revolved around the personality of the principal, as in the case with Pike and Bonsall. Sometimes it was caused by disagreement over the management of the college, as appeared to be the case with Meyer. Sometimes it arose because of uncertainty over the college's viability and rationale, as happened with M'Caw.

As each new principal was appointed, each had his own ideas about the purpose of the college and the kind of training it should provide. Some maintained a strong emphasis on training for missionary service overseas, while others seemed to be more concerned to train men for Christian ministry at home. It was this uncertainty about the distinctive role and purpose of the college which surfaced in the closing years of M'Caw's principalship and had to be resolved by his successor.

5.3 DOCTRINAL BASIS AND CHARACTER

Four factors guided the council as they took the momentous step to open a Bible college in 1923. Firstly, it was to be an evangelical college, so that 'missionaries in their training may be free from the enervating influence of modern theology and religious rationalism.'[66] Secondly, it was to be an interdenominational college, based in the south of England and preferably in the home counties. Thirdly, its primary function was to be the preparation of men and women for overseas missionary service: 'The institution should be of a distinctive missionary character, for the training of men and women who would ultimately be welcomed into the ranks of missionary societies and other departments of missionary work.'[67] Fourthly, it would provide practical preparation for Christian ministry rather than a highly academic programme. It would accept all those who were deemed to be suitable for evangelistic or missionary work, whether or not they had been fortunate enough to

66. B.I. Greenwood, 'The great need for the All Nations Bible College', in: *MRAN* 62 (April 1922), p. 222.
67. G. Thomas, 'A short account of the foundation of the ANBC', in: *MRAN* 147 (April 1939), p. 16.

have tertiary education. It would develop their character and equip them for a life of hard work and sacrificial service.

5.3.1 Evangelical and scriptural religion

From the outset, F. B. Meyer made the doctrinal position of the college clear. It was 'for the training of the servants of Christ in evangelical and scriptural religion.'[68]

The doctrinal position of the college was given careful consideration. A committee, consisting of Anglicans, Baptists, Brethren and members of other Free Churches, was appointed to draw up a statement of faith. This committee held two conferences and submitted a doctrinal statement which was subsequently adopted by the full council.[69] This statement of faith remained unchanged for the next sixteen years and was retained when the college reopened after the Second World War.[70] It was read out every year at the annual meeting, and all members of staff and the council were required to give their assent to it in writing. A framed copy of the doctrinal basis was always exhibited in the entrance hall of the college (appendix 1).[71]

The basis of faith reflected the evangelical stance of the college. Particular emphasis was laid on the inspiration, trustworthiness and authority of the Scriptures. Liberal scholarship and modernism were frequently criticised in the *Missionary Review*. Dr Cunningham Pike, the second principal of the college, gave a strong critique of Arthur S. Peake's commentary of the Bible because 'of the plain errors and mistakes honeycombed right through the book from beginning to end.'[72]

The founders of the college were aware of the influence of liberal scholarship in theological education in Britain at this time. 'It would be difficult to name a single college in this country in which students are being trained for the Christian ministry in which the modern view of the Old Testament is not assumed as a matter of course.'[73] One article refers to two new students at All Nations, who had previously attended another missionary training college. There they had been told that the Bible contained many errors and Jesus 'was a great teacher and liable to be mistaken.'[74] It was the determination of the founders of All Nations that those whom they trained should have a high view of Scripture and know how to communicate it effectively to others.

The college was sometimes critical of other traditions of the Christian Church. Arthur H. Forbes, who served as a lecturer and tutor from 1923 to 1936, wrote a long article on Roman Catholicism, which was published over two issues of the *Missionary Review.*[75] He accepted that Christians are to love one another and avoid

68. Quoted in *NAN* (Winter 1957), p. 3.
69. See appendix 1 for the doctrinal statement.
70. 'Doctrinal Basis of the All Nations Bible College', in: *MRAN*ns 1 (1947), p. 12.
71. G. Thomas, 'A short account of the foundation of the ANBC,' *MRAN* 147 (April 1939), p. 17.
72. W.J. Cunningham Pike, 'Conference on the all-inspired Word of God', in: *MRANs* 73 (July 1924), p. XVIII.
73. Dr G. Jackson, quoted by F.B. Meyer, 'How All Nations Bible College is helping', in: *MRANs* 69 (October 1923), p. 184.
74. 'The teaching of error in a missionary training college', in: *MRANs* 72 (April 1924), p. X.
75. A.V. Forbes, 'Romish Controversy', in: *MRANs* 85 (December 1926), pp. LXXXV-LXXXVIII and 86 (February 1927), pp. 99-100.

controversy, but argued that sometimes controversy is unavoidable. He recognised that many Roman Catholic clergy are 'sincere, earnest and conscientious,' but he felt obliged to point out those elements of their creed that he considered to be wrong. Such articles did not appear very frequently in the *Missionary Review,* but they reflect attitudes that were not uncommon among British evangelical Christians during this period.

5.3.2 Interdenominationalism

The founders of ANBC were motivated by a desire to establish an interdenominational Bible college in England and, more specifically, in the vicinity of London. There was no such college in the country and, as Charles Inwood had observed, the growth in the number of interdenominational missionary societies created an urgent need for a college where their candidates could be trained.

The All Nations Missionary Union appointed a council for the new college in June and July 1922.[76] The council was deliberately interdenominational in character and was composed of clergymen and laymen, both from the Church of England and of the Free Churches.[77] The first council included two medical doctors, two Justices of the Peace, and others with experience in business, finance and education.

The members of the council were all well-known evangelical leaders, committed to mission. They also were knowledgeable about the needs of the mission fields. Several served with different missionary organisations. Some of them travelled extensively. Francis Brading, the secretary of the Scripture Gift Mission, travelled to America, Japan, China, Korea and India. W.J. Ervine travelled twice around the world. Once they joined the council, the members took their obligation to the college very seriously. Many of them remained on the council until their death. Several of them gave large donations.

In 1924, a ladies' committee was appointed. In its composition, this also reflected the interdenominational character of the college. Geoffrey Thomas acted as Chairman and his wife as the secretary. The committee also included: Miss E. B. Whitfield, principal of Mount Hermon, as acting chairman; Mrs Cunningham Pike, the wife of the principal of All Nations; and three other ladies. It is unclear what were their specific duties but they may have been concerned with the domestic side of the college.

While the staff and council members enjoyed good relationships with evangelicals of all denominations, they differed in their attitude towards other Christian traditions. Meyer was at home among a wide spectrum of Christian leaders. Poole-Connor, on the other hand, was unhappy about any association with non-evangelicals and was highly critically of the ecumenical movement. Those who succeeded him were not as outspoken as he was, but his attitude of suspicion and mistrust dominated the college thinking well into the 1960s.

76. G. Thomas, 'A short account of the foundation of the ANBC', in: *MRAN* 147 (April 1939), p. 17.
77. 'The All Nations Bible College: why it was founded', in: *ANBC prospectus* (1926), p. 3.

5.3.3 Preparation for missionary service

Charles Inwood wrote: ‘The large and increasing number of interdenominational missionary societies calls loudly for such a college where missionary candidates may be equipped for their life work.’[78] Miss Emily Whitfield, superintendent of Mount Hermon Missionary Training College, which was situated nearby to the proposed site for the new college, wrote: ‘We are most thankful to God that the ANBC is now actually being started for the training of men for the mission field... The sisters of Mount Hermon prayerfully welcome the brother students of ANBC to their neighbourhood and ask for great blessing.’[79]

An editorial of MRAN claimed that ‘ANBC is the only interdenominational college in England for the special training of men for the foreign mission field.’[80] Soon after he assumed the principalship, Henry Curr wrote that ‘the purpose of the college is to prepare missionaries.’[81] Only a year later he described it as ‘designed for the training of evangelists.’[82] Men were accepted to train as evangelists, or even pastors in the home country, but the primary focus of the college was the overseas mission field. Within a few years, the secretary of the college was able to assert that the college had gained a ‘strong reputation for solid specialised missionary training.’[83]

ANBC was not established to provide a theological education equal to that which would be found in a denominational theological college or a university. The course was designed to last only two years and was geared specifically to the requirements of the mission field. Men were welcome at the college whatever their educational background, or, in Henry Curr’s words, ‘even though they had not enjoyed a finished education.’[84] F. B. Meyer was convinced that tertiary education was not a prerequisite for success on the mission field. On the contrary, he believed that less well educated men might be more adaptable and successful in rugged pioneering contexts. He was saddened when many fine missionary candidates were debarred from the field simply because of their inability to pass the tests of missionary societies. At the dedication of the college buildings on June 24th 1922, he said, ‘I believe for the opening up of new enterprises the humbler man is often the best. In such places a man must know how to do a certain amount of manual work and be willing to rough it and live in a life of toil and sacrifice.’[85] Consequently it became the policy of the college never to turn away any applicant through lack of educational qualifications.[86]

Thirty years later, Principal M’Caw was able to look back and reflect on the kind of men that had been trained at the college: ‘Over four hundred have trained

78. C. Inwood, in a letter dated October 6 1921.
79. E.B. Whitfield, in: *MRAN* 62 (April 1922), p. 225.
80. Editorial, in: *MRANs* 76 (Feburary 1925), p. XLVI.
81. H. Curr, ‘Principal’s report and statement of the aims and purposes of ANBC’, in: *MRANs* 80 (November 1925), p. 76.
82. H. Curr, ‘The purpose of ANBC’, in: *MRANs* 83 (July 1926), p. 113.
83. G. Thomas, in a statement made to the college council and quoted in: *MRANs* 94 (September 1928), p. 49.
84. H. Curr, ‘The ANBC curriculum’, in: *MRANs* 79 (September 1925), p. LXIII.
85. F.B.Meyer, quoted in *NAN* (summer 1955), p. 2.
86. G. Thomas, in a statement to the council, in: *MRANs* 94 (September 1928), p. 49.

here: men from varied homes and occupations, indeed from many countries, some with no educational advantages or lacking almost all resources, others with a university background and ample means; carpenters, clerks, salesmen, sailors, nurserymen and mechanics.'[87]

Although it was the original intention of the council to train men and women for missionary service, it remained an all male institution throughout this period of its history. Ridgelands and Mount Hermon were situated only a few miles away, and it may have been felt that further provision for the training of women was unnecessary. In the event, strong links developed between All Nations and Mount Hermon. Miss Whitfield, founder and principal of Mount Hermon, always welcomed close co-operation between the two colleges, and Mount Hermon students often attended the Friday night prayer meetings at ANBC. By 1926, at least two marriages had resulted from the proximity of the two institutions.[88]

5.3.5 Conclusion

All Nations Bible College was founded as an evangelical college. It upheld the plenary inspiration of the Scriptures and rejected contemporary scholarship that appeared to undermine its authority. It sought to provide its students with a basic knowledge of the Bible and with confidence in its reliability. Its narrow and critical stance towards those who held different views was typical of conservative evangelicals of this period. Only in the decades after the Second World War did evangelical scholarship grow in stature and respectability, with the result that evangelical colleges could feel more confident to engage in debate with modern scholarship. By 1962, ANBC was barely effected by that development.

As an interdenominational college, the college welcomed Christians from a wide spectrum of denominations. This was no mean achievement as students held widely divergent views on such topics as worship, baptism, the Holy Communion, church government and predestination. However, this spirit of ecumenicity was limited to evangelicals. There were marked differences of opinion, especially among the principals, towards those who belonged to different traditions of the Christian Church. While the founding principal took a more positive stance towards non-evangelicals, the dominant spirit of the college, during most of these years, was one of suspicion and mistrust towards those outside its own constituency, and especially towards those involved in the ecumenical movement.

The college was founded in London with the purpose of training missionaries. Although it did train some for evangelistic work at home, its primary focus was overseas ministry. Its aim was to provide not an academic theological education but personal preparation for Christian service. It was willing to accept any candidates who had a genuine call to mission service whatever their educational background. In consequence, the academic qualifications of students who came to ANBC was not very high, but the college did not see this as a barrier to effective service. On the

87. L.S. M'Caw, 'Editorial', in: *NAN* (Summer 1955), p. 3.
88. 'College notes', in: *MRANs* 81 (February 1926), p. 93.

contrary, in the view of many of the staff, men with humbler qualifications often proved to be more effective missionaries.

5.4 The programme

'We are concentrating on one thing – the training of adaptable, dependable men who know the Scriptures, are experienced in faith and prayer, and who have that growing love, irrepressible joy, and deep humility which indicate both the presence of the Lord Himself and the anointing of the Spirit for effective service.'[89]

'The curriculum of ANBC is geared to prepare thoroughly in two years those who are going overseas. It includes a systematic study of the English Bible and practical equipment for service so that they are ready to face any situation.'[90]

These quotations reflect the desire of the staff and council of ANBC to provide a holistic programme of missionary preparation. That programme was designed to include spiritual preparation, character formation, practical training and academic study.

5.4.1 Spiritual preparation

Spiritual preparation was undoubtedly seen as the single most important facet of the training. Regular times were set aside for both collective and corporate prayer, and these were 'long enough to enable the lessons which such experiences endue to be grasped.'[91] Dr Curr believed that the value of appointing set times for prayer was to provide a stimulus, and create a pattern, which students might subsequently follow for the rest of their lives. 'If we only ate when we felt disposed to do so, we should not derive as much benefit as we do from regular meals.'[92]

Lectures were given on prayer, and students were encouraged to read appropriate devotional literature. Curr was convinced that the best way to learn to pray was to pray. 'A man will learn to pray more quickly on his knees with the Holy Spirit as his tutor than by reading devotional books on the subject.'[93]

Each new session began with a prolonged time of worship, biblical exposition and testimony, which would set the tone for the term ahead. On one such occasion in April 1923, 'the presence of God was manifest in the meeting' and many spoke of it afterwards 'as a meeting they will always remember.'[94]

Regular weekly prayer meetings were held to which the public, and the young ladies of Mount Hermon, were invited. Geoffrey Thomas observed of these meet-

89. *All Nations Brochure* (c. 1955), p. 1.
90. Henry Curr, 'The ANBC curriculum', in: *MRANs* 79 (September 1925), p. LXIII.
91. Henry Curr,' 'The importance of prayer', in: *MRANs* 132 (April 1936), p. 7.
92. *Ibid.*
93. *Ibid.*
94. 'Editorial', in: *MRANs* 76 (April 1925), p. LIV.

ings: 'The spirit of prayer which invariably characterises the meeting is something for which no friend of the college can be too grateful. No sooner has one voice ceased than another takes up the petition, and thus the blessed moments fly.'[95] On one occasion, Henry Curr commented that the students of their own initiative were holding brief prayer meetings on every available night of the week to intercede for the nations of the world.[96] On another, he wrote that the students had been let off their usual Friday afternoon routine for a half day of prayer. He remarked, 'We have never had so much prayer and so much football.'[97]

The Keswick Convention exerted a considerable influence on the spiritual life of the college. The idea for the college had been born at the convention in 1921 and many staff and students attended subsequent conventions. In 1955, Principal M'Caw commented: 'The college stands for Keswick principles applied to the training of young men for Christian service, especially those going overseas.'[98] In later years the college was also affected by the teaching of the East African Revival and the teaching of men like Dr Joseph. E. Church, who worked with the Ruanda Mission.[99]

5.4.2 Character formation

A college prospectus published in the 1950s compared the college to a whetstone, which could sharpen the cutting edge of the church. It was the policy of the college to put the students under 'balanced pressure' so that they would become more conformed to the image of Christ.[100] The training of character was as important as the imparting of academic knowledge.

Curr believed that the impress that men receive during their time at college would remain with them for the rest of their lives. He was realistic enough to admit that the lectures and sermons might soon be forgotten but 'the stamp put upon a man will remain to the end of his days.'[101]

The college did not seek to mass-produce identical missionaries, or encourage each student to reach the same academic standard. Rather the aim was to enable each man to reach his own potential and develop his own gifts.

The residential nature of the training enhanced character formation. Staff and students learned a great deal from one another as they lived together in close community. Henry Curr believed that residential training offered the closest parallel to the pattern of discipling followed by Jesus as he trained the twelve. 'Nobody, who has any experience of such an institution would refuse to acknowledge at once that close contact and intercourse with his fellows meant a great deal to him, and, it may

95. G. Thomas, 'College notes', in: *MRANs* 81 (February 1926), p. 86.
96. H. Curr, 'Principal's Report' at the Third Anniversary Celebration, held on February 13 1926, and quoted in: *MRANs* 81 (February 1926), p. 86.
97. H. Curr, 'Principal's speech,' end of term meeting, March 1928, quoted in: *MRANs* 92 (May 1928), p. 15.
98. L.S. M'Caw, 'Editorial', in: *NAN* (Summer, 1955), p.3.
99. J.E. Church, 'Oneness', in: *ANMR* ns 7(Summer 1949), p. 12f.
100. *ANBC Prospectus* (c.1955), p. 1.
101. *Ibid.*

be ... that he will prize more than anything the lessons which he learned not from the printed page, but from communion with his fellows.'[102]

Twenty five years later, Principal M'Caw made a similar observation: 'It is sometimes forgotten how great is the influence which the life of a whole community can have upon the faith and even the unbelief of a new member. Trustfulness is contagious and prayerfulness can be a constant challenge.'[103]

5.4.3 Technical skills

From the outset, the training offered at All Nations was intensely practical. Ten hours a week were devoted to the developing of technical skills. Men were being prepared for pioneer evangelism in some of the least developed parts of the world. They needed to be able to turn their hands to anything, and the aim of the course was to equip the students to be competent to cope with any situation they might face. As A. G. Watson, the first technical instructor in the college, wrote: 'The pioneer missionary especially needs to know how to choose the site for a house or mission room, how to plan and build; often it is very useful if he knows how to make bricks, the use of wood-working and other tools, and in addition, how to adapt himself to the task when many of the tools and even ordinary tools are lacking.'[104]

Carpentry tools, metalwork tools, an anvil, a forge and a printing press were all slowly acquired by the college. Under the watchful eye of Mr Watson, students built easels, bookshelves, benches, desks, a duck house and a technical workshop.[105] They made a set of front gates for the college and learned to turn treacle tins into tin kettles.[106]

Courses were also provided in book-keeping[107] and the understanding of oriental languages.[108] A basic course was offered in elementary physiology, anatomy, the elements of first aid and surgery, and tropical health. The aim of this course was 'to teach essentials, not to create a number of dental surgeons.'[109] Some students were encouraged to attend a month-long vacation medical course at the Islington Medical Mission.

5.4.4 Instruction and practice in ministry skills

Another essential component of the All Nations training was to give instruction in various aspects of Christian ministry, and to provide students with an opportunity to put into practice what they had learned. Lectures were given on how to speak to

---

102. H.S. Curr, 'Principal's letter', in: *MRANs* 100 (December 1929), p. 126.
103. L.S. M'Caw, 'Editorial', in: *News from All Nations* (Autumn 1955), p. 3.
104. A.G. Watson, 'Technical preparation of the missionary', in: *MRANs* 71(February 1924), p. II.
105. 'A.G. Watson, Technical instructor (1926-1931)', in: *MRANs* 107 (May 1931), p. 59.
106. 'Editorial', in: *MRANs* 68 (August 1923), p. 157.
107. 'College notes', in: *MRANs* 75 (November 1924), p. XXXI.
108. 'College notes', in: *MRANs* 79 (September 1925), p. LXVI.
109. E. White, quoted in 'College notes', in: *MRANs* 89 (April 1927), p. 133. An sample examination for this course is given in appendix 2.

different age groups of children, and how to make use of visual aids, such as flannelgraph.[110] In 1935, Henry Curr instituted a preachers' class, in which a brief devotional service was led by one of the students and then another student preached a sermon. 'The performance of all those concerned is then freely criticised by those present,' wrote Curr.[111] He was aware that young preachers quickly developed mannerisms and hoped that they might be eradicated of they were pointed out in time.

Every weekend students were involved in evangelism and other forms of ministry. One group held evangelistic meetings in a London City Mission hall,[112] while others travelled to speak, sing or give testimonies in other churches and clubs in the vicinity. When the college was re-established in Taplow after the Second World War, the new generation of students were just as ardent in their desire to reach out in local evangelism. The class of 1948 determined to evangelise every village that lay within a 35 mile radius of Taplow.[113]

Vacations offered opportunities for more sustained periods of experience in Christian ministry. Many students were involved in rural evangelism, using a caravan or cart, which was often pulled by hand. One student went to France and wrote of his experience when he handed out a copy of Mark's gospel to a French housewife in the village of Tilly. 'Oh, St Mark,' she said,' We pray to him for the gooseberries.'[114] Another student gained experience by working with a fishing fleet from the port of Lowestoft. 'I can now speak with feeling of the ups and downs of a fisherman's life,' he wrote.[115]

In some instances the evangelistic efforts of the students were richly rewarded. In March 1937, they were involved in six separate campaigns, and more than 'fifty conversions were recorded among children, young people and adults.'[116] Later the same year, one student team trekked over 400 miles to Durham, where '200 stood in the pouring rain for one and a half hours to hear the preaching of the Word, and the following night nearly 400 stood for two hours.'[117]

5.4.5 Academic studies

As we have noted, ANBC could not pretend to offer a course on a par with that of a university or theological college. Nonetheless academic studies were considered to be important and a major part of the programme was devoted to them. It was the aim of the staff not simply to cram the students full of facts but to teach them how to learn, so that they continued learning throughout their lives and ministry.[118]

---

110. G.F. Vallance, 'How to make and use the flannelgraph', in: *ANMR* ns 3 (Spring 1948), p. 11f. and 4 (Summer 1948), p. 5f.
111. H.S. Curr, 'Editorial', in: *MRANs* 127 (April 1935), p. 303.
112. *MRANs* 85 (December 1926), p. LXXXV,
113. 'Student evangelistic drive going well', in: *ANMR*ns 3 (Spring 1948), p. 9.
114. *MRANs* 71 (February 1924), p. II.
115. *The College's Review* (1934), p. 235.
116. H. Bates, 'Students' spiritual work', in: *MRANs* 137 (April 1937), p. 91.
117. H. Bates, 'Students' spiritual work', in: *MRANs* 139 (September 1937), p. 117.
118. H.S. Curr, 'Principal's letter', in: *MRANs* 93 (June 1928), p. 29.

Priority was given to a systematic study of the English Bible. In the view of Principal Curr, that was the best textbook to be the base of a two year programme of missionary training.[119] The first year was devoted to a study of the Pentateuch, historical books, prophets and wisdom literature; the second year to the gospels, Acts, epistles and Revelation. Each term a course was given on one of the major Christian doctrines: the nature of God, the person and work of Christ, etc., so that students acquired a comprehensive overview of Christian fundamentals. Greek, Hebrew and advanced biblical studies were also available for those students who wished to take additional subjects.[120] Termly courses were also presented on church history, with extensive attention being paid to the 'Romish controversy' and the 'Counter Reformation.'

Visiting lecturers gave missionary addresses and, during the second year, courses were offered on comparative religion. That appears to have been the only instruction given which could have been called missionary or missiological studies. The strong appeal made at the Edinburgh Conference of 1910 that missionary candidates should be trained in the science of missions, or in the understanding of culture, appears to have remained largely unheeded.

The other regular component of the programme was the study of English literature. The students were introduced to the works of Chaucer, Shakespeare, Spencer, Milton, Byron and Tennyson, as well as the great English novelists. This was considered to be an integral part of missionary preparation.

In the post-war period, the syllabus appears to have remained much as it was in the early days. 40% of lectures were given to a 'careful and prayerful study of the text of the Bible', 30% to its historical background and to doctrine, and around 20% to church history, homiletics, modern heresies, etc.[121]

5.4.6 Conclusion

ANBC was established to provide practical and holistic missionary training for men, most of whom had not had the benefit of higher education. To some extent it was attempting to compensate for the lack of higher education among many of its students.

The most striking feature of the curriculum was the absence of any serious missiological and cultural study. There was no course on the theology or practice of mission, on the study of culture, or on cross-cultural communication. The history of missions received brief mention under church history, and relatively little time was given to the study of other religions. These seem to be strange omissions for a college that was founded to train missionaries.

On the other hand, the range of technical training that was offered, particularly in the pre-war years, was impressive. The ANBC student was taught many practical skills that would stand him in great stead in primitive situations. He was equipped

119. H.S. Curr, from his opening address given on September 15th, 1926, at the beginning of a new academic year, quoted in *MRANs* 84 (October 1926), p. LXXVI.
120. A complete curriculum dated c.1935 is given in appendix 4.
121. 'Prospectus,' (c. 1955), p. 3.

not only to survive but also to pass on to others many of the skills he had learned.

Great attention was paid to the development of the spiritual life and this was reflected in the ethos of the college and the lives of both staff and students. The nature of this spirituality was distinctly evangelical and strongly individualistic. This individualism led to a highly personalised view of mission. There was little understanding of the role of the church in mission and, at the same time, an instinctive suspicion of other spiritual traditions.

The staff were concerned with the development of the students' characters. Curr was aware of the value of living in a small Christian community and the impression that a period of two years in the college could make on the lives of students. He further recognised the responsibility of the staff to set a good example of Christian living.

The academic level at the college was inevitably rather low, since lecturers faced the challenge of teaching students with a wide range of ability and knowledge. While the academic standard was below tertiary level, the course appeared to offer a reasonable introduction to biblical and theological studies from an evangelical perspective. The method of teaching by the dictating of notes did not encourage students to think for themselves. The failure of the course to include the views of less conservative scholars deprived students of the opportunity to learn from them or interact with them.

The principals disagreed about the content and length of the course. Pike insisted that all that was necessary was for the students to become conversant with the biblical languages. Curr saw the systematic study of the Bible as the one essential of missionary training. Brash Bonsall believed that missionaries needed to be as well trained as ministers. He broadened the course content and expanded its length to three years.

5.5 THE STUDENTS

When the college opened in February 1923 there were eight students. These eight, to whom two more were added after a few weeks, constituted the first group to be trained at the college. They completed their course together in 1924.

As the reputation of the college grew, the number of candidates began to increase. Principal Curr hoped that one day there would be a hundred students at All Nations but, although there seemed to be no shortage of women applying to Mount Hermon, there was not a corresponding number of men wanting to come to All Nations. A special meeting was held at the Eccleston Hall on March 7th, 1927 to present the challenge of missionary work to young men and to boost the number of applicants to the college.[122] A deputation secretary was appointed, the Rev J.R. Hayman. Friends of the college were encouraged to hold 'drawing room meetings' so that the work of the college could become more widely known. In spite of all that

122. It was entitled 'The need of men for the foreign field, and the work of All Nations Bible College.' A report of the meeting appeared in *MRANs* 88 (June 1927), pp. 106-113.

effort, numbers increased very slowly. Most years, there were twenty four students. and the largest number was thirty in 1933.

Between 1923 and 1939, two hundred and forty eight students registered at the college.[123] The majority completed a two year programme running from September to July. However, the college adopted a flexible policy on admission and departure dates to suit the needs of the candidates and mission boards. Some students were unable to join the programme until the middle of the academic year, while others were required to leave for the mission field during the course of a term. In the years 1945 to 1962, a further 251 men were trained at the college.[124]

5.5.1 Academic requirements

All Nations Bible College was initially intended for those who had not had the advantage of higher education. The decision taken by the council in September 1921 stated 'that the candidates to be received should be those who had only the advantage of an elementary school education.'[125]

As it turned out, a number of men who had received tertiary education also began to apply for training at the college and in consequence the academic level began to rise. As G. Thomas wrote in 1939, 'When the college was actually established the range of candidates was found to include many who had had the advantage of higher education, so that these, also, were admitted as students, and thus the influence of the college widened.'[126] It is also true to say that many of the students who had only completed secondary education, were capable of studies at tertiary level, as their subsequent achievements demonstrated. They had been prevented from proceeding to tertiary education by their family circumstances or the limited accessibility of university places.

In the post-war years, the majority of students continued to be non-graduates. Their occupations varied from concrete maker, joiner, shoe repairer, window cleaner and grocer's assistant, to plumber, watchmaker, telephone engineer and printer. However, the college register also included medical doctors, research scientists, and an architect.

5.5.2 Denominational and national background

From the outset it was resolved that the college should be interdenominational, so students were accepted from many different denominations. The representation of denominations in the student body in the pre-war years was as follows: Baptists 37%, Anglicans 20%, Independent Evangelical 10%, Brethren 7%, Methodists 6%, Presbyterian and Congregational 5%. Other denominations and overseas students represented the remaining 15%.[127]

---

123. G. Thomas, 'A short account of the foundation of the ANBC', in: *MRAN* 147 (April 1939), p. 118.
124. *Register of Students, ANBC.*
125. G. Thomas, 'A short account of the foundation of the ANBC,' in: *MRAN* 147 (April 1939), p. 16.
126. *Ibid.*
127. *Register of students, ANBC.*

In the post-war period, the denominational representation was similar, but with a slight decline in the number of Anglican, Methodist and Presbyterian students. The percentages were: Baptist 39%, Independent Evangelical 14%, Anglicans 12%, Brethren 6%, Methodist 4%, Presbyterians 3%. The remaining 22% belonged to other denominations or came from overseas.[128]

Although the students came from such a wide diversity of denominational backgrounds, they seemed to have got on well together. After the college closed at the beginning of the Second World War, G. Thomas, the Honorary Secretary of ANBC, was able to write: 'We have always had happily studying together men from the Church of England, the various denominations and the Brethren.'[129]

The majority of students came from the British Isles: 85% of the pre-war students were British; 13% came from continental Europe;[130] 2% came from other parts of the world, notably Japan, India and Egypt. In the period after the war, 87% came for the United Kingdom, 11% from Europe. 2% from other countries, including Ethiopia, Nigeria and Malaysia.[131]

5.5.3 Societies and countries of service

The *ANBC Registry of Students* gives brief but incomplete details of what students did after they left college. In the period from 1923 to 1939, there are no records of forty students. Of the remainder, 58% went overseas as missionaries, 22% went into pastoral work in the home country, while the rest went on to further study or returned to secular work.

In the post-war years, 60% went abroad as missionaries, while 15% went into pastoral or evangelistic work at home. The remaining 25% took up secular work or undertook further studies. There is no record of 17 students.

The students went to many different countries and continents. In 1929, the *Missionary Review* published a list of former All Nations students and the countries where they were serving.[132] Forty names are given and their areas of service are stated as follows: Africa 13, Europe (including Latvia, Poland and Lithuania) 13, Asia 7, Middle East 2, United Kingdom 2, Canada 1, Jamaica 1, South America 1. 30% of the graduates were working in countries which had close associations with the British Crown (Nigeria, Gold Coast, Kenya, S. Africa, India, Burma, Jamaica and Canada). Two others were serving in the British mandated territory of Palestine.

Four years later, a similar list appeared in the *Missionary Review*, giving the names of forty-seven men who were serving overseas.[133] The figures given are as

128. *Ibid.*
129. G. Thomas, 'Temporary closing for the war time of the All Nations Bible College', in: *MRAN* 150 (November 1939), p. 118.
130. The numbers of students coming from European countries during these years were as follows: Norway 6, Germany 6, Poland 5, Russia 4, Switzerland 4, France 3, Latvia 3, Sweden 3, Ukraine 2, Demnark 2, Finland 1, Austria 1, Italy 1, Holland 1, Estonia 1, Czechoslovakia 1, Lithuania 1.
131. *Register of students, ANBC.*
132. 'Prayer list for ANBC missionaries', in: *MRANs* 99 (October 1929), p. 117.
133. 'Some of the past students trained at ANBC', in: *MRANs* 116 (January 1933), pp. 160f.

follows: Africa 18, Europe 13, Asia 11, Middle East 3, Jamaica 1, South America 1. These figures show a large number of students going to the African continent, while only one is serving in South America.

The college prepared students for work with a great variety of missionary societies. In the sixteen years from 1923, students went out with more than thirty different missionary organisations. Some of these were interdenominational in character, such as the China Inland Mission, the Sudan Interior Mission, the North Africa Mission and the Regions Beyond Missionary Union. Several were denominational missions such as the Baptist Missionary Society, the Church Missionary Society, the Bible Churchmens' Missionary Society and the South America Missionary Society. The last three were Anglican missions.[134]

5.5.4 Conclusion

Five observations may be drawn from the statistics mentioned in the previous sections. First, the students at ANBC were mainly British, with a small minority coming from other European countries, and a handful from elsewhere. Secondly, the majority of students came from Baptist or Free Evangelical backgrounds, with the rest representing a wider cross-section of Protestant denominations. Thirdly, most of the students came from the working class and had only had the benefit of elementary education. Fourthly, while just over half of the student body did go overseas as missionaries, nearly forty percent did not. Fifthly, among those who did go overseas, a high proportion went to Africa or Europe. A significant number served in countries in Asia and Africa which had strong links to the British crown.

5.6 Conclusion

In 1923, the year of the establishment of ANBC, the impact of the Edinburgh Conference of 1910 was still being felt and the IMC had just been established. The missionary task of the church was high on the agenda of many Protestant denominations, and the importance of the thorough preparation of missionaries had been widely recognised. ANBC was founded to provide such training but it only served a small section of the Christian Church.

The college had an auspicious beginning under the leadership of F. B. Meyer but suffered under frequent changes of principal. Indeed the council found it extraordinarily difficult to find a suitable principal who would remain for any length of time. Meyer stayed for little over a year, Cunningham-Pike for only seven months. Curr provided a period of stable leadership for fourteen years, but while he was an able scholar he was something of an eccentric, and weak in the area of personal relationships. After the Second World War, Poole-Connor lent his name and his reputation to re-establish the college, but he only remained for three years. Brash Bonsall

134. See appendix 5 for a list of missionary societies with which All Nations students served during this period.

brought new vision and energy to the college, but clashed both with the council and his own staff. M'Caw, though gifted as a scholar and teacher, was ineffective in promoting the public image of the college, and eventually the Council had to ask him to leave.

Similarly to the two sister colleges, the staff and council of ANBC were strongly influenced by Keswick. They emphasised the authority of the Bible. They were suspicious of other Christian traditions and critical of much contemporary biblical scholarship. The college accepted men of differing ability, including many who had not had the advantage of tertiary education. The course was geared to prepare men for missionary life and work. It recognised that a degree was not a prerequisite for effective missionary service and that many non-graduates proved to be more effective as missionaries than those who had been to university.

Whether by accident or design, the programme of training incorporated a number of suggestions which had been suggested at Edinburgh and subsequent conferences. The nurturing of a strong independent spiritual life, singled out at Edinburgh as the first prerequisite of a missionary training programme, was an important component of the ANBC training.[135] Equally strong was the emphasis on character training, particularly the developing of Christ-likeness and the dogged perseverance which pioneer evangelism would necessitate. The training in technical and practical skills was another notable feature of ANBC. By contrast, the content of the academic courses was limited in scope, particularly in the area of missiology. In many ways the ANBC syllabus was a pale reflection of courses offered by denominational theological colleges.

In July 1910, the All Nations Missionary Union published a glowing report of the Edinburgh conference: 'This great assembly of the missionary forces of the Church of Christ is now a thing of the past, but that its influence will live, and, in countless ways, affect the future of our great enterprise, there can be no doubt.'[136] The article pointed out the spirit of unity that was seen among high church Bishops and evangelical leaders, between Anglicans and non-conformists. It stated the conviction, that was expressed repeatedly at the conference, that only a united church could hope to succeed in the task of evangelizing the world.

In view of this affirmative review of Edinburgh 1910, and its call for ecumenical co-operation in the task of mission, it is surprising that in subsequent publications by the ANMU, produced before and after the founding of ANBC, no further reference can be found either to Edinburgh or to any of the conferences organised by the IMC or the CWME. This striking omission reflects the ambivalence which evangelicals felt towards the emerging ecumenical movement. Some principals of ANBC, like F. B. Meyer viewed this development positively. He was equally at home with Anglican bishops as he was among fellow evangelical non-conformists. Others, notably E. J. Poole-Connor, were strongly opposed to the ecumenical movement. He criticised 'the inadequacy of its doctrinal base, its ultimate objective of the re-establishment of one visible church and its interpretation of Christianity as an eth-

135. WMC, *Report on Commission V* (1910), p. 100.
136. J. Jackson, 'The World Missionary Conference: the impressions of a delegate', in: ANMR (July, 1910), p. 1f.

ical way of life rather than a gospel of redemption of fallen man.'[137] Those who followed Poole-Connor were less vociferous in their criticism and less enthusiastic about the separation of evangelicals which he advocated. When M'Caw came to the college, he had been involved in several different churches and this gave him an appreciation of differing Christian traditions. Even so, the influence of Poole-Connor gave the college a certain reputation, and this was reflected in student admissions. Whereas before the Second World War, one third of students came from Anglican, Methodist, Presbyterian and Congregational churches, that figure was almost halved after the war. At that stage of its history, ANBC was perceived to be serving the independent evangelical constituency, and to have further distanced itself from the ecumenical movement.

The task of mission in the post-colonial world created a new set of problems. As African, Asian and Latin American countries sought political independence, Christians in those countries expressed a desire for ecclesiastical independence. They did not want to serve under foreign leadership, or be dependent on Western finances and personnel. They wanted to addresses issues which concerned them rather than pursue an agenda which was imposed from the West. They were aware of the enormous social, political and economic problems that confronted their countries and recognised the urgent need for the appropriate contextualisation of the church and its message.

The impression that is gained from the archives of ANBC is that the college was slow to understand the significance of these changes or respond to these challenges. In spite of the recommendation from Edinburgh that the science of missions should have a major place in any training curriculum,[138] little attention appears to have been given to the theology and practice of missions, or to the study of non-western cultures and cross-cultural communication. The isolation of the college from the ecumenical movement meant that it was removed from the debate on the nature of the church's role in the world. The college's commitment to the primacy of evangelism meant that little attention was paid to the place of social, let alone political, action in the life of the church.[139]

Yet in spite of its shortcomings, ANBC trained almost five hundred men between 1923 and 1962, providing them with spiritual, practical and academic preparation for Christian service. More than half of them went overseas and many spent their whole working lives in missionary service.

---

137. E.J. Poole-Connor, *The WCC: whence and whither?* (1962), p. 11.
138. WMC, *Report on Commission V* (1910), p. 161f.
139. This had not always been the case, however. According to D.J. Tidball, *Who are the evangelicals* (1994), p. 44, 'Meyer specifically applied the gospel to society and argued for social righteousness from a theological platform.'

6. All Nations Missionary College (1962-1971) All Nations Christian College (1971-1981)

6.1 Introduction

This chapter considers the history of All Nations Missionary College (ANMC) from 1962 to 1971 and All Nations Christian College (ANCC) from 1971 to 1981. It explores the role of David Morris, whose personality and theory of training had such a formative influence on the ethos of the new college and the design of its programme (6.2). It examines the doctrinal basis of both colleges (6.3) and the major components of their curricula (6.4). It surveys the background of the students and their subsequent areas of service (6.5), and concludes with an evaluation of the college, by staff and students, and by external critics (6.6).

6.2 History and development

Between 1962 and 1981 All Nations was transformed from a small, struggling Bible college training single men for ministry at home and overseas into a flourishing co-educational institution, preparing single men, single women and married couples for cross-cultural missionary work. This transformation is largely attributable to the vision and effort of one man.

6.2.1 David Morris (1962-1981)

David Morris was born in 1919, the son of a director of Barclay's Bank. He grew up in the Oxfordshire countryside and in many ways enjoyed an idyllic childhood. His mother adored him, favouring him above his brother and sister. His father was a perfectionist, who never gave him a single word of encouragement. Morris was initially educated by a governess, and then was sent to school at the age of 8. He was not a very diligent pupil, and preferred hunting and shooting to studying books. Later, at Magdalen College School in Oxford, he would often sneak away to find bird's nests, when he should have been playing cricket. He was often beaten for his misdemeanours.

When he left school, his father told him that he must work for three years in Barclay's Bank. After that, he would be allowed to follow whatever career he chose with his father's blessing, though not with his money! David Morris hated the bank and was only saved from dismissal by the position of his father.

With the growing threat of war, Morris applied to join the Territorial Army. His parents assumed that he would not be accepted as he had suffered from Talipes Equinus in his childhood and had not been expected to walk. However, at his medical examination, the doctor, an aged colonel, gave him a gentle prod on his chest and declared him to be perfectly fit for service.

From childhood, Morris had attended the same Brethren Assembly as his parents, but he had long reacted against the sterile Christianity he perceived there. In his first few months in the army he encountered what his Brethren colleagues would have called 'the world.' He became desperately aware of his need for moral guidance. For the first time in his life he wanted to find Christ. On March 7th, 1939, he called at the home of a Territorial Army chaplain and blurted out, 'I'm not right with God and I won't leave this house until I am.'[1] Initially the chaplain was somewhat amused by this serious young man, asking him why he needed such a dramatic conversion. He then left the room to find a suitable book to lend him, and in his absence, David Morris found the peace that he was looking for. He remembers that, 'the room lit up and I knew that I had passed from death to life.'[2]

It was one thing to be a Christian. It was quite another to try to live as a Christian in such a secular environment. Morris found it extremely difficult to sustain his Christian life in an army barracks. Twice he tried to give up his faith. On the first occasion, he received a telegram from the War Office. It commended him for 'his known moral stand,' and despatched him to another unit where morale and morals had collapsed. On the second occasion, when he was about to abandon this Christian faith, he happened to go into the officers' mess carrying a Bible. An attractive female officer came over to him and asked if he believed in the Bible. She was a young Christian looking for someone who could help her to understand it better.[3] Three months later, David Morris and Trenna Heard were married.

Morris' time in the army had a profound impact on his future career as a missionary trainer. He was appointed as a training officer with the Royal Artillery and was given the responsibility of training those who would train others. He was determined to make that training as realistic as possible, devising a number of mock scenarios to simulate crises that the gunners might face.[4] In later years, he used this experience of providing realistic training for soldiers in developing practical training for missionaries.

In April 1945, Morris was sent to the National Institute for Industrial Psychologists to attend a course on selection. He then spent twelve months interviewing British returning prisoners-of-war with the aim of re-settling them into civilian life. With the rank of acting major, Morris was in charge of a team of twenty captains, who interviewed each returnee and twenty sergeants, who gave them a series of intelligence and aptitude tests. The team had to assess the mental and emotional state of each man to decide whether they should be discharged or continue in the army. During this year, Morris learned a great deal about how to interview men and to assess their fitness for continuing service. He also learned how easy it was to make mistakes. This 'caused me to turn my team into a kind of club, where we could meet and discuss as friends and, when I was uncertain what I should do, I

1. Interview with David Morris, March 14 1994.
2. Interview with David Morris, March 14 1994.
3. Interview with David Morris, May 21 1996.
4. These exercises were known as T.E.W.T. (Tactical exercises without troops).

would seek their advice.'[5] The interviewing techniques and the lessons learned about leading a team were to stand Morris in good stead when years later he was leading a missionary training college.

After the war, he studied at Oxford University and graduated with an honours degree in geography. While he was at university, he was deeply challenged by the need for educational work in Nigeria. He was eager to respond to God's call, but patiently waited for six months until his wife also became convinced that God was calling them to the mission field. They went to Nigeria with the Sudan United Mission[6] in 1949.

After three years, they returned to Oxford, so that Morris could take a full-time course in education. The course was focussed on overseas education in backward areas and problems connected with missionary work in colonial territories. He obtained his Diploma in Education with distinction.

There followed a second period of service in Nigeria with the Sudan United Mission. He became principal of the Teacher Training College at Gindiri and was able to use all his knowledge and experience in the training of future teachers, pastors and evangelists. As Morris commented later, 'It was here that the vital importance of training husbands and wives together was realised and put into practice – against the local custom and wishes.'[7]

During his time in Nigeria, Morris was appalled by the actions and attitudes of some of his fellow missionaries. They seemed to have little appreciation of Nigerian culture or respect for African people. They demonstrated an air of racial superiority inappropriate in the days of the Empire and completely out of place in a nation rapidly moving towards independence.[8] This left a deep impression on Morris, and in later years influenced his own attitude towards the selection and training of missionaries.

In 1956, the ill-health of one of his daughters brought him back to the United Kingdom. He taught for three years as housemaster of a preparatory school in Yorkshire, while he continued theological studies under the tutelage of Dr F.F. Bruce, Professor of Biblical History and Literature at the University of Sheffield.

6.2.2 All Nations Missionary College

Morris joined the staff of All Nations Bible College in 1959 as resident tutor. During the course of his first year, he had the misfortune to fracture a femur and was hospitalised for seven weeks. After Morris had spent three years at the college, the previous principal left and Morris was invited to take his place. It was a daunting task. The number of returning students was thirteen and only three new students had been accepted for the next academic year.

---

5. Personal correspondence, February 18 1998.
6. Now called Action Partners. For an account of their work in Nigeria, see J. B. Grimley & G. E. Robinson, *Church growth in central and southern Nigeria* (1966).
7. Personal correspondence, February 18 1998.
8. Nigeria became an independent nation on October 1 1960.

Morris was convinced that the college must sharpen its focus on missionary training and develop a programme to meet the needs of contemporary missionaries. He spent a great deal of time discussing with missionaries and mission leaders about the type of training they felt was necessary in the closing decades of the twentieth century. He drew up plans for the new college and asked the council to give him three years to develop these ideas. They deliberated for some time whether they should go along with his radical proposals, but capitulated after a prolonged council meeting.

One of his first requests was that the name of the college should be changed. When ANBC was founded there had been a strong emphasis on the training of missionaries. Morris felt this should be reflected in the name of the college. His proposal, duly accepted by the council, was that the name should be changed to 'All Nations Missionary College.'[9]

For some time, the council had been considering the possibility of moving the college to new premises, preferably nearer London. Taplow Hill House was not entirely suited to the needs of the college. The building required considerable maintenance and was in need of extensive repair. This fact was emphasised one Sunday afternoon when the principal and his wife were having tea and 'part of the top floor fell at their feet.'[10] The council considered a number of premises, but none seemed to be suitable. Morris records the memorable day when the possibility of moving to a house in Hertfordshire was first suggested: 'A grey haired member of the council, Captain Godfrey Buxton (founder of the Missionary Training Colony), somewhat slowly pulled from his brief case a faded sepia photograph of a country house. Would the council be interested in a house in Hertfordshire which his grandfather had built? It was now vacant as the London County Council had closed the children's home there.'[11] Captain Buxton explained that the house would be available for rent rather than purchase.

The country house in question had been built in 1869 by Thomas Fowell Buxton, son of Sir Thomas Fowell Buxton, who was nicknamed 'The Liberator' on account of his work with William Wilberforce for the abolition of the slave trade in the British Empire. A few weeks after the family had moved into their new home, Lady Hannah Buxton, the widow of Sir Thomas Fowell Buxton, wrote the following letter to her grandson, John Henry Buxton on May 8 1969:

> *Dearest John Henry,*
>
> *I opened my testament on a text with your initials written at the side, and this induced me to tell you myself how much I have desired a simple dedication service on the entrance into the new abode.*
> *I feel this is a residence given by God, and I would trace His hand in the important transaction in your lives. This may be a residence of Buxtons for how long, or how short a time also; but we look on to generations yet to*

9. Minutes of the Council, September 18 1962, minute 702.
10. D. Morris, *The story of Easneye* (1973), p. 14.
11. *Ibid.*, p. 14. The Council meeting in question met on June 25 1963.

come, and you may suppose what are my desires and hopes concerning it. That it may ever be inhabited by faithful servants of God in and through Christ Jesus, and that it may ever be a habitation of God in the hearts of the inhabitants by the Holy Spirit, and Christ be honoured, confessed and served, and this place be a fountain of blessing in the church and to the world. Consider what I say, and the Lord give thee understanding in all things. Your most affectionate Grandmother,

Hannah Buxton.[12]

These words proved prophetic, for less than a hundred years after they were penned, the building became the home of a missionary training college, committed to being 'a fount of blessing in the church and to the world.' So it was that in 1963, the council members, aware of the strong Christian associations of the house, were encouraged to think that this might indeed be the place they were looking for. They decided at once to go and visit it, both to assess its suitability and to discuss the possibility of a lease agreement with its current owner, Mr John Buxton.

While they were impressed with the property, they realised that a number of repairs and alterations would need to be carried out, before it would be suitable for the college's needs.[13] They were also aware of the need to sell the Taplow property before they could proceed to a new site. It took over a year to reach agreement on the terms of the lease and to finalise the sale of Taplow Hill House. Late in July 1964, the college left Taplow and moved to its new home at Easneye.

In addition to the lease of the main house, the college also agreed to rent the cricket ground, the North Lodge and the stables at a rental of £250 per annum.[14]

The numbers of students slowly began to rise. In 1963, 26 men enrolled for the autumn term. By 1965, there were 41 students. Additional tutorial staff were appointed: the Rev. and Mrs Ron Waine, formerly missionaries in North Africa, in 1962: the Rev. Ronald Davies in 1964; and Mr Stan Bruce in 1968.[15]

6.2.3 The merger

A number of married students had begun to apply to the college and in 1966 study courses were developed for a group of seven students' wives.[16] This was a beginning but it was clearly inadequate. 'It seemed ridiculous to the principal that men could be trained and not their wives. After all, were not the wives also going out to serve God with their husbands?'[17]

---

12. A copy of this letter still hangs in the entrance hall of ANCC.
13. The London County Council had previously used the building for evacuees during the war. They submitted a ninety one page dilapidations schedule, listing over 1900 items that needed repair. Minutes of the Council of ANMU, January 14 1964, minute 793.
14. Minutes of the Council of ANMU, October 29 1963, minute 780.
15. Minutes of the Council of ANMU, July 21 1965 and March 25 1968.
16. Minutes of the Council of ANMU, November 28 1966, minute 926.
17. N. W. Oakley, *The story of Easneye* (1997), p. 16.

Morris had long been of the opinion that single men and women should also train together, since they would have to work together in mission contexts. When Meg Foote visited ANMC soon after her appointment as principal of MHMTC, the possibility of a merger between the two institutions was raised. 'How would you feel about a merger and a new approach to combine training for men and women,' Morris asked.[18] Miss Foote had already made it clear to her council that she had every intention of developing co-educational training, and she responded to Morris' suggestion with enthusiasm.

The two principals began to meet on a regular basis to discuss possible ways forward. They began to merge their curricula, and lecturers began to give courses at both colleges. Mission leaders were consulted and the possibility of a merger was raised with their respective councils. Not everyone was convinced about the proposal. Some council members felt it was inappropriate, while only two of the students at ANMC were in favour of the idea. The ladies at MHMTC were more enthusiastic. For a while it seemed uncertain whether the merger would ever become a reality.

By 1966, specific proposals were tabled and the date of July 1971 suggested to effect the merger. So far only two colleges had been involved, but the council of RBC then began to express interest in such a merger. In 1968, a Formation Committee was established with representatives from all three institutions.[19]

First a Memorandum of Association was adopted by all three college councils. Then an administrative sub-committee was appointed to finalise the details of the Articles of Association.[20] Morris was invited to become the first principal, and Miss Foote, the vice-principal.[21] Over the next eighteen months, other staff appointments were made. Some former staff members of ANMC and MHMTC were invited to join the new college. Mr Martin Goldsmith and his wife, Elizabeth (nèe Hoyte), former missionaries with the Overseas Missionary Fellowship, were also appointed to the staff.

Different names were proposed for the united college, including the 'Evangelical Training College' and 'All Nations College.' Some past students of ANMC wished to retain the word 'missionary,' but the general consensus was to adopt the name 'All Nations Christian College.' One Sudanese student said that he would die as a Christian but not as a missionary, for in his country missionaries were often mistaken for mercenaries.[22] The councils of MHMTC and RBC gave their approval to the new name,[23] and it was formally adopted on April 29th, 1970.

---

18. *Ibid.*, p. 17.
19. This was composed of four members of the Council of the respective colleges, together with the college principals. The first meeting of the Formation Committee of All Nations, Mount Hermon and Ridgelands Colleges was held in London on December 3 1970. Mr Ernest Oliver was appointed chairman of the committee.
20. The ANMU ceased to function as a company in the summer of 1971, as did RBC and MHMTC. The assets and liabilities of the merging colleges were transferred to ANCC. ANMU continued as dormant company for a while as matters were being wound up and was finally deleted from the Companies Register in 1974. From private notes supplied by D. J. Syratt, bursar from 1973 to 1993.
21. Minutes of the Formation Committee, 45/69, December 3 1969.
22. D. Morris, from personal correspondence, February 18 1998.
23. Minutes of the Formation Committee, 3/70, February 10 1970, and 12/70, April 29 1970.

With regard to the location of the united college, it was agreed that a site in the home counties would be preferable. Such had been the opinion of the Conference of British Missionary Societies fifty years earlier, when they considered setting up a Central College of Missionary Studies.

A search committee viewed a large number of properties, but all were rejected on the grounds of their poor state of repair. 'I had no idea,' comments Morris, 'that so many dreadful old buildings could be found in the ten mile belt surrounding London.'[24]

Easneye, the site of ANMC, had been rejected on the grounds that it was only a rented property, but when John Buxton, the owner died, the Buxton family decided to sell the house to meet death duties. A group from the three colleges met the land agent, representing the Buxton family, and bought the house together with nine acres of the estate for £31,500.

One hundred and twenty students were expected for the first year of the new college. Additional space was needed to accommodate such a large number and to provide adequate facilities for lecture halls, seminar rooms and tutors' studies. Plans were drawn up to build an academic block and a three-storey hostel for the women at a cost of £328,000.[25] It was a vast financial undertaking. The council hoped that an educational trust, or a generous benefactor, might make a large contribution to the project. In this they were to be disappointed. Money did start to come in, but 'it was through small, sacrificial gifts rather than large donations.'[26]

At the council meeting of February 4th, 1971, £150,000 was still needed to cover the cost of the building work. It was a defining moment in the life of the college. If they failed to proceed with the contract, they would not be able to accept the large number of students they anticipated. If they went ahead with the contract, they might find themselves with an intolerable burden of debt. After some time of prayer and discussion, Captain Godfrey Buxton proposed that the council should take a step of faith and place the contract. His proposal was accepted unanimously and the decision was made.[27] The members of the council were confident that the Lord would supply all they needed. Their confidence was fully justified. By June 30 1972, all the necessary funds had been obtained through loans, an overdraft and outright gifts.[28]

As the news of the new united college became public, prospective students began to apply. By September 1971, 128 had been accepted. Thirty five were single men, fifty eight were single women and thiere were eighteen married couples.

6.2.4 Growth of the united college

As the time for the opening of the college drew near, it was evident that the building work would not be completed on time. The start of the term was delayed by two

24. N. W. Oakley, *The story of* Easneye (1997), p. 18.
25. Equivalent to £3.5 million in 1999.
26. N. W. Oakley, *The story of Easneye* (1997), p. 19.
27. *Ibid.*
28. D. J. Syratt, personal correspondence, February 13 1998.

weeks, and letters were sent to the students warning them of the conditions that would confront them on their arrival. Morris and Miss Foote wrote: 'There will be certain inconveniences – e.g. only two floors of the new hostel being in use for the first fortnight of term, certain decorating of corridors and offices etc. being left for the Christmas vacation ... The academic block will not be ready until next term. Some staff are still waiting to move and others will be in temporary accommodation.'[29]

Far from being put off, the new students were more determined than ever to make the best of things. After all it was good missionary training. 'I'll sleep in a bath if I can come,' wrote one. 'I'll come and move things until there's room to begin,' said another.[30]

By all accounts the first few weeks of the new college were chaotic. When students arrived, they found the main hall of the college piled high with the furniture, which had come from the two ladies colleges. There was water on the floor of the new residential block and, with the academic block still under construction, there was mud everywhere. The only place for a hot bath was in the principal's house. All day long a stream of students arrived for a bath – for which they were allowed 20 minutes.

Such a disastrous start to the new college could have had a very negative impact on the community. In fact, the reverse was the case. Everyone had to help to sort out the chaos. As people worked together to make the place habitable, natural barriers of shyness and embarrassment were broken down and friendships quickly made. At the end of that first year, the members of the community had learned a great deal about themselves, about each other and about the Lord. As Oakley says, 'It was, in many respects, the best start they could have had.'[31]

Over the first few years of the college's life, there was a constant stream of applications, particularly from single women and married couples. The vacancies for single men were always the last to be filled.

The pressure for the college to grow in size increased year by year. Morris believed that a ceiling on the number of students should be maintained at 130, so as to 'provide true pastoral concern, which is the object of our existence.'[32] He was concerned at the growing pastoral demands being made on the staff. He spoke of 'the considerable pressure experienced by the staff because of the personal tuition system and the continuing need for personal counselling.'[33] He felt that it was imperative that staff should receive adequate training in counselling and should not be required to carry an excessive pastoral load.[34]

As more missionary candidates chose to marry before they went overseas, the question of providing more accommodation for married students at ANCC became an urgent topic of discussion at council meetings. One proposal was to add a new

29. Letter written to new students by the principal and vice-principal on September 14 1971.
30. N. W. Oakley, *The story of Easneye* (1997), p. 19.
31. *Ibid.*
32. Minutes of the ANCC Council, May 25 1973, 73/21.
33. Minutes of the ANCC Council, May 22 1975, 75/8.
34. Minutes of the ANCC Council, October 14 1974, 74/18.

wing for married couples to the existing hostel. Another was to purchase houses in the local village and convert them into apartments.[35]

In 1974, a house was purchased in King Edward Road in the nearby town of Ware, and this was converted into three flats for staff or married students. In 1976 a building project was launched to enable the college to raise the size of the student body to 150. Under the title 'Growing Pains,' an appeal was made for £90,000 to provide more housing, a nursery, and a recording studio.[36] Three years later, a second appeal raised a further £135,000 for the purchase of the estate manager's house and for the conversion of the garage block into staff studies and accommodation.[37]

While much attention was concentrated on the finance for buildings, the re-structuring of the college income and expenditure for the day to day running was also important. John Syratt, who served as Bursar from 1973 to 1993, wrote: 'All Nations was no longer in the pattern of a 1930's college, but the leader in this field of education and missionary training. It was vital to improve the student/staff ratio in view of the successful introduction of the tutorial system, and also to improve remuneration generally. At a council meeting in January 1973, it was reported that there was some financial hardship among the staff. A decision to improve the salary scales was taken, and by 1980 the college moved on to the Lichfield Scale for Anglican colleges.'[38]

The rejuvenation of the former All Nations Bible College, the bringing together of the three institutions, and the rapid development of the united college had taken a heavy toll on the health of the principal. In the autumn of 1980, he was advised to rest by his medical consultant.[39] He consequently took a period of sick leave, hoping to return to college at the commencement of the summer term, at least on a part-time basis. It was clear, however, that he would not be able to continue in office, and he retired as principal in July 1981.[40]

During the ten years in which ANCC had been in existence, Morris had been ably supported by an outstanding staff team. One of his strengths that he had the ability to attract the right people onto his staff. He took great care before making any appointment. Although he usually engaged university graduates, he was more concerned that his staff had pastoral and teaching gifts and, preferably, some experience of cross-cultural ministry. While it is impossible to include all those who served under him, it is appropriate to mention some who made a particular contribution to the development of the burgeoning college.

Meg Foote, former principal of MHMTC and vice-principal of ANCC, shared Morris' vision for the united college and worked closely with him for the realisation of that vision. Her wise and measured counsel often served as the ideal antidote to his more imaginative ideas and occasionally bizarre sense of humour. John Syratt, who joined the college as Bursar in 1973, brought with him his considerable experience as chief accountant of a retail grocery chain. His wise management of the finan-

35. Minutes of the ANCC Council, March 24 1973, 73/20.
36. This was later dedicated in memory of Colin Grant, a member of staff who was tragically killed in a road accident.
37. N. W. Oakley, *The story of Easneye* (1997), p. 22.
38. D. J. Syratt, private correspondence, February 13 1998.
39. Minutes of the ANCC Council, October 30 1980, 80/23.
40. Minutes of the ANCC Council, June 9 1981, 81/22.

cial affairs of the college meant that the college accounts remained in the black, and major building contracts were completed without debt. Martin Goldsmith had served as a missionary in south-east Asia for ten years. He had a sharp mind, was an excellent communicator and had a limitless fund of missiological anecdotes. Morris entrusted him with the task of re-writing the college syllabus from scratch, which he proceeded to do on the back of an envelope. Ron Davies, an ordained Baptist minister with a particular interest in Eastern Europe, had joined the staff of ANMC in 1964. He served as director of studies for ANCC from 1971 to 1984. Stan Bruce, appointed in 1968, had the unenviable task of amalgamating the libraries of the three colleges. Doreen Peck, who had served for many years with the Rwanda Mission in Africa, joined ANCC from MHMTC. So did Margaret Jones, who developed the pastoral studies course which became a significant feature of the All Nations training. Bob Hunt, another Baptist minister with mission experience in Zaire, came to the college in 1973 to be director of the Christian ministries department. Along with Ruth Giesner, he had the responsibility of seeing that the academic side of the training was balanced by adequate field experience. In 1978, David and Rosemary Harley came on the staff. As theological graduates, they had studied mission and practical subjects at ANMC before going to Ethiopia. David was the first ordained Anglican to study at the college and was to be a future principal.

Morris saw no division between academic and administrative staff. They were all serving God and all playing key roles in the process of training students for missionary service. A close friend and colleague of Morris was Thomas W. Paget. Tom Paget had first joined the staff as head gardener in 1958. When Morris became a tutor a year later, the two men became firm friends. For the next thirty years, Paget supervised the afternoon chores that the students were required to do around the house and garden. He also organised a wide range of practical courses, in such subjects as carpentry, building, photography, food production etc., which were an integral part of the college course. His spiritual influence was very real. His statement, 'it's the life that counts,' which later evolved into 'it's the wife that counts,' was long remembered.

Each of these staff members, and the many others who are not mentioned by name, were carefully and prayerfully appointed by Morris. He looked for men and women[41] who would make a significant contribution to the holistic training he was seeking to develop, and who would fit well into the team he was endeavouring to establish. But he always made new appointments in consultation with the other staff. Unless all the staff felt that the interviewee was the right person, he or she would not be invited to join the team.

6.2.5 Conclusion

The reputation of All Nations Christian College as a missionary training college is largely the result of the foresight and labour of Morris. When he came to the col-

41. From the start Morris was determined that there should be an equal number of men and women on the academic staff.

lege, he brought with him practical experience from his missionary work in Africa, and insights gained from his time training gunnery officers in the army. He had a clear understanding of the kind of missionary preparation needed in the contemporary world, and of the ways in which men and women could best be trained to perform specific tasks. Initially, he convinced the council of ANBC to accept his radical proposals for missionary training. Subsequently, he persuaded the councils of the three colleges to pool their resources so that his vision could be realised. Without his leadership and foresight, it is doubtful whether ANCC would ever have come into existence.

A significant factor in the development of the college was Morris's personality. It was his warmth of character, his openness, his humility and his outlandish sense of humour which attracted people to him. It was enthusiasm, his strength of character and his ability to communicate his ideas that made them pay attention to what he said. He had the ability not only to get church leaders and mission statesmen to listen to him, but also to attract on to his staff a committed and gifted group of men and women, whom he moulded into a harmonious and united team.

Morris was the first to admit his own mistakes and weaknesses. He sometimes came into a classroom, wearing an 'L' plate[42] to indicate to the students that although he was the principal, he still had much to earn. He had a tendency to judge people too quickly, which led to occasional errors of judgement.[43] He also was prone to exaggeration, when he recounted stories from the war or his time in Africa. As his wife remarked 'I enjoy his stories, but I don't always recognise them.'[44]

Though he consulted his staff widely, Morris exerted a strong authority over the college. He knew the value of decisive leadership and, while he listened carefully to the views of others, he would then make up his own mind on the right course of action. He was viewed by some as a benign dictator who, in Goldsmith's words, 'was undoubtedly the leader of the college.'[45]

Morris found it difficult to delegate responsibility. Even when the college had grown from a few students to more than 150, he still felt pastorally responsible for the whole community. He continued to spend a great deal of time in helping students or staff members struggling with a problem. He believed it was his duty to set an example to the rest of the staff, so he tried to be at his desk before anyone else. He wanted to be at the forefront of everything that was going on, though he realised too late that was not always possible or desirable.[46]

The merger of the three colleges exacted a heavy toll on his health. Some months before the amalgamation was achieved, he was warned by his doctor that unless he took a complete rest he was heading for a physical or mental breakdown. He consulted a friend who told him that there was noone else who could see the project through, and that perhaps this was the price he would have to pay to see its successful conclusion. Morris decided that he was willing to pay that price. The merger

42. 'L' plates are used to signify learner drivers in the U.K.
43. Personal interview with David Morris, July 20 1999.
44. Personal interview with Trenna Morris, July 20 1999.
45. M. Goldsmith, *Life's tapestry* (1997), p. 180.
46. Interview with David Morris, July 20 1999.

went ahead, but within six months he suffered a complete breakdown of his health from which he never fully recovered.

6.3 Doctrinal basis and character

It is to be regretted that Morris did not write extensively about his theory of effective missionary training. However, there is enough extant material to determine the principles he considered of fundamental importance. First, there is the document that he authored as a discussion paper when the idea of a merger was first muted.[47] Secondly, there are some personal reflections on missionary training, written during the time he was principal.[48] Finally there are four pages of manuscript that he kindly wrote when he knew this dissertation was being undertaken.[49]

Morris' principalship brought both continuity and discontinuity with the past. He built on the foundations of the three merging institutions, but he narrowed the focus of the training. This section will consider how he built on those foundations and how he developed his training programme. It will examine the maintenance of the evangelical tradition of the three colleges (6.3.1), the beginnings of a wider engagement with the ecumenical movement (6.3.2), the response to the challenges of mission in a post-colonial era (6.3.3), the preparation of men, women, and families (6.3.4), the development of personal and spiritual gifts (6.3.5), the designing of tailor-made courses (6.3.6), the introduction of the tutorial system (6.3.7) and the role of women (6.3.8).

6.3.1 The maintenance of the evangelical tradition

Morris was determined that the new college would maintain the evangelical tradition of the three uniting colleges. He wrote: 'The basis of belief (of the new college) will be that commonly called conservative evangelical and will be the same as that of the existing colleges.'[50]

Each institution had retained similar doctrinal statements from the time of their foundation and, in preparation for the merger, the respective councils agreed on a common statement of faith which reflected the same basic doctrinal position (see appendix 6). This reflected a continuing commitment to the authority of Scripture and the traditional doctrines of the Christian faith.

Since the beginning of the century, however, there had been a significant change of attitude among evangelical Christians in Britain. The level of academic scholarship among conservative theologians had advanced considerably and evangelicals no longer felt that they were fighting with their backs to the wall. They were more

47. D. Morris, *Proposed missionary training campus: proposals for discussion and amendment* (1967), 7pp.
48. D. Morris. *Personal reflections* (unpublished ms., nd), 4pp.
49. D. Morris, *Training principles* (unpublished ms., 1998), 4pp.
50. D. Morris, *Proposed missionary training campus* (1967), p. 1.

ready to learn from other Christian traditions and to acknowledge the value and necessity of critical scholarship.

This new outlook was reflected in the ethos of the new institution, for although ANCC was firmly committed to the Scriptures as the final authority for the church in all matters of faith and doctrine, there was an absence of the harsher dogmatism which had occasionally characterised the earlier institutions.

One addition to the doctrinal statement of the college refers to the 'one, holy universal Church, which is the body of Christ and to which all true believers belong.'[51] This appears in the 1970 doctrinal statement of ANCC but is absent in the earlier doctrinal statements of the three colleges. Its absence up to this point reflects the low priority given to the doctrine of the church by most evangelicals.

The doctrine of the church became a contentious issue in the first term of the united college. A number of students were asking for more frequent services of Holy Communion. This raised the issue of the relationship between the denominations and a parachurch organisation like a Bible college. For others, it also raised the question as to whether they could take communion with Christians whose denominations did not enjoy intercommunion with their own. In the ensuing debate, it was made clear that the college was not a church and did not desire to undermine the commitment of the students to their own denominations. It was recognised that at interdenominational conferences, such as Keswick, the practice of holding an occasional communion service had become acceptable. All those who were communicant members of their own church were welcome to attend. This was seen as an exception rather than a matter of regular practice. This policy was subsequently adopted at the college. It did not satisfy everyone, and some students refused to attend these Communion services.

Two other doctrinal issues were the cause of some controversy. A number of students, including a couple from Africa, were shocked that a staff member at the college could believe in and practice infant baptism.[52] Coming from a church where only adult believers were baptised, they had assumed that all evangelicals held the same view. The resultant discussion with a staff member did not change their beliefs, but it did widen their perspective.

Another issue, over which students had strongly divergent views, was the work of the Holy Spirit. Some students came from charismatic churches, while others belonged to denominations or congregations which condemned the charismatic movement. The college was sometimes criticised by the latter group for not condemning charismatic teaching. It was also condemned on occasions for not being sufficiently open to the work of the Spirit. In these and other controversies, the policy of the college was to foster free discussion over issues where evangelicals held different opinions, and to encourage students to understand and respect the views of others.

51. This wording was taken from the doctrinal statement of the Inter-Varsity Fellowship of Evangelical Unions (1959).
52. Personal interview with Martin Goldsmith, August 20 1999.

6.3.2 The beginnings of engagement with the ecumenical movement

Since the days of Poole-Connor, All Nations had taken a negative stance towards the ecumenical movement. Even in 1968, according to Morris, 'anything to do with the World Council of Churches was anathema to many members of the council.'[53] Morris felt that this attitude was counterproductive and unhelpful, depriving the college of a number of benefits it might gain from association with other Christians and preventing it from making a contribution to the wider Christian community. He encouraged the staff to become familiar with ecumenical and Roman Catholic literature on mission, and to play an active part in missiological debate outside the narrow conservative evangelical confines within which they had operated.

During his time in Nigeria, Morris had developed a close friendship with a leading Catholic educationalist. Later, he attended meetings both of the International Missionary Council and the Conference of British Missionary Societies. He had the opportunity to interact with a number of leading missiologists and was particularly impressed by his conversations with M. A. C. Warren. Morris was convinced that it was important for him and other staff members to be involved at this level of debate but he was criticised by some council members.

When Ron Davies was invited to become the director of studies in the new college in 1971, he was given the opportunity to visit a number of colleges in America that were known for their strong missions programmes. He initially went to evangelical institutions, such as Wheaton and Fuller, and met a number of leading evangelical missiologists, such as Arthur Glasser, Donald McGavran and Alan Tippett. On Glasser's recommendation, he also visited the Marynoll Fathers, Yale Divinity School and the ecumenical missionary training centre at Stoney Point. These contacts made Davies aware of current ecumenical and Catholic thinking about mission, and significantly influenced him in the design of the new syllabus at All Nations.

A number of staff attended the conferences of the Evangelical Fellowship for Missionary Studies (EFMS), which was formed in 1968. The EFMS sponsored an annual conference for twelve years, usually held at the Selly Oak Colleges or All Nations, which brought together a broad spectrum of British missiologists. Professor Andrew Walls served as chairman for many years, and speakers included Kenneth Cracknell, Simon Barrington Ward, Andrew Kirk and Sister Mary Hall. Four or five papers were presented at each conference, covering such topics as contextualisation, the theology of revolution, creation and redemption, church growth, the role of women in mission, the theology of M. M. Thomas and G. Gutierrez.

One member of ANCC staff, Martin Goldsmith, took part in the Evangelical Roman Catholic Dialogue on Mission (ERCDOM), which first met in Venice in April, 1977. ERCDOM developed out of the shared concern for mission, expressed both by Evangelicals (at the Lausanne Congress of 1974) and by Roman Catholics (in the publication by Pope Paul VI of his exhortation entitled *Evangelii nuntiandi* in 1975). The main purpose of ERCDOM was to make a theological investigation

---

53. Personal interview with David Morris, July 20 1999.

into areas of convergence and divergence in evangelical and Catholic understandings of mission, with a view to establishing whether some common witness might be possible. There were eight Catholic participants in these discussions, including Sister Joan Chatfield and Father Thomas Stransky, and eight Evangelicals, including John Stott and Dr. Peter Beyerhaus.

The participation in such conferences by Morris and other ANCC staff indicated their desire to be more constructively engaged in the wider ecumenical community, and to play an active part in contemporary debate on the nature and theology of mission. This represented a significant step forward from the ghetto mentality of the previous generation.

This development was not welcomed by all the college supporters. Morris received a number of critical letters after Roman Catholic and Russian Orthodox visitors had been invited to address the student body.[54]

6.3.3 The challenge of mission in the post-colonial era

Morris had served as a missionary in Nigeria during its closing years as a British colony. He realised there would need to be many changes in the style and practice of missionary work in the post-colonial era. First, he knew that the evangelisation of the world would only be achieved through a partnership between Christians of every continent. He realised that those going out as missionaries from the West would need to work in partnership with, and under the leadership of, national Christians. He wanted to encourage the development of national leaders in Africa and Asia and to foster the growth of indigenous missionary movements in those continents. He also wanted to make Western missionary candidates more aware of the abilities and perspectives of Christians in other parts of the world. One of his first objectives, therefore, was to attract more students to the college from Africa and Asia.

Secondly, Morris believed a radical change was necessary in the attitude of Western missionaries. He had observed that 'missionaries went out with the assumption that British ways were best and that every African was inferior.'[55] Furthermore, he felt that they demonstrated 'a total non-appreciation of the culture and religion of the people to whom they go.'[56]

In developing the programme at the college, Morris was determined to change these attitudes. He wanted the students to spend much more time studying and learning to appreciate the culture and religion of the people to whom they would go. He wanted them to understand as much as possible the political, social and economic condition of the country where they would serve. He insisted that each student should undertake an extensive project on the country where they expected to serve.

In 1999, Morris was awarded an honorary doctorate by the Open University in recognition of his contribution in the field of adult education. The citation includes

54. Letters written to D. Morris from the Rev. W.V. Vernon and the Rev E.W. Walton-Lewsey, dated October 8 1975 and October 27 1975, respectively.
55. Personal interview with David Morris, July 20 1999.
56. Ibid.

the following: 'He had long nurtured plans to modernise and radicalise the preparation of missionary recruits and the rapid changes he saw going on at that time within, for instance, African countries as they achieved their independence gave impetus to that vision.'[57]

6.3.4 The preparation of men, women and families

Both Morris and Miss Foote were convinced that in the second half of the twentieth century men and women should be trained for missionary service together. They also believed that married couples should undergo the same preparation before embarking on a career of cross-cultural ministry. As stated by Morris: 'Wives *must* always be seen as partners in mission – they *must* have equal training.'[58] When ANCC opened in 1971, married couples were only accepted if both husband and wife were full-time students. Both attended lectures, and were expected to complete assignments, to do practical courses etc.

As Morris observed: 'Wives often have babies.' Therefore he concluded that a nursery must be provided so that children could be looked after while parents were attending lectures. This idea met with considerable criticism even within the college council, but he persisted in implementing this vision. In 1978, a purpose built nursery was opened for twenty babies and infants.

6.3.5 The development of personal and spiritual gifts

In his discussions with mission leaders, Morris had discovered a common concern at the lack of adequate training for missionary candidates. It was generally agreed that there were insufficient places to meet the demand for missionary training, that there was a lack of adequate teachers, who could provide personal supervision and guidance of students, and that there was a lack of specialist staff who could provide the breadth of specialised courses needed.[59]

The three antecedent colleges had been founded with the purpose of training missionaries. More than half of the students from MHMTC had gone overseas. Many from ANBC also had become missionaries, although in the latter years of the college's life, there was an equal emphasis on training for the home ministry. At RBC too, students were trained both for work in their home countries and for cross-cultural ministry overseas. Morris' vision for the united college was to narrow the focus of the college's training to the point where it was almost exclusively training people for cross-cultural ministry.

Fundamental to the training offered in the new college was the development of character and spiritual maturity. As Morris stated: 'This must be done on a person to person basis with the aim of training men and women to develop their own personal and spiritual gifts in such a way that they can contribute constructively to a

57. This was presented to David Morris by the vice-chancellor of the Open University at ANCC on February 27 1999.
58. D. Morris, private notes, dated February 18 1998.
59. D. Morris, *Proposed missionary training campus* (1967), p. 1.

team effort.'[60] Morris believed that personal devotional life, corporate worship and prayer, real concern for others, and self- discipline were all vital in a holistic training programme. Furthermore he believed that the kind of programme he envisaged with constant and close staff-student interaction, was possible in a larger institution, provided there was a commitment to such a programme and an adequate ratio of staff to students.

It was axiomatic for Morris that missionary training should be practical, not theoretical. It must equip people for the job they were going to do. So he was insistent that practical training should form a major component of the course. That meant practice both in developing the art of effective communication, and in acquiring such technical skills as might be necessary in the future.

As a Regimental Gunnery Officer, he learned to invent games and exercises which created as realistic a battle scenario as possible. The more his troops practised in this way, the more competent they would be in real crises. He applied the same principle to the training of missionaries. He aimed to make the training as realistic and practical as possible. He wanted them to imagine the situation they might face and see how they would react to it.

Morris also believed that training should be fun. In the army he organised games, quizzes and competitions. He awarded prizes for the best kept hut of the week. He allowed a degree of larking about, where men could shower each other with water hoses. He involved them in dramatic mock battles where men were designated to die on cue, and often did so in most dramatic fashion. The conclusion he reached from these experiences was that such approaches to training lifted the morale of the troops and made them more responsive to the training and more effective as soldiers. He believed the same approach could be applied to the training of the servants of Christ.

Morris was convinced that ANCC should be training for the future rather than for the present. There was a need for constant curriculum review. Would the substance of the lecture courses being taught now be relevant in five or ten years time? Did the questions discussed in seminars reflect the concerns of the past, or the issues facing the contemporary church in Asia and Africa? Were the practical courses providing relevant technical skills for students, who might work in an air-conditioned city office rather than in the jungle?

In his view, it was vital that the students were prepared for the challenges and problems they were likely to encounter during the course of their missionary career. They had to be provided with the right exegetical tools to enable them to think biblically and missiologically when they faced a future crisis. They must develop a flexibility of approach and procedures, which would prepare them to adapt easily in a world where change was the only constant.

Morris was also concerned that the new college should become a centre for advanced missionary studies and mission research.[61] As the college library developed, evangelical scholars and mission leaders could be invited to the campus for a

60. *Ibid.*, p. 7.
61. *Ibid.*

period of sabbatical research and reflection. Missionaries on home assignment could also be invited to spend time evaluating their ministry and planning future strategy. Refresher courses and extra-mural studies could also be offered.

6.3.6 The designing of tailor-made courses

Morris had great respect for the individual. He recognised that each student came to college with their own agenda and that they had widely differing gifts, temperaments, backgrounds and needs. He wanted that to be reflected in the life of the college and in the structure of the curriculum.

When Morris was interviewing a potential student, he would not simply assess their present level of gifts and maturity. He would always look for indications of further potential and latent gifts. He often compared students to barrels of oil, which benefit no-one as long as the oil remains inside them, but which become a rich resource of energy and power when the oil is released. The task of the trainer, in his view, was to perceive the potential of each trainee, and enable that potential to be released into the world. The aim of the personalised training he introduced was to discover and develop that potential.

Since the tutors (the term that Morris used for academic staff) carried the major responsibility for the implementation of that training, he took exceptional care to choose those who would provide good pastoral care and individual supervision for each student. It was axiomatic in his theory of training that above all else the tutors should be people persons. There were, of course, other criteria used in their selection: they were expected to be mature and committed Christians, with mission experience, good qualifications and real gifts of communication. But first and foremost, they had to be approachable. They had to have the ability to relate with ease both to their fellows members of staff and to the students.

Morris' respect for people also affected his own attitude towards his staff. So far as he was concerned, they were all of equal importance, whether they were secretaries, cooks, maintenance staff or faculty. He saw the total staff as a microcosm of the body of Christ, in which there were many members, but where each member had a vital and equally important function. Weekly staff and prayer meetings, therefore, involved the whole staff. All major decisions of college policy were made only after the widest consultation. Morris wanted 'all staff to be happy about the methods and aims of the college.'[62] He also insisted that student references, sent out in the name of the college, were approved at the plenary staff meeting, and that new staff members were vetted by the whole staff.

He made it his business to know how each member of staff was getting on and what they were thinking. He would spend several hours each week just walking around the college, visiting staff in their offices or places of work. It was a principle that he had first learned in the army, where he began to understand the importance of a strong relationship between an officer and his troops.

62. D. Morris, *Personal reflections* (nd), p. 2.

6.3.7 The introduction of the tutorial system

At the heart of Morris' understanding of missionary training lay the role of the college tutors. As an undergraduate at Oxford, he had studied under the supervision of a personal tutor. He realised the potential value of such a system for the training of missionaries, but wanted to extend the scope of the tutors' responsibility to include personal and practical matters as well as academic studies. He saw the tutor not just as an academic adviser, but as a pastor, counsellor and friend.

Members of the faculty were chosen as much for their proven pastoral ability and relational skills as for the academic qualifications and mission experience. On their appointment they were required to fulfil the role of tutor to a group of about eighteen students.[63] They met with this group three times each week for a time of worship and at other times for informal coffee parties. They were encouraged to eat their lunch with the student body, and to schedule evening social gatherings once or twice a term with their own tutorial group.

Three or four times each term,[64] the tutors met with the students on an individual basis for about an hour to discuss their academic work, their practical work in a local church, their own personal development and spiritual growth, and any other area that they wished to raise (e.g. guidance for the future, personal relationships etc.).

Dr Bob Ferris of Columbia International University, who made a study of innovative programmes in ten seminaries and Bible colleges around the world, made the following observation about the tutorial system at ANCC:

> The tutor is responsible to weave the various aspects of the college program into an integrated – and individualised – curriculum for the student's personal and professional development.[65]

The ethos of the tutorial system was one of mutual friendship and trust. The tutors were respected for their experience and maturity, but they regarded themselves as fellow disciples of the same Lord, able to learn from their students. They tried not to intrude into the students' lives by asking insensitive questions, but sought to earn the students' trust. When a student shared something of a confidential nature, the tutors respected that confidentiality.

The faculty members were expected to devote a large amount of their time to this interaction with the students. It was an attempt to model the training on the pattern which Jesus used with his disciples. It was very costly in terms of time and emotional energy, and several minutes of ANCC council meetings contain references to the pastoral demands that were made on the staff.[66] It also meant that staff had less time for the pursuit of private studies or the writing of articles for learned

63. This figure was reduced gradually as the staff/student ratio improved. In 1978, the normative number for each tutor was sixteen. By 1981, it had been reduced to twelve.
64. The academic year was divided into three ten week terms.
65. R.W. Ferris, *Renewal in theological education* (1990), p. 102.
66. The minutes of ANCC Council, January 24 1974, 74/7, and January 23 1975, 75/8.

journals. In essence, it was a reflection of Morris' commitment to holistic training that the tutorial system was given such high priority.

6.3.8 The role of women

In his book on the history of faith missions, K. Fiedler points out the significant pioneering role in evangelistic and missionary work played by women. Mount Hermon and Ridgelands were both influenced by the faith missions movement and both were founded by women.[67] In the appointment of successive principals, women were always chosen rather than men, though in the case of RBC there was a time when the appointment of a married couple was considered.

When the three colleges merged in 1971, the leadership was shared by David Morris, as principal, and Meg Foote, as vice-principal. When Morris was absent through ill-health, Miss Foote took over his responsibilities. It was agreed from the outset that, since ANCC had been formed by the merger of two women's colleges and one men's college, the principal should try to maintain parity between the number of male and female lecturers on the faculty. This was a progressive policy for an evangelical college, especially at a time when there were relatively few women theological lecturers in Britain.

Some of the students, especially those from churches which did not allow women to teach or exercise leadership, found it difficult to be instructed or counselled by a woman. Some requested they should have a male tutor for both their first and second years, but they were not allowed to do so. The policy of the college was clear. Students who chose to come to ANCC must be willing to be taught by women and to be under their spiritual direction.

6.3.9 Conclusion

Morris built the new college firmly on the foundations of its predecessors. He maintained the conservative evangelical position and the early emphasis on personal devotion which characterised the earlier institutions. At the same time he realised that many changes were needed. He wanted the college to move out of its evangelical isolationism, and be more involved in missiological debate within the wider ecumenical context. He wanted to provide appropriate training for missionary service in a post-colonial era, and to challenge the incipient racial superiority that characterised so many Western missionary candidates.

Morris deliberately spurned the purely academic curriculum which characterised many theological institutions. He set out to provide a relevant, practical and holistic course of training, where issues of spirituality and character formation were given equal emphasis with academic study. He developed an innovative model of missionary training which others have sought to emulate.

---

67. At Ridgelands, Mrs Hooker had the initial support and encouragement of her husband, but she had the full responsibility of running the institution, while Mr Hooker continued his work as a solicitor. After his premature death in 1923, Mrs Hooker ran the college entirely on her own.

The decision to develop a holistic rather than a purely academic programme did have some negative consequences. Alumni who subsequently wished to proceed to post-graduate theological studies were not able to do so. Those who wished to enter the ordained ministry were required by their denominations to undergo a prolonged period of further training.

Morris treated each student as an individual and sought as far as was possible to provide them with a tailor-made course. He saw the tutorial system as the key to effective missionary training and structured the whole curriculum around it. His insistence that husbands and wives train together, while criticised initially, has been vindicated by the passage of time and has provided a pattern which other theological institutions have sought to adopt.

Finally, Morris had a high regard for the gifts and ministry of women. He encouraged wives to realise and develop their own gifts, observing that they were often more gifted than their husbands. He enjoyed sharing the leadership of the college with Meg Foote and greatly appreciated her wisdom and advice. He had equal regard for the women on his staff as for the men. His policy of maintaining an equal number of male and female lecturers was in direct contrast with other similar institutions.

6.4 THE PROGRAMME

The training programme at ANCC represented the culmination of an evolutionary process in missionary training. It combined the wisdom of three institutions which between them had been engaged in the training of missionaries for 160 years. To that wisdom was added the insights and experience of a trained educationalist, who had served as a missionary himself and who brought together a team of like-minded, experienced, missionary practitioners. The net result was the emergence of a distinctive model of missionary training.

This section examines the major components of the programme, adopting the same categories as used in previous chapters but considering each in greater detail.

6.4.1 Spiritual life

The three colleges which united in 1971 had all emphasised the development of the spiritual life, and this tradition was maintained in the united college. The fostering of a vigorous prayer life and the development of Christian character were perceived as primary objectives of the training.[68]

Each weekday morning began with a time of worship. Three times a week the community divided into the tutorial groups for worship, led by each student in turn. On Wednesdays and Thursdays, the whole college met together for worship. The style of worship, both in small groups and in the communal celebrations, reflected the cultural and denominational diversity within the community. The leader was

68. *All Nations Christian College* brochure (1971), p. 2f.

encouraged to use the traditions or patterns of worship to which they were accustomed. The objective was that the services would be varied in style, and that students would learn to appreciate patterns of worship different from their own. In this way some had their first encounter with liturgical services, some had their first experience of charismatic worship, some realised the value of silence and meditation.

It was a deliberate policy on the part of the college to encourage a wide appreciation of the full spectrum of evangelical Christianity, not only so that the students would be enriched but also that they might be prepared in the future to work alongside those whose doctrinal emphases or patterns of worship were at variance with their own.

Three times a year, a day was set aside as a quiet day. There were no lectures on that day and silence was observed on the campus. The purpose of the day was to enable each student to devote the day to prayer and listening to God. The day began with a morning devotional session and ended with an evening communion service. The rest of the time was left for private prayer. The third quiet day in the year was sometimes left free of communal worship. Some students were unfamiliar with this form of spiritual discipline and struggled with this novel experience. By the end of two years, however, most had come to appreciate these opportunities for prayer and quiet reflection and hoped to build in such personal retreats into the pattern of their future ministry.

The staff often made reference in their lectures to different aspects of the Christian life. In due course a series of lectures was offered on the spiritual disciplines. Students were encouraged to read some of the great classics of Christian spirituality and to appreciate expressions of religious faith in art and music. There was a growing appreciation of the spiritual riches to be found in the other great traditions of the Christian church, though there was still some suspicion of authors who did not come from an evangelical background.

Any residential Christian community runs the danger of becoming a religious hothouse and that was the last thing that Morris wanted. He could not stand any kind of pretence or hypocrisy in a Christian. If he thought he saw any one pretending to be holier than other people, he would gently poke fun at them. He did not want students to behave in an unnatural way just because they were living in a Bible college, but he did want them to be wholeheartedly committed to Christ. As a soldier he had read widely in the field of military literature and had been impressed by the life of the Field Marshall Rommel. He urged the students to be as committed to their service of Jesus Christ as Rommel was to his profession as a soldier.

6.4.2 Character formation

'It's the life that counts,' quoted earlier as one of the favourite sayings of Tom Paget, reflects a conviction that was shared by all the staff: in the training of missionaries, the development of Christlikeness is as important as the acquisition of theological knowledge or ministerial skills.

Before students were accepted into the course they had to undergo a thorough selection process.[69] Those who appeared to be insensitive towards other people and intolerant of any opinions other than their own were not usually accepted. It was expected even before they came to college that they showed some evidence of personal godliness and 'a mature attitude to life.'[70]

The staff members were aware that students would have flaws in their character and that some would have emotional problems needing to be worked through. They did not expect them to be perfect but they did want to see some evidence of growth and personal development in their lives.

The staff monitored the students' development. Over the course of a year, they prayed for each student in turn. At their weekly staff meetings, they discussed their progress and shared matters of a less confidential nature. When a reference was required for a particular student, both academic and administrative staff had an opportunity to express their opinion. This provided a more balanced picture of the student than would have been the case if the reference had only been written by the academic staff. The latter might be pleased with the assignments of a student and their attentiveness in class, but the administrative staff might have discovered that the same student was troublesome and unco-operative in fulfilling their domestic chores.

Living in a close-knit community was a challenge in itself. Most students were required to share a room, which was a particular hardship for those who had enjoyed living in their own accommodation prior to coming to college. The staff tried to place people together who had some common point of interest, or who shared similar sleeping habits. Some room-mates got on extremely well and became life-long friends. Others could not get on at all and moved to another room as soon as possible. This interaction often revealed important traits in students' characters, sometimes unexpected patience or depth of compassion, sometimes poor relational skills.

Students were required to perform domestic chores and do regular maintenance work in the house and grounds. This was a practical way of keeping the fees down, but it was also an effective means of fostering a spirit of service among the students. Some of the male students came from cultures where 'the women did all that sort of work,' but they learned to do even the most menial tasks in the spirit with which Jesus washed the disciples' feet.

For some students, who had spent some years in a successful career, the experience of coming to ANCC brought an additional challenge. Whereas in their profession they enjoyed a very high status and were treated with respect, in college they were just another student. This often caused a loss of role and identity, which was disconcerting and humbling. At the same time, it provided an opportunity for students to learn that their value as a person did not depend on their status within society or on their professional or academic achievements, but on their relationship and standing with God. It also prepared them for the loss of role and identity when

69. The selection process is described in more detail later in this chapter.
70. *All Nations Christian College* brochure (1971).

they first arrived as missionaries in a new culture and found they were unable to communicate with those around them.

Sometimes a serious character weakness was obvious to others, but not to the person concerned. In that case, the tutor would endeavour gently to point this out to the individual. The students were often genuinely surprised since they had not realised how others perceived them. Some students found it painful to face their weakness, but they were usually grateful that their fault had been pointed out. The tutors did not intend to upset or embarrass the students, but to help them face up to some aspect of their personality which might cause more serious problems in their future ministry if it was not addressed.

6.4.3 Academic studies – approach

As has been already noted, one of the principles that Morris followed in developing the curriculum was that each student should be able to follow a tailor-made course. Since they came from different backgrounds, with different experiences, gifts and qualifications, and since they were going to serve in varied forms of ministry and service, in a variety of professions and in a great diversity of cultures, it was self-evident that they did not need a uniform course of training. Morris proposed that the course should be divided between those subjects which were considered to be essential for everyone, and those which were optional and could be selected by students according to their particular needs, abilities, and interests. The aim was to 'enable the curriculum to serve each student, not squeeze all students through an identical programme.'[71] Students had considerable discretion to decide in discussion with their tutor which subjects they wished to follow and to plan their own personal route through the course.

6.4.3.1 Core courses and electives

The course was divided into five major fields: biblical studies, doctrinal studies, missiological studies, pastoral studies and practical studies. Within each field, certain courses were core. All students taking the two year course were required to attend the core courses, unless they had covered the same material prior to coming to the college. These core courses did not clash with any other courses in the timetable.

All other subjects were designated as electives and students were free to choose as many of these as they wished. Several electives were offered at the same time on the timetable and the students had to decide which would be most pertinent for their future ministry. Often a core subject would provide an introduction to a field of study which could then be taken further in an elective. So *Introduction to world religions*, a core subject, provided the foundation for several electives which specialised on individual world religions.

71. ANCC, *Certificate and Diploma in Biblical and Cross-cultural studies* (1993), p. 4. This was a document that was submitted to the Open University and which reflects the institutional aims and ethos that had been established in 1971.

6.4.3.2 Coherence and progression

The curriculum was designed to provide both coherence and progression. There was a deliberate attempt to create links between the five fields of study and to correlate the material that was being covered in the core subjects. So in the same term, students found themselves studying the nature of humanity from a biblical perspective in *Genesis*, from a theological perspective in the *Doctrine of Man*, and from a psychological perspective in *Pastoral Studies*.

Because of the missiological emphasis in the curriculum of the college, an effort was made to bring a cross-cultural hermeneutical dimension to the biblical and theological studies. Scripture and doctrine were not only studied from a Western and historical perspective but also from the cultural perspectives of the developing world.

The subjects covered in each term sought to build on those that had been covered during the previous term. So, for example, students began their study of Christianity and culture with a basic introduction to the study of culture (*Understanding Culture*). They then examined ways in which Christianity has interacted with culture *(Christianity and Culture)*. Finally they explored selected models of non-western, culturally contextualised theologies (*Non-western Theologies*). Similarly, students began their missiological courses with a basic biblical foundation, proceeded to explore a range of current missiological theological issues, and concluded with a study of selected contemporary documents from different Christian traditions.

6.4.3.3 Educational methodology

The bulk of the course was taught through lectures. Faculty members were encouraged to give time for questions and class interaction. A number of subjects were studied through seminars, led either by staff or students. Students also took part in role plays and organised group presentations in class. Case studies taken or adapted from real mission situations confronted students with the hard decisions that might face them in their ministry.

During the course of each ten week term, students were required to complete two major writing assignments. These assignments were published at the beginning of every term, and students made a selection, with the advice and guidance of their tutors, of those assignments which they aimed to complete.[72] The students were not required to give a specific view in their assignments but rather to show that they had understood the issues involved and had formulated their own opinion. While the college was firmly committed to historic Christianity as communicated through the Scriptures and the catholic creeds, there was no set college position on those areas of sincere debate among Christians. The staff sought to avoid giving simplistic or dogmatic answers to complex and controversial issues. They encouraged the students to reach their own convictions and to be content with a certain level of ambiguity.

In addition to regular assignments, every student was expected to undertake a project on a specific culture, country, ministry or missionary society. This could be in the form of a written report from field observation or specific research into a

72. Examples of these assignments are given in appendix 7.

particular area of study. In many cases, students used this opportunity to familiarise themselves with the people or geographical location in which they hoped to work.

All two year students were required to spend eight weeks in a ministry placement, either in the UK or overseas, in which they could gain practical exposure to Christian work, preferably of a cross-cultural nature. They were also required to reflect on this experience and produce a written report.

6.4.3.4 Visiting lecturers

One of the distinct advantages of the united college was that the combined faculty was able to offer a wider range of subjects than would have been possible in a single smaller institution. Even so, there were some topics which the staff did not feel competent to handle and they were grateful for visiting lecturers who came to share their expertise. Initially these visiting lectures tended to be pastors or mission leaders from the UK, but occasionally church leaders from the non-western world visited the school and shared their distinctive cultural and contextual perspectives.

6.4.3.5 Evaluation and assessment

One of the first decisions taken by the staff of the united college was to abolish exams. This decision was influenced by the staff who came from Mount Hermon, who had already concluded that exams were not the most relevant way to test missionary potential. It was decided instead to operate a system of continuous assessment, whereby the work of students would be appraised on the basis of their written assignments and their class participation. Since many of the assignments were of a general theological or missiological nature, all tutors were expected to be competent to evaluate them and make appropriate comments. When an essay was written on a more specialised subject, it was passed to the specialist lecturer for his, or her, assessment. Thus, the progress and achievement of each student was monitored, quantified and recorded by their tutor.

This system preserved the flexibility for each student 'to pursue their learning objectives and interests as individually as possible.'[73] It enabled the tutors to treat each student on the basis of their previous educational experience, their ability and their rate of progress. It avoided the need for grades and removed the temptation for students to 'give priority only to that which would be examined and graded, at the expense of other worthwhile work.'[74] The students were able to audit a wide range of lecture courses without the pressure of facing a host of exams at the end of the term. They also learned to assume greater responsibility for evaluating their own work and progress.

6.4.3.6 Accreditation

During the first ten years of the new college, considerable discussion was given to the question of accreditation. Prior to amalgamation, all three colleges had entered some of their brighter students for external examinations, but the staff were uncer-

73. ANCC, *Certificate and Diploma in Biblical and Cross-cultural Studies* (1993), p. 8.
74. *Ibid.*

tain what the policy of the new institution should be. Initially some students were encouraged to take the Diploma of Theology from the University of London,[75] which gave students the opportunity to obtain an accredited theological qualification within two years.

In 1975, a staff study group was appointed to consider whether ANCC should seek accreditation either from the Council for National Academic Awards (CNAA) or from the World Evangelical Fellowship (WEF).[76] It was recognised that ANCC was as well placed as many other colleges to offer an accredited diploma in theology or biblical studies. It was also acknowledged that association with other academic bodies could bring many benefits to the college and provide a valuable stimulus to the development of the course. On the other hand, a great deal of work would be involved in preparing the submission for such accreditation and some staff queried the value of such a diploma. Eventually it was agreed not to proceed with accreditation with either the CNAA or WEF. As Ron Davies, the Director of Studies, reported in the newsletter: 'It was felt that such exams would cut across the whole purpose and ethos of the college.'[77]

The majority of students continued to follow the college diploma course and, even though it had no external accreditation, there was still no shortage of applicants. The reputation of the school for practical, relevant, contemporary missionary training proved incentive enough for a constant stream of new students. Many of these had all the degrees and professional qualifications they needed. They were not looking for more. They simply wanted to be prepared as well as possible for their future service overseas.

For those students who wished to teach or translate the Bible, however, an accredited theological qualification was deemed necessary. The problem with the Diploma of Theology from London University was that it offered no paper in missiology, which was the discipline in which the college had the greatest interest. So the decision was taken to look for a more suitable external diploma course for the small number of students who needed to study for an accredited award. This proved to be the Certificate and Diploma in Religious Studies (CDRS) that was offered by Cambridge University. It was a respected theological course, which had a missiological option. The only disadvantage for students who wished to proceed was that Cambridge did not allow it to be upgraded to a degree.[78]

6.4.4 Academic studies – content

The ANCC Diploma was based on a two year course. The academic year ran from September to the end of June, and was divided into three terms of approximately

75. *All Nations Christian College* brochure (1971).
76. Minutes of the Council of ANCC, January 22 1976.
77. Ron Davies, 'Inside information', in: *ANCC Newsletter* (1976), p. 7.
78. In 1989, ANCC did apply to the CNAA for accreditation for a Diploma in Higher Education in Biblical and Cross-cultural Studies. In 1995, this was upgraded to a B.A. degree. In 1992, an M.A. in Aspects of Christian Missiology, the college's first higher degree, was validated. In 1996, the Open University accepted the college registration for M.Phil. and Ph.D. programmes. However, in 1998, 75 percent of the students at All Nations preferred to follow the college diploma course, which is not accredited.

ten weeks. The curriculum was arranged in five major fields: biblical studies (6.4.4.1); theological studies (6.4.4.2); missiological studies (6.4.4.3); pastoral studies (6.4.4.4) and practical studies (6.4.4.5).

6.4.4.1 Biblical studies

Just over one third of the timetable was devoted to biblical studies. This embraced a study of biblical languages, principles of interpretation, expositions of key texts and an integrated study week. The teaching of biblical studies was characterised by a strong emphasis on the cross-cultural application of biblical truth.

Biblical languages

The foundation for detailed study of the biblical text must be the biblical languages. Therefore, courses were offered in both *Greek* and *Hebrew.* Not all students were required or even advised to take these courses, but those who were preparing to be Bible translators or theological educators were expected to do so.

Principles of interpretation

All students were required to take the course which dealt with biblical interpretation. They were introduced to the basic principles of *Hermeneutics* and shown how these principles could be applied, through a study of selected areas of the biblical literature. The aim of the course was to sharpen their ability, so that they could interpret different types of biblical literature correctly and apply their truths appropriately in a contemporary context. It was hoped that the course would strengthen them in their convictions and, at the same time, challenge them in their prejudices.

Exposition of key texts

A large proportion of the ANCC course was devoted to the expository study of key biblical texts. There was no attempt to cover the whole Bible, as was often the case in Bible colleges. Rather a number of the books were selected as being of particular importance or as representative of different literary genre. The aim was to provide a model for approaching, interpreting and applying biblical passages.

The initial core course in the area of Old Testament studies offered an introduction to the history and religion of Israel. Its aim was to enable students to appreciate the value and importance of these scriptures, their place in the Christian canon, and their relevance to the contemporary mission of the church.

Core lecture courses were given on *Genesis, Exodus, Deuteronomy, Isaiah and Psalms*. Electives were also offered on the *Minor prophets* and *Wisdom literature*. These courses dealt with the critical issues of literary pedigree, historical reliability and moral behaviour that inevitably arose from a study of the text. The primary concern, however, was to examine the theological intent of the author and to provide models of exposition and application.

The New Testament studies also began with an introductory course, followed by detailed studies of the *Gospels, Romans, Corinthians, Ephesians,* and *Hebrews*. Students did their own detailed study of *Acts*, and electives were offered on *1 Thessalonians* and *Revelation*.

By the end of the course, students had considered the background and literature of most of the New Testament. They had learned to appreciate the value of contemporary scholarship, and had been introduced to both Johannine and Pauline theology. More importantly, they had learned how to express the central message of each book and to expound them accurately and meaningfully for today.

Integrated study week

One of the more innovative elements that was introduced into the study of biblical literature was the *Integrated study week*. Once a year, a week was set aside for the study of one Bible book. No other lectures or seminars were held during that week. The regular programme was set aside. The whole community just focused on the one text.

The book that was selected had to be short enough to be handled over five days. The most common choices were 1 Peter, Habakkuk and Nehemiah. The aim was to examine the background of the book, study its content and consider its contemporary application. Some lectures and devotional talks were given during the week, but the bulk of the work was done by the students on their own and in small groups.

This study week proved to be a welcome and enjoyable break in the regular routine of college life. Many appreciated the opportunity to spend a whole week on only one subject. The impact and effectiveness of this mode of teaching may be seen in the fact that many students used the materials from the week in their teaching in local churches and in their future ministry.

The multicultural hermeneutic

The lecturers at ANCC sought to avoid approaching the text from a monocultural perspective or relying too exclusively on biblical commentaries written by scholars from the West. The students came from diverse cultural backgrounds and were going to serve all over the world. It was important that their insights were heard and that different perspectives were presented. It was equally desirable that those who were going to another culture began to address the issue of how the biblical text might be understood and interpreted in that culture. So as they studied a particular passage of the Bible they were asked to consider how a particular chapter related to their future work as missionaries or how it might be taught in a different cultural context.

The book of Genesis provides a good example of the approach that was taken. The early chapters of that book present the foundations of the biblical worldview: the creation of the world by God, the creation of men and women 'in His image,' and the account of the fall. This biblical perspective differs from many of the worldviews which students would encounter in their future work. In the Genesis account God is portrayed as a personal God, who exhibits personal characteristics and enters into personal relationships with humankind. He is the creator of everything though he is distinct from his creation and his creatures. This view of a personal creator God is very different from the monistic faith of Hinduism, for example, or the atheism of Buddhism.

The author of Genesis proclaims that there is only one God, who created the heavens and the earth. Those who follow traditional religion often believe in a high creator God but are more immediately concerned with a hierarchy of lesser deities and spirits, who are the objects of their worship.

Genesis chapter three describes the events of the fall, a concept that is found in the folklore of many cultures. Among the Ashanti in Ghana, for example, it is believed that God once lived close to human beings but that he has now gone away because a woman poked his eye with a pestle.[79] Among the Maasai in East Africa it is said that there used to be a bridge connecting heaven and earth but that a Maasai warrior cut it down because he was angry with God.

The course on Genesis challenged the students to consider how they would cross the hermeneutical bridge between the worldview of the Bible and that of the people to whom they would go. How would they teach these chapters to people who already have their own understanding about God, their own set of values, their own stories of creation, their own perception of the fall?

So with all the lecture courses in the field of biblical studies, the purpose was not simply to provide the students with a summary of the contents or the theological perspectives of the book, but to challenge them to consider how each book could be taught and applied in other cultures.

6.4.4.2 Theological studies

The field of theological studies was divided into three areas: doctrinal studies covered the major doctrines of the Christian faith; historical and ecumenical studies concentrated on the Roman Catholic and Orthodox Churches, the rise of Protestantism and the growth of the ecumenical movement; applied and contextualised studies focused on ethics and non-western theological developments.

Doctrinal studies

The doctrinal studies provided an introduction to the basic tenets of the Christian faith: *God, Humanity, Christology, Pneumatology, Ecclesiology and Eschatology*. The lecture courses sought to familiarise the students with the biblical teaching on each doctrine and the ways in which the church down the centuries had sought to understand and develop them.

In the case of Christology, the lecture course was supplemented by group study on some of the key Christological texts in the New Testament. Students were required to do their own private study on these passages with the help of commentaries, and using the Greek text if possible, before taking part in a small group discussion, led by a member of staff.

Particular emphasis was given to a consideration of the missiological implications of each doctrine. So the course on *Humanity* addressed the implications of a fully biblical understanding of humanity for the various aspects of Christian ministry and mission. The course on the *Holy Spirit* examined the vital importance of the Spirit in enabling the Church to fulfil its mission. The study of the *Last things* examined the motivation for mission which resulted from the different millennial perspectives.

---

79. John S. Mbiti, *Concepts of God in Africa* (1970), p. 71.

As with biblical studies, students were challenged not only to understand each doctrine from its biblical or historical perspective, but were also encouraged to reflect on how it could be presented most effectively in another cultural context. This is reflected in the assignments that were set for these lecture courses, e.g. 'Give an account of the Christian doctrine of the Trinity, its biblical foundation and historical formation. What difficulties are you likely to encounter in seeking to present this truth in the particular religious and cultural context in which you expect to work in the future, e.g. Islam, Judaism, Hinduism, Western materialism?'[80]

Historical and ecumenical studies

The historical and ecumenical studies included a lecture course on the *Roman Catholic Church*. This covered the historical development of the doctrines of the Catholic Church and the theological developments since the Second Vatican Council. The course examined the sources of authority within the church. It also prepared the students to relate with greater sensitivity to those within the Roman Catholic Church with whom they might have contact or among whom they might work. Courses were also offered on the *Ecumenical movement* and on the theology and spirituality of the *Eastern Orthodox churches*.

A series of lectures was offered on the *Independency movements,* which have flourished particularly in Africa. The aim of this series was to enable students to identify the cultural, economic and socio-political context which gave rise to these new religious movements.

In a two year training course which was designed to prepare missionaries, it was not possible to offer a comprehensive study of ecclesiastical history. Courses were given on early church history, the Reformation and the modern period. Particular attention was paid to the story of the expansion of the church through the centuries (see under *Missiological studies).*

Applied and contextualised studies

Almost three quarters of the students at All Nations came from the UK and continental Europe. They were strongly influenced by the ethical values of the secular society in which they grew up. A lecture course on *Christian ethics* presented them with a survey of representative non-Christian ethical systems, and offered them the criteria with which to evaluate the strengths and inadequacies of those systems. The course also aimed to equip the students to analyse ethical problems, to apply appropriate Scriptural principles and to formulate their own personal stance.

In preparation for their ministry in the non-western world, students were introduced to significant non-European theological developments. They were reminded that they could not simply impose a Western perspective on the Christian faith on Asia or Africa. They needed to look at Scripture through the eyes of others. They needed to start learning their theology from the Two-Thirds World.

The course on *Non-western theologies* considered the works of writers like Kitamori with his emphasis on the pain of God, Koyama and his teaching on the wrath

80. *Bible Study Assignments and Other Work* (1980).

of God, Mbiti and his view of the African concept of time, Gutierrez, Boff and Miranda on the theology of liberation. In each case the students were asked to consider the different context in which these theologies arose, and the ways in which they addressed the pressing sociological, emotional and spiritual needs of that context. Each student taking this course was required to read and to critique one book by an important non-western theologian.

6.4.4.3 Missiological studies

Missiological studies received almost as much class time as biblical studies (360 class hours compared to 390 class hours). Half of these were devoted to core courses, the rest were given to electives course, where students could pursue more specialised missiological studies pertinent to their future vocation. In the following section we look at a few courses in more detail.

Theology of mission

The study of the theology of mission began with an introductory course on the *Biblical Basis of Mission*, which traced the God's concern for the nations of the world from the early chapters of Genesis to the eschatological climax in Revelation. Particular attention was paid to the universality of the Abrahamic covenant, the role of Israel as a light to the nations and the distinctive missiological perspectives of the different New Testament writers. A compulsory assignment for all students was 'to write a brief summary of the main stages of the spread of the gospel in the book of Acts, classifying the different obstacles which the early Christians encountered and how they overcame those obstacles' and 'to make a comparison of the form and content of the sermons in Acts, noting the similarities and differences related to the varying audiences and explaining the implications for mission.' The students were also required to read Roland Allen's missionary classic *Missionary methods, St Paul's or ours?* (1912)[81]

In the second year a more advanced course, the *Theology of mission*, explored major areas of debate in the modern missiological scene, and examined how Christians from differing traditions have developed their understanding of mission. The nature of mission, its motives and aim, general revelation, the theology of religion, salvation and its socio-political implications, dialogue and proclamation, witness and proselytism, syncretism and accommodation, were all considered in turn, and in considerable depth.

Finally students were introduced to the key Roman Catholic, Ecumenical and Evangelical statements on mission produced in recent years. The purpose of the course was to broaden their horizons, to enable them to appreciate the distinctive emphases and developments within the various traditions, and to give them a greater understanding of those they might meet in the course of their ministry.

Culture and worldview

In a series of lectures on understanding culture and cultural anthropology, students were made aware of their own culture and its influence on them. They were warned

81. *Bible Study assignments and other work* (1980).

of the dangers of ethnocentricity, of making the assumption that their cultural way of doing things was normative and superior to other patterns of behaviour. They were forewarned of the syndrome of culture shock and were encouraged to become bi-cultural people, capable of appreciating another culture as much as their own. They were also reminded of the importance of language learning in identifying with a host culture. Furthermore they were shown the value of cultural anthropology as a tool for discerning the functional role of rituals and cultural practices, and understanding the dynamics of cultural change.

A course entitled *Gospel and culture* explored the importance and role of culture within the Bible, and examined the extent to which the Scriptures provided guidelines for the contextualisation of the gospel. Many were asking, for example, how far could ideas, illustrations or religious practices be adapted from the recipient culture without running the risk of syncretism? The course considered the meaning of conversion and the nature of the church, and how they might find expression in a new context. It also investigated ways in which theologians and missiologists have sought to apply anthropological insights to mission strategy, in such areas as church growth and the homogeneous unit principle.

World religions

All students received a basic introduction to the *Major world religions*, and were then encouraged to attend a specialist course on the religion, or religions, dominant in the area where they hoped to serve. The aim of these specialist courses was to enable them to understand and appreciate the beliefs and practices of that religion, so that they could relate to its adherents intelligently and sympathetically, and could make mature and sensitive comparisons between that faith and their own Christian faith.

An introductory course on *New religious movements* examined the history, beliefs and practices of some of the religious groups which emerged in the West in the nineteenth century, such as Jehovah's Witnesses and Mormons, and some of the new religious groups of the 1960s and 1970s, influenced by Eastern religions.

Historical and contemporary studies

A ten lecture course on the *History of Christian mission* was based on Stephen C. Neill's book of the same name (1964). The course examined the expansion of the early church, the Celtic missionary movement, the work of the Jesuits, the story of the Moravians and the growth of the Protestant missionary movement during the past two centuries. As students considered each period of history, they were asked to consider what principles could be drawn from the experience of the church that could be applied to the work of Christian mission today.

Every week a lecture was presented under the title *Christianity in today's world.* The speaker was usually a guest, often from overseas. Occasionally it might be a member of staff or a student. They would address some topic of the church's life and ministry of which they had particular knowledge or expertise. They might cover anything from the contextualisation of theological education in Africa to the work of Afro-Caribbean churches in Britain, from the potential of radio for world mission to the need for the conversion of Europe, from the effect of urbanisation on the role and status of women to life under tension in the Sudan. These lecturers came from a wide variety of ethnic and denominational backgrounds. They included speakers like Bishop J. E. Lesslie Newbigin, Bishop Stephen C. Neill, Thomas F. Stransky (President of the Paulist Fathers), Metropolitan Anthony of the Russian Orthodox Church, Gottfried Osei-Mensah (General Secretary of the Lausanne Committee for World Evangelisation), Bishop John Reid from the diocese of Sydney, Daniel Ho from the National Evangelical Christian Fellowship in Malaysia, Heather Wraight (Director, Radio Worldwide) and Sister Rita Rosario, a Roman Catholic Sister from South India. The breadth of this list indicates the desire of the staff that their evangelical students should have a broader understanding of what was happening throughout the world, and should not operate from a blinkered or uninformed perspective.

Missionary methodology and practice
A variety of courses were offered on the implementation of missiological theory in practice. These included principles of evangelism and church growth, leadership training, theological education by extension, development work and medical missions.

Missionary life and work gave practical guidelines on issues like the packing and shipping of goods, the choice of a library to take, the bringing up children in a different culture, the education of children, and the writing of effective prayer letters.

Every week students met in small groups for *Current mission discussion*. The aim of these discussions was to introduce them to the kind of issues they might face in the future. At what standard should they live? Should they employ servants, own a car or use air-conditioning? How should they respond to those who ask them for food or for bribes? In a political crisis, how should they decide whether they should leave the country?

6.4.4.4 Pastoral studies
During the first ten years of united college increasing recognition was given to the importance of courses on *Pastoral studies* and *Christian spirituality*. These lectures provided a biblical basis for and understanding of personhood and pastoral care. They reminded students of the importance of their own personal development and introduced them to different traditions of Christian spirituality.

Pastoral studies
The course on *Pastoral studies* encompassed such topics as stress and transition, patterns of reaction, and the dynamics of loss, change and growth. Issues of sexuality, sexual abuse and homosexuality were also tackled. The objectives of the course were that students should grow in personal insight and maturity in Christ, acquire an ability to facilitate others towards greater self-awareness and growth, and develop the ability to use and teach these pastoral skills in their own or another culture.

Christian spirituality
In the course on *Christian spirituality* students examined the spiritual disciplines and some common motifs of the spiritual walk, such as the desert and pilgrimage. They were introduced to some of the spiritual classics and to a broad spectrum of Christian traditions. They were recommended to develop an appreciation for these traditions and to cultivate their own spirituality. They studied the relationship between self-knowledge and the knowledge of God, between spiritual friendship and spiritual direction, and between temperament and spirituality.

A further lecture series examined the question of *Spiritual warfare*, as it is understood in the various world religions and in different traditions within the Christian church. The issue of theodicy was also considered from a biblical perspective, and scriptural teaching on Satan and demons was examined. The objective of the course was to enable students to formulate their own theological understanding of the spiritual warfare in which Christians are engaged and to learn how to minister in those contexts where people are acutely aware of the presence and power of evil spirits.

6.4.4.5 Practical studies
Practical studies at ANCC were divided into two categories*: communication techniques* and *technical knowledge*. The first of these concentrated on developing students' ministerial gifts and speaking abilities. The second equipped students with technical skills that they might use or teach others in their future work.

Communications techniques
First there were courses dealing with communication skills and the exercise of Christian ministry. The aim of these courses was to enable the students to communicate their Christian faith effectively to others, in a way that was both acceptable and appropriate to the age, culture, background and ability of those whom they were addressing. Lectures on the theory of communication, formed the foundation for subsequent sessions on work among children and teenagers, leading group Bible studies and preparing sermons.

Every week students met in *Speakers groups* where they gained practical experience in sharing their testimony, and giving a brief explanation of the gospel, or short talk, to a specific audience. In their second year they learned how to develop their expository skills, and do other specialised courses. In addition, a ten week *Communications practical course* was offered twice a year . This provided instruction in street evangelism, sketchboard evangelism, drama, the use of visual aids, the use of an overhead projector, and the designing of leaflets.

Each student was involved in *Weekly Christian ministry* in a local church, mission or secular club. Most students were engaged in ministry within a few miles of the college, but a few travelled further so that they could attend one of the ethnic and multi-racial churches in London.

All students doing the college two-year diploma course had to spend four weeks in their first year and four weeks in their second year on block placements. Many travelled overseas to gain further experience of Christian ministry in a cross-cultural environment. On their return they were required to present a report on what they had learned about ministry from their experience. A debriefing session conducted in small groups also enabled them to share their observations with students and a tutor.

A brief course on *Linguistics* introduced students to the basics of phonetics, grammar and phonemics, to facilitate their learning of a new language. Lectures were also given on *Creative writing* to enable students to explore the dynamics of contemporary writing and develop their own writing skills.

Technical knowledge
The second area of practical studies were those providing technical skills. These varied from *Car maintenance* to *Tropical health and hygiene*, from *Basic cookery* to *Emergency dentistry*, from *Photography* to *Hairdressing*. These course were usually held in the afternoons or at weekends. Students selected which courses to take depending on their own preference and previous experience. The primary purpose of the courses was to enable students to acquire new skills which might be valuable in their future ministry, particularly if they were going to a remote or isolated context.

6.4.5 Conclusion

Morris's philosophy of training left its mark on every aspect of the college course. The tutorial system which he introduced provided the framework in which all students planned and pursued their personalised curriculum.

Every encouragement was given to the students to cultivate their own spiritual development. Though the college was evangelical, Morris had little time for superficial or hypocritical spirituality. He wanted his students to be real in their religion and sincere in their worship. He encouraged serious commitment to Jesus Christ, practical Christian living, and respect for those who held different religious convictions.

The college was committed to the development of Christian character. The communal life of the college meant that any flaws of character, or failure in relational skills, came to light. The tutorial system provided the natural framework in which such weaknesses could be addressed.

Several aspects of the academic course are noteworthy: the coherence fostered between disciplines; the progression encouraged by the system of core and elective courses; the serious attempt to look at Scripture and Christian doctrine through non-western eyes; the constant application of lessons learned to future ministry; the practice of continuous assessment in preference to exams, and the refusal to seek accreditation at the cost of effective training. The students at ANCC were not given pat answers, but they were equipped with the hermeneutical tools to enable them to draw their own conclusions from the text. Above all, the students were encouraged to think for themselves, to realise how little they knew and to commit themselves to a lifetime of learning.

The academic curriculum marked a significant step forward from those of the precedent colleges, but there were some important areas of study which received little or no attention in the timetable. There was no specialist course on medical mission, although nearly one third of the students came from the medical profession. There was, therefore, no opportunity for extensive discussion on the relative merits of Western and traditional medicine. There was no course on urban ministry, in spite of the massive migration to the cities happening around the world. Relatively little time was given to a discussion of the relationship between evangelism and development work, or to the social and political implications of the gospel. Insufficient time was devoted to Pastoral studies, and the course on the history of Christian mission was too short to deal adequately with the important issues about the theory and practice of mission which it raised. These omissions were corrected in later years as new staff members with expertise in these areas joined the faculty, but at this early stage they represent serious gaps in the curriculum.

The teaching style was still largely confined to the lecture method, though some work was done in discussion and small study groups. Some staff were creative in their teaching and insisted on plenty of interaction with students, but most seemed to be unaware of contemporary developments in the field of adult education.

The college made a serious attempt to complement the academic studies with practical training. The courses on technical skills provided a light diversion during the week, as well as useful preparation for the future. Considerable time was also allotted to the teaching and development of communication skills. The weekly placements provided a regular opportunity for the students to develop their own gifts of preaching, teaching, evangelism, and the leading of worship. One of the weaknesses of this aspect of the training, however, lay in the college's location. East Hertfordshire was essentially a rural area offering students little in the way of experience in urban ministry. It was also mono-cultural. The population consisted almost entirely of anglo-saxons with no significant ethnic communities. This deprived the students of the opportunity of working among people of different cultural backgrounds, which would have been a helpful preparation for their future ministry. Some students chose to travel to London for their placements, so that they could minister among one of the ethnic communities in the city. A large number of students also went overseas for at least one of their ministry placements to gain further experience in cross-cultural service.

Notwithstanding these weaknesses mentioned above, the training offered at ANCC provided a good model of holistic missionary preparation. It embraced the spiritual life, character formation, academic rigour, practical tuition and ministerial experience. In its comprehensiveness it went some way towards the pattern envisioned at the Edinburgh Conference (1910).

6.5 THE STUDENTS

This section explores the process of student selection (6.5.1) and the criteria used in that selection (6.5.2). It reviews the national, denominational and professional background of the students (6.5.3), and continues with an analysis of the countries where they served after the completion of their training (6.5.4).

6.5.1 The selection process

Early in the life of the college, it became necessary to distinguish between casual enquirers and serious applicants. The selection process was developed into five stages: enquiry, preliminary application, full application, references, and interview.

When initial enquiries were received through letters, telephone calls or personal visits, the principal, vice-principal, and their respective secretaries, tried to discern whether the person in question was seriously interested in coming to ANCC and would be the sort of person whom they might accept. If there were obvious reasons why the enquirers would not be suitable at ANCC, or ANCC would not be the right place for them, they would not be encouraged to proceed any further with their application. However, if there was no obvious reason at this stage why they should not be considered more seriously, they would be given a preliminary application form.

This application form requested from the persons involved basic information about educational background, work experience, church membership and involvement, missionary call, anticipated future service and financial situation. The applicants were asked to give some indication of their ability in English[82] and also to write a brief account of their personal history, including their conversion experience and the steps leading towards this initial application.

The preliminary form usually gave a good indication of whether or not the applicants would be suitable candidates for ANCC. If they did not match up to the college's criteria (see 6.5.2) or if their knowledge of English was inadequate to cope with the course, they would be informed that the college did not think ANCC was the right place for them.

If the preliminary forms revealed no apparent grounds why the applicants should not study at the college, they were sent the full application papers. These required more detailed information about academic qualifications, work experience, gifts and calling. The applicants were required to write a doctrinal statement,[83] and to indicate if they held any views that differed from those usually held by evangelical Christians. They were asked to supply the names of three people who would be willing to write references on their behalf. At this stage, they were also requested to complete a medical form and undergo a medical examination.

Referees were asked to comment on the applicant's character, spiritual life, missionary call, academic potential, relational skills, and ability to cope under pressure. They were also asked if they had any reservations about the candidate's suitability for college and community life, or for work in any climate in stressful conditions. Those who gave references were encouraged to be absolutely honest, and their comments were treated as confidential to the college staff.

---

82. Applicants whose first language was not English were usually required to pass the British Council English Test at Grade 5.5 or to obtain a similar qualification.
83. They were asked to state in their own words what they believed about the deity of Jesus, the work of the Holy Spirit, the atonement, the Bible and the Christian's role in society.

Once the full application papers, the medical forms and the references had been received, the applicant would usually be invited for an interview at the college.[84] This would involve spending at least half a day at Easneye, giving the opportunity for the candidate to look round the college and meet a number of students informally. A mature student, responsible for hosting the applicant, sometimes volunteered significant information and became a useful sounding board in borderline decisions. The interview lasted about one hour and was conducted by two members of staff. Initially the principal (in the case of single men or married couples), or the vice-principal (in the case of single women), were always involved in these interviews. As the college grew this became impracticable and the interviewing was shared out among all the academic staff.

The aim of the interview was to enable the applicants to discover the next step in God's will for their life. The desire of the interviewers was not so much to see if the interviewees passed a certain test and made the grade for acceptance at ANCC, but rather to discover whether God was calling them to cross-cultural ministry and, if so, whether ANCC was the right place for them to train. Meg Foote comments: 'It was made very clear to the applicant that non-acceptance was not a negative experience of rejection but a positive step forward in discovering God's will. Many wrote appreciatively of this months later.'[85]

In some ways the selection procedure followed at the college was as thorough as that pursued by the missionary societies . The time of preparation at an institution like ANCC was the first major step in a path that would lead to overseas service. The staff were concerned only to encourage those along that path who were likely to reach that goal.

6.5.2 The selection criteria

As the reputation of the united college grew, the number of applicants increased rapidly. By 1981, more than one thousand letters of inquiry were being received each year from potential applicants. Over this first decade of the college's life, the staff were forced to adopt a more rigid selection procedure and to clarify the criteria on which they would accept students.

6.5.2.1 Spiritual maturity

Candidates were expected to be committed Christians with a personal and growing relationship with God. Usually they were not accepted if they had been Christians for less than three years. Regular attendance and faithful service in a local congregation was usually looked for as one mark of spiritual maturity and commitment.

It was assumed that those who were coming to the college were in sympathy with its evangelical position, but they were not required to sign the college's statement of faith. While students were encouraged to hold their own convictions, they

84. As the numbers of overseas applicants increased, a number of alumni and friends of the college were asked to conduct interviews in the countries where they were living.
85. M. Foote, personal correspondence, April 16 1998.

were discouraged from trying to force their views on others. Those who made clear at interview their determination to convert the rest of the college to their way of thinking were not usually accepted.

6.5.2.2 Missionary vocation

While other Bible colleges offered training for pastoral work or evangelism in the home country, the distinct focus of ANCC was to train men and women for cross-cultural ministry. Consequently students were only accepted if they had a strong sense of call to this kind of ministry. It did not matter if they were unsure about the country to which they might go, or the missionary society with which they might serve. Those details could be clarified later. At this stage it was important that their sense of vocation matched the kind of training that the college offered.

In some cases applicants felt called to cross-cultural ministry within their own country, to work among a specific tribal group in Kenya, for example, or among one of the Asian communities in Britain. That was felt to be consistent with the rationale of the college.

Occasionally there were students who came with a clear intention of serving in cross-cultural ministry, but whose sense of vocation changed during their time at ANCC. Sometimes ill-health made it impossible for them to proceed with a career overseas. Sometimes a latent gift was discovered that would be more fully utilised if they stayed at home rather than went abroad. Sometimes marriage led them into a different kind of Christian service. On completion of their training at ANCC, some felt called to train for the ordained ministry in their own country. None of these were seen as failures from the perspective of the college. Rather the staff rejoiced with the students that they had discovered God's will for their lives. However, these were the exceptions rather than the rule. The vast majority of ANCC students came with a clear missionary call and proceeded to serve in cross-cultural ministry when they left.

Morris believed that husbands and wives should train together. He also believed that they should both be convinced that they were called to missionary work. When he had first felt called to Africa, he had waited for several months until his wife came to share his conviction. Now as college principal, he would not encourage a married couple to proceed to work overseas unless they both believed that this was God's will for their lives.

6.5.2.3 Church endorsement

In his book *Transforming mission*[86] (1991), David F. Bosch cites a long list of motives that have led men and women into missionary service. Those who have counselled potential missionary candidates will be aware of the wide variety of motives that may lie behind their sense of call. While it is vital that the individual does have an inner conviction of his or her calling, it is equally important that their calling is endorsed by the local church.

Those who applied to come to ANCC were expected to have the full backing of their local congregation. A reference was required from the pastor indicating that

86. D.F. Bosch, *Transforming mission* (1991), p. 5.

the elders of the church believed that the students involved were called to missionary service. An assurance of prayerful and, preferably, financial support from the church was also expected.

Sometimes a newly appointed pastor did not know the potential missionary candidate well enough to provide a satisfactory reference. Sometimes the church was not in the least interested in missionary work or felt that it was no longer appropriate. Sometimes the pastor was more concerned to retain gifted and dedicated young people in his own congregation than to encourage them to go to some distant corner of the world. In spite of these exceptions, the college sought as far as possible to follow the biblical precedent set by the church in Antioch (Acts 13: 1-3) and to accept only those applicants who came with the approval and blessing of their home church.

6.5.2.4 Proven gifts

The local church plays a major role in the preparation of missionary candidates. It is the context in which most come to faith in Christ and receive their initial discipling. It is also the place where they may receive their missionary call and begin to develop their gifts of ministry. Members of the local church can observe their growth and development. They are able to judge better than anyone else whether an individual has the ability to make an effective contribution to the life of a local congregation.

One of the criteria used at interview by the faculty at ANCC was whether the potential candidate gave 'evidence of potential usefulness to the work of Christ in the world through the fellowship of church and mission.'[87] The interviewers worked on the premise that if people had made a useful contribution to the life of the church in their own country, there was at least the possibility they might make a similar contribution in another country. But if they had not exercised any significant ministry at home among people whom they knew, in a context with which they were familiar, there were little grounds for optimism that they would do so among people who were totally strange to them and in a context that was completely foreign.

6.5.2.5 Personal maturity

Personal maturity was another criterion which was used in student selection. In the words of the college brochure: 'Applicants are expected to show a mature attitude to life.'[88] The staff were not looking for perfect people. They were aware both of their own weaknesses and of the failures of some prominent characters in the Bible. Rather, they were looking for applicants who had reached some level of self-understanding and were seeking to grow and develop.

References were required from a personal friend of the applicant of the same sex and from their present or recent employer, as well as from their pastor. Although the referees were asked to be as honest as possible they tended to write in glowing terms. Those reading the references had to be adept at spotting any sugges-

87. *All Nations Christian College* brochure, (1972).
88. *Ibid.*

tion of weakness and following that up either through a telephone call to the referee or during the course of the interview.

The reference from the student's employer, usually a non-Christian, was often the most telling, either because of what it did not say or because of what it did say. One employer drew a line through several questions on the reference form, complaining that he did not understand them. He then went on to write, 'I do not understand half of these questions, but if this man is a Christian, I wish all my employees were Christian.'[89] Needless to say, that applicant was accepted.

Relational skills are an important quality for those who may have to live and work within a small team in isolated and pressurised conditions. Both through the references and in the personal interview, the staff would try to assess how well the applicant would relate to others and, in particular, how well they might work alongside those who came from a different denominational or cultural background. On the top of the interview assessment form, which the interviewers used but which the interviewees did not see, was printed the question, 'Would I be willing to work with this person?'

6.5.2.6 Physical and emotional health

Students were required to fill in a comprehensive questionnaire about their medical history and undergo a medical examination. There was little point in their embarking on a course of missionary preparation if they were never going to be fit enough for overseas service.

They were asked if they, or any close relatives, had suffered from a depressive illness. It was not the policy of the college to exclude such people from the course. Morris himself struggled with severe depression for much of his life. He demonstrated how effectively such a person can be used in the service of God and be a constant source of blessing and encouragement to many. The staff knew that depression was no bar to fruitful Christian ministry. At the same time, they felt that special care should be taken in cases where there was a history of mental illness, to ascertain whether the person in question would be able to cope with the pressures of missionary service.

6.5.2.7 Gifts and academic qualifications

When the three colleges merged there was considerable disparity between the academic level of the incoming students. Early in the first year the principal reported to the college council that one of the problems they faced was 'the wide range of ability among the students in academic status, especially as generally speaking the standard among the women tended to be higher than that among the men.'[90]

As the reputation of the new college grew, an increasing number of graduates began to apply. By 1975, 50% of the student body held university degrees or an equivalent qualification. Inevitably the academic standard of the lectures rose, as did the level of debate and interaction within classes and seminars.

89. Interview with David Morris, March 14 1984.
90. Minutes of the ANCC Council, October 21 1971.

It was the conviction of the principal, shared by his staff, that lack of academic ability was no barrier to effective Christian service. The question which needed to be asked was not whether the applicants had a degree but whether they had some recognisable skill or ability which would be relevant to the needs of the people whom they wished to serve. Among some of the most gifted students in those early years was a blacksmith, a pig-farmer and an organ builder. Some from Africa had lacked the opportunity for higher study but they had proved their effectiveness in ministry and leadership.

The aim of the college was to offer appropriate training to all students whatever their academic background. Yet the staff were aware that there had to be some minimum requirement. If students were accepted who could not cope with the course they might feel frustrated themselves or frustrate others by their constant questions and requests for clarification. The criterion eventually adopted was that applicants should normally have a degree or the equivalent, but that others would be accepted onto the course providing it was felt that they would be able to handle the academic level.

6.5.2.8 Secular and cross-cultural experience
Morris wanted his students to be able to survive the pressures of their future ministry. He knew that many had grown up in the sheltered environment of a Christian home. He knew the value of experience gained from a period of work in the secular world. Those accepted as students at ANCC were normally expected to have had some work experience after completing their education. This often meant that students delayed their coming to ANCC, and, in consequence, the average age of the student body was between twenty eight and thirty.

It also became increasingly apparent that those who had work experience in another culture benefited more from the course than those who hadn't had that opportunity. They were already aware of the pressures of cross-cultural life and the critical issues facing the church in other lands. They tended to be less naive in outlook and more appreciative of other cultures.

In later years, when places were oversubscribed, those with cross-cultural experience were usually preferred to those who had similar gifts and calling, but lacked that experience. Where applicants stated that they had never been outside their own culture they were encouraged to go overseas for at least three months before coming to ANCC. Often they went for one or more years.

6.5.3 The background of the students

At the beginning of each academic year a list of students was produced giving details of their nationality, denomination, profession and anticipated field of service. These annual lists provide the statistics, which are illustrated on appendices 8 to 12, and described in the following paragraphs.

6.5.3.1 Student numbers
Appendix 8 indicates the steady growth of the college during the decade. Starting with 128 students in 1971, the student population rose to 157 by 1980. During this

period, the number of single men remained fairly constant whereas the number of single women increased from 58 to 70. The greatest increase was seen in the number of married students, rising from 36 married students in 1971 (18 couples) to 56 in 1980.

6.5.3.2 Nationality

Appendix 9 illustrates how the composition of the college changed during the course of this decade. In 1971, 86% of the student body (110 out of 128 students) came from within the United Kingdom. At that time, ANCC was largely a college for British students, with a small group (18), who came form other parts of the world. Nine years later, ANCC had become an international college, where overseas students constituted 52% of the student body, outnumbering the British students by a margin of 82 to 75.

The increase among foreign students was particularly noticeable among those coming from European countries. These numbered 14 in 1971, but 47 in 1980. The largest representation from a single country occurred in 1980 with 21 students coming from the Netherlands. Scandinavian countries were usually well represented, 10 coming from Sweden and Norway in 1978. In the same year, there were 8 students from Switzerland, another country that always sent some students to the college. Most West European nations had occasional representatives in the college, and some came from communist countries, such as Yugoslavia (2 in 1974) and Czechoslovakia (1980).

There were always some students from Asian countries, the largest number being the 17 who came in 1979. These included 4 from Malaysia, 2 from Thailand, 2 from the Philippines and others from Singapore, Hong Kong, India, Pakistan and Korea. In other years, students also came from Japan and Sri Lanka.

Over this first decade of the new college, 13 African nations were represented among the student body: Nigeria, Ethiopia, Tanzania, Zambia, Zimbabwe, South Africa, Malawi, Burundi, Rwanda, Ghana, Uganda, Egypt and Kenya. The biggest single group (9 students) came from South Africa in 1978.

Relatively few came from the Americas. Occasionally there were students from the USA, Canada or the Caribbean. In 1973 and 1980, there were students from Brazil. From 1976 to 1980, there was always at least one student from Australia and most years someone from New Zealand.

6.5.3.3 Denominational affiliation

The statistics for denominational affiliation (appendix 10) show that two denominations were dominant among the ANCC students, the Anglican and Baptist Churches. More than 60% of the students belonged to these denominations, which is a fair reflection of the numerical strength of evangelicals within British churches at this time.

There was usually a smaller representation of the Christian Brethren, Independent Evangelical, Presbyterian, Methodist and Pentecostal Churches.

As the numbers of students from the European continent grew, so did the number of members of Lutheran and Reformed Churches. Occasionally students were accepted from the Moravians and the Quakers, and even from the Roman Catholic Church.

6.5.3.4 Professional background

As appendix 11 indicates, 53% of the students came from the medical or teaching professions. 25% were doctors, nurses, midwives, physiotherapists, dentist etc., while 28% were teachers.[91] Among the single women, the percentage from these two professions was particularly high. In 1979, 90% (56 out of 62 two single women) were medics or teachers, 58% (36) in the medical profession and 32% (20) in education. 6% had been engaged in full-time evangelistic or pastoral work prior to coming to the college.

The remaining students came from a wide spectrum of professions and occupations, ranging from solicitor to secretary, agriculturalist to architect, blacksmith to banker, chemist to carpenter, pilot to plumber, confectioner to computer programmer.

What is clear is that over these ten years the academic standard of applicants steadily rose. By 1980, it was estimated that between 70 and 80% of the student body were university graduates or had completed a tertiary education qualification.

6.5.4 Fields of service

Many of those who came to ANCC were uncertain about their future field of service. In 1976, more than a quarter of the students (36 out of 137) said that they did not know where they were going to work.

Some had already chosen their missionary society or had come to the college as an accepted candidate of a specific society. They knew the general area of the world to which they would go, but the specific country was as yet undecided.

The remainder came with a definite country in mind, though by the time of leaving college their ideas had often changed. A clearer understanding of the needs and opportunities in different parts of the world, together with a more realistic assessment of their own gifts, often caused them to review their chosen field of service.

Complete statistics are not available on where the students eventually went but their anticipated field of service, recorded when they first came to the college, gives some indication of where they hoped to go (appendix 12).

In 1971, 32% expected to go to Africa. Nigeria (8), Ethiopia (7) and Rwanda (4) were the most popular destinations. 29% anticipated service in Asia, particularly in India (6), Pakistan (4), Thailand (4) and Indonesia (3). 5% intended to go to the Middle East (4 students were hoping to go to the Lebanon). 8% chose to go to the Americas (Peru, Chile, Paraguay and Argentina, with two going to the USA). 26% expected to serve in continental Europe or the United Kingdom.

Five years later, the most significant change was the decline in the numbers of those who expected to stay in Europe for their ministry. This figure had dropped to

91. This includes every category of teachers from nursery teachers to university lecturers.

8%, whereas the number of those who hoped to go to Asia had increased to 39%.[92]

By the end of the decade, the interest in Asia had increased further. In 1980, 56% of the students expressed a hope to serve in Asia, with Pakistan (7), Nepal (7), India (4) and Korea (6) being the most popular destinations. In the same year, only 22% felt that they were being called to Africa. 7% were interested in Latin America, particularly Brazil (6 students). The degree of interest in the Middle East remained constant at 7%, though there were more students (3) who were hoping to work in Israel. 10% were considering service within Europe, which represents a small rise on 1976, but is a much lower figure than the 26% of 1971.

ANCC always did receive a few students who felt called to the pastoral ministry in Britain, but as the pressure on places grew it was felt that less people in this category should be accepted, and that priority should be given to those with a specific call to cross-cultural ministry.

The consistent popularity of Nigeria was in part due to the enthusiasm of Morris for that country, since he had served there as a missionary. The decline in interest in Africa, and the corresponding increase in the focus on Asia, reflected the influence of Martin Goldsmith. He had spent many years in south-east Asia as a missionary and made students aware of the needs of the church and the opportunities for Christian service in that region of the world.

It is noticeable that several of the most popular destinations were those having close historic ties with Britain (India, Nigeria, Ghana, Pakistan, Malaysia) or with another colonial power (Rwanda, Indonesia, Brazil). In the cases of Thailand, Ethiopia and Korea there was no such historic association, but each of these countries presented considerable scope for missionary service.

A further important factor in the choice of a field of service lay in the image of the various missionary agencies. Those agencies which produced attractive publicity and communicated an approach to mission coinciding with that held by the students inevitably attracted more applications. During these ten years, societies like WBT, OMF and BMMF (later InterServe) became increasingly popular. In 1976, they accounted for 17% of the student population. In 1980 that had risen to 27%.

6.5.5 *Conclusion*

The demand for places at ANCC forced the staff to sharpen their criteria for acceptance. The focus of the college on missionary training dictated the kind of people who would be accepted: those who had a clear missionary call, who gave sufficient evidence of appropriate gifts and character necessary for missionary service in the contemporary world, and who would be most likely to benefit from the kind of training ANCC provided.

As the reputation of the college grew, the number of applications increased dramatically. One of the reasons behind this increase was the recognition that ANCC

92. The remaining figures are Africa 34% (Nigeria again being the most popular destination with 6 students expecting to go there), Middle East 7%, Americas 12% (including 3 students aiming for Peru, and 2 for Brazil).

was one of the few colleges in the United Kingdom, or even in the whole of Europe, which focused exclusively on missionary training.

Initially the college was little known outside the British Isles, a fact reflected in the small number of students from overseas in the early years. This soon changed, so that by the end of the decade, overseas students formed the majority. Those from continental Europe made up almost a third. This led to an increase in the representation of students from Lutheran and Reformed churches. Numbers coming from Africa and Asia also increased during the same period, due in considerable measure to the itinerant teaching ministry of Martin Goldsmith, a faculty member. He travelled extensively throughout Asia and in other parts of the world, attracting many students to come to the college. The strong historical ties which Britain had with many countries in Asia and Africa was also a significant factor in attracting students from those continents. By contrast the historical ties with Latin America and the Caribbean were weaker. This may account, in part, for the small number of applicants who came from that area of the world, who could also obtain training more easily from North America.

There was always a greater demand for places for single women. The vacancies for single men were the last to be filled. In 1980, the number of single women students outnumbered those of the single men by more than two to one. This reflected the experience of many missionary societies, who often complained that too few men were willing to consider overseas service, preferring instead to enter the ordained ministry at home.

The number of married students also rose sharply. This was largely due to the college's insistence on comprehensive training for both husbands and wives and the provision of nursery care for children so that both parents could study.

The staff did not believe that high academic qualifications were the 'sine qua non' of effective missionary service and were always ready to accept students whom they believed would make a significant contribution to the church overseas. Nevertheless the academic standard of successful applicants did rise, with an increasing number coming from the medical and educational professions.

Insufficient data is available regarding the students' fields of service to draw too many conclusions. Some students were clearly influenced in their choice by the interests and enthusiasm of staff members. Many went to places that had historical or cultural ties with their own country. The decline in those going to Africa may reflect the growing maturity of a church which had less need of missionary personnel. The increasing number of students who opted for Asia may indicate new opportunities for service particularly in South Asia.

6.6 EVALUATION

It is not easy to obtain an unbiased evaluation of any institution since those who approve of it are often fulsome in their praise while those who do not are often silent. This section reviews comments, good and bad, which have been made about the college's training programme. The evaluation of students while they were still at college is considered first, followed by opinions expressed by alumni. The section concludes with the comments of faculty members and the evaluation of some from outside the institution.

6.6.1 Evaluation by students

Although students were regularly asked for their feed-back on individual courses, the first known evaluation of the whole course by those studying at ANCC was conducted by a second year student in 1977.[93] Although no details of this research remain, two of the findings were recorded.

The first was the discovery that 70% of the students had come to the college on the basis of 'the personal recommendation of friends or missionary organisations and that advertising had played no part at all in their choosing ANCC.'[94] Clearly, within a few years of its foundation, the college was already gaining a good reputation as a missionary training centre. Both those who had trained there, and the mission agencies who sent them, appeared to have been satisfied with the training given. This discovery convinced the college that no more money should be spent on advertising, as it was deemed unnecessary.

The second finding of the 1977 survey was that between 75 and 80% of leaving students still intended to serve overseas.[95] Their time at the college had both equipped them for service and confirmed their sense of vocation.

A second and more comprehensive student survey was carried out in June 1982.[96] Although this was the year after Morris had resigned from the principalship, more than half of those taking part in this survey spent their first year under his leadership. Also, the shape and content of the course had changed little in the course of that year.

Students were asked to comment on each lecture course they attended and to indicate its relevance and value to their future ministry. The overwhelming response was positive. While a few courses received a relatively low rating, most were rated highly and appeared to be greatly appreciated.

Students also appreciated the tutorial system, which gave the opportunity to discuss both academic matters and personal issues with their tutor. They did, however, feel that some tutors were often preoccupied with other things and that college life seemed to be dominated by a general air of busy-ness. D. Foster expressed this view: 'One of the big enemies at college is a sense of rush and business. We students need help in discerning and only doing the important (as opposed to the 'urgent') and college routine needs to be reviewed so that it doesn't foster unnecessary over-activity.'[97]

93. Hunt, R., *An evaluation of the adequacy and effectiveness of a cross-cultural missionary training programme* (1995), p. 41.
94. *Ibid.*
95. Hunt points out that this figure included students from overseas (e.g. from Asia and Africa) who were returning home to work among their own people or those of another culture.
96. 121 out of 154 students completed this extensive survey.
97. D. Foster, *Student evaluation questionnaire* (1982).

Overseas students also expressed their deep appreciation of the course but commented that they found it difficult to understand the accents of some of the faculty and to comprehend some of technical vocabulary used in lectures. They also criticised the course for being too Euro-centric and urged the college to appoint a lecturer from the Third World.[98]

6.6.2 Evaluation by alumni

Between 1993 and 1995, Bob Hunt, the vice-principal, conducted a survey of those who had studied at ANCC and its three antecedent colleges. Survey instruments were returned by more than a thousand alumni.

There were 256 respondents who had studied at ANCC between 1971 and 1981. A few of their comments give some indication of how they felt about the training they received:

> 'At every turn I've thanked God for the training received at ANCC.'[99]

> 'There can be few colleges that give a better cross-cultural training than ANCC.'[100]

> 'I am grateful for the fact that its holistic and integrated training was well ahead of its time.'[101]

> 'It was the first place where I was allowed to think through issues of faith and practice in quite radical ways. I have found the cross-cultural training almost as valuable for Liverpool as I did in Arabia.'[102]

> 'My time at ANCC was one of the most formative times of my life, where for the first time I felt really accepted as who I was and I learned to accept myself as who I was.'[103]

The consistent picture gained from students who studied at ANCC between 1971 and 1981 is that they would choose ANCC again. A number of them stated that the college had played a significant role in their choice of country or society, while some who decided not to go overseas felt that the college did not pressurise them into cross-cultural ministry.

They did identify a number of weaknesses in the programme. They felt that there was inadequate instruction in the areas of management and administration. They also wanted more emphasis on the teaching of spiritual disciplines and spirit-

98. This request was initially met with the appointment of visiting lecturers from overseas.
99. Margaret Leppard (1974-76), a curriculum development adviser, Interserve, Bangladesh.
100. Roger Senior (1979-81), area director OMF, Korea.
101. Fred Olney (1975-77), pastor, Evangelical Protestant Church, France.
102. Pat Bond (1976-8), research technician in Riyadh, later Liverpool.
103. Hanna Faust (1975-77), personnel administrator, WBT.

ual warfare.[104] One student asked whether the college was fulfilling its avowed aim, to produce men and women who were truly spiritual and Christ-like.[105]

The practical courses also were the subject of some negative criticism. Some expressed the need for these courses to be constantly reviewed and changed so that they provided necessary and relevant skills for the contemporary missionary scene.

6.6.3 Evaluation by staff

The staff sought to evaluate the training programme on a frequent basis both at their regular staff meetings and through periodic reviews. This led on occasions to a radical surgery being carried out on the curriculum, with some courses being cut out and new courses being transplanted in.

When Ray Windsor was invited to come to ANCC as Morris' successor, he was impressed with the pattern of training that had been established. He expressed his appreciation of the ethos of All Nations and its life as a Christian community. However, he found that the life at the college was dominated by English culture and needed to become more truly international. He saw the lack of non-western faculty members as a serious weakness of the college and immediately set about inviting lectureres from Asia, Africa and Latin America to spend at least one term at ANCC. He recognised the value of the practice of continual assessment adopted at ANCC and its advantages when compared to the setting of exams.[106] He saw the writing of long essays as a product of a British educational system and queried its relevance in a programme of missionary training. He felt that students devoted a disproportionate amount of energy producing long papers on a few subjects and had little time to reflect on many other important issues that were being addressed in lecture courses.

The fact that most of the staff remained on the faculty for a long time probably does indicate their approval of the college's educational approach. They stayed at ANCC because they enjoyed being there and wholeheartedly approved of the way students were being prepared for future service.

Few of the staff, however, actually committed themselves in writing to express their evaluation of the course. One who did so was Martin Goldsmith. Together with his wife Elizabeth, he served under Morris' leadership for ten years. He was one of the first faculty members to be appointed to the united college and he made a major contribution to the development of its syllabus. In his autobiography *Life's tapestry*, he writes of his experience. When he was first invited to join the staff in 1971, one Christian friend warned against it. 'Don't join All Nations,' he warned. 'They will be bankrupt within eighteen months and you will be put out of a job. They are buying their property and putting up new buildings too, but they don't have the money for it. In our present financial crisis in Britain there just isn't that sort of money around.'[107]

---

104. Hunt, R., *An evaluation of the adequacy and effectiveness of a cross-cultural missionary training programme* (1995), p. 78.
105. Rosie Kopecek (1971-3), midwife, AWM, Morocco.
106. R. Windsor, 'The Manila Consultation and the Missions Commission International Missionary Training Project', in: *Internationalising missionary training* (1991), p. 17.
107. M. Goldsmith, *Life's tapestry* (1997), p. 168.

Far from being put off by such comments, the Goldsmiths felt increasingly this was where they were meant to be. They accepted the invitation to join the staff and remained there for nearly twenty five years. He writes, 'What a privilege it has proved to be! We have seen the college grow in numbers, in the quality of its training, in its academic standards and in the high calibre of its students. We have been thrilled to play a small part in training such men and women of God for service overseas.'[108]

Goldsmith comments on some of the strengths which characterised the All Nations training from the very beginning of the united college: the importance of holistic preparation and the need to integrate the missiological, practical, pastoral and spiritual components of the course: the necessity of studying scripture through non-western eyes and including the story of the church in Asia and Africa in any course on church history; the significance of the tutorial system and the provision of training for husbands and wives.

For Goldsmith, the cultural diversity of the college was enriching and challenging. He also appreciated the warmth of fellowship between staff and students. He would set aside twelve hours each week for personal talks with students[109] but he would also love to engage students in conversation over lunch or a cup of coffee. In his view, this informal interaction was one of the important components of the training at ANCC.

6.6.4 External evaluation

Emmanuel Oladipo, the International Secretary of Scripture Union, was a student of All Nations during Morris' principalship. He also sent a number of Scripture Union workers from Nigeria to attend the college during these years. He commented, 'I think one of the great strengths of ANCC was the way it was able to gear training to the level of the individual. Twenty years ago I found just what was required at All Nations and other Scripture Union staff from all over the world have found the same. In an atmosphere of sensible practical spirituality, each individual was intellectually challenged and stretched.'[110]

Those who received All Nations graduates as fresh recruits for overseas ministry also commented favourably on the effectiveness of their preparation. Karen Lampinen, language consultant with OMF in the Philippines was impressed 'with the quality of students from ANCC who have come to the Philippines.'[111] Margaret Adams, the OMF Language Centre co-ordinator found that 'those who had trained at ANCC were of a high standard – very well prepared.'[112]

Others complained that those who had been trained at ANCC gave the impression that they have little to learn. To quote Joyce Odell, a language supervisor in

108. *Ibid.*, p. 169.
109. *Ibid.*, p. 175.
110. *Ibid.*
111. Karen Lampinen, language consultant, OMF Philippines.
112. Margaret Adams, language centre coordinator, OMF Philippines.

Nepal: 'I've seen several couples (from ANCC) come out to Nepal who have been very sure that they have all the answers.'[113]

The most comprehensive critique of the college, written by someone from outside, is found in R. Ferris' *Renewal in theological education.*[114] He never had the opportunity of meeting Morris personally, but he interviewed a number of staff about the foundation and development of the college under Morris' leadership. His critique can be taken as a fair description of the institution as it was established by Morris.

Ferris described ANCC as 'a British, university level, interdenominational missionary training college which demonstrates spiritual formation, holistic curricularising and a developmental focus.'[115] He then went on to say, 'The entire program of the college reflects a creative adaptation of traditional training patterns for the specific purpose of preparing students for effective missionary service.'[116]

Ferris observed that the very smallness of the college when Morris took over made it easier to implement change. Either the college had to change or it was doomed to probable closure. Ferris wondered whether change of the magnitude which Morris introduced could have been undertaken if the college was the size it is today, with nearly 200 students. He commented that there is 'an inertia inherent in largeness that is resistant to change.'[117]

He remarked on the role played by the principal in effecting change. He believed that 'it is totally incredible that ANCC should have become the institution it is today if God had not raised up Mr Morris,'[118] and concluded that this highlights the determinative role of institutional leadership in the change process.

Ferris identified four other factors which contributed to the college's success and distinctiveness, each of which were integral to Morris' understanding of missionary training: first, its clearly defined focus – to train missionaries; second, its employment of successful practitioners as faculty members – the belief that missionaries make the best missionary trainers; third, its commitment to the holistic development of its students; and fourth, its refusal to compromise purpose for growth – the college refused to expand even though it received 1000 enquiries every year.[119]

6.6.5 Conclusion

Those who studied at ANCC, those who have served on the faculty and those who have just observed the college from the outside, each bring their own distinctive critique.

While students were still at the college, they appeared to appreciate the balance between the academic, the pastoral, the spiritual and the practical elements of the

113. Joyce Odell, language supervisor, Nepal.
114. R. Ferris, *Renewal in theological education* (1990), p. 99-105.
115. *Ibid.*, p. 99.
116. *Ibid.*
117. *Ibid.*, p. 103.
118. *Ibid.*, p. 104.
119. *Ibid.*, p. 104-105.

course. Their major criticism was that the staff were often too busy to offer as much pastoral care as the students would like.

Alumni were able to speak with the wisdom of hindsight. They described most of the training they received as being of direct relevance to their chosen ministry, but they would like to have had more teaching on leadership and more instruction in the spiritual disciplines.

Few of the faculty have expressed their evaluation of ANCC in writing, though in the opinion of the writer, the views expressed by Goldsmith accurately reflect those of his colleagues.

Ferris' has written the most thorough external evaluation of the college. The pattern of training he observed at the college was much as it was in Morris' day. His assessment of Morris' role in its development is certainly valid.

All Nations had its fair share of weaknesses and these will be considered in the final chapter. Nonetheless, the consensus appears to be that it did the job it set out to do. It aimed to provide holistic training for cross-cultural ministry in a balanced programme of academic, practical, pastoral and spiritual preparation. It would appear that students, staff and outside observers believe that it achieved that goal.

6.7 Conclusion

Morris assumed the leadership of All Nations at a time when one nation after another in the developing world was achieving independence. From his own experience in Nigeria, he had a good idea of the way in which the change from colonialism to post-colonialism would impact the missionary activity of the church. He realised that the ways in which Western missionaries operated in the days of Empire, and the attitudes which they often demonstrated would no longer be appropriate or acceptable. He recognised that the preparation of missionary recruits had to be radically changed and modernised, and he determined to develop the training at ANCC accordingly.

Along with most other evangelical institutions, All Nations had had little contact with the ecumenical movement. Unlike its sister colleges of Mount Hermon and Ridgelands, ANBC had little association with the established church. Under Poole-Connor, it had taken a very hostile stance towards the World Council of Churches. Morris was not happy with this spirit of isolationism. While remaining faithful to the conservative evangelical heritage of the college, he sought to forge links with a broader spectrum of Christian traditions and to involve the staff in missiological debate with ecumenical and Catholic scholars. Under his leadership, the college had come full circle, returning to the more eirenic and positive attitude towards all Christians that had been demonstrated by the first principal, F.B. Meyer.

When he was invited to assume its leadership, he had a clear idea of the kind of college he wanted it to become. In the space of less than twenty years he turned a dying establishment into a well-known and respected missionary training institution. It was his clear-sightedness, his perseverance, and his ability to draw a gifted team of like-minded people around him that enabled him to turn his vision into reality. The price that he paid to achieve his goal was a breakdown in his health and the disappointment of early retirement. The lasting memorial to his achievement is the institution that he left behind.

Morris built on the foundation of the antecedent colleges. In some ways he changed little: the doctrinal basis, the interdenominational ethos of the college, the focus on missionary training, the stress on spiritual life, the accent on Christian character, the importance of community living – all these things had been part and parcel of the life of the earlier institutions. In other ways, he changed everything: the exclusive focus on missionary training, the training of men and women together, the provision of a nursery, the employment of tutors with missionary experience, the development of a truly holistic programme, and the design of a curriculum drawn from the perceived needs of missionary service in a post-colonial world.

Morris' own attitude to missionary training shaped the whole programme. In a way, All Nations was David Morris and vice versa. His respect for his staff, his decision-making by consensus, his bizarre sense of humour, his strong dislike of hypocrisy and false piety, his discernment of the potential of each student, his encouragement to each person to be themselves, all these contributed to create the distinctive ethos of the college. His training as an army officer influenced his style of leadership and he could appear to be authoritarian. His weakness was his inability to set parameters on his pastoral care of staff and students, and this probably contributed to the breakdown of his health and to his early retirement.

The holistic emphasis of the training was not just talked about theoretically. It was incorporated into the structure of the curriculum. Personal spiritual growth and the formation of a more Christ-like character were encouraged both by the times for private and corporate worship, but also by the provision within the tutorial system of someone akin to a mentor or a spiritual adviser. The practical side of the training was provided by the many courses offered in afternoons and weekends. The academic stimulus was provided by a broad selection of core and elective courses, all aimed at relating scriptural truth to the practical issues of cross-cultural ministry in the twentieth century. This amalgam of the spiritual, the pastoral, the practical and the academic could not satisfy all of the people all the time, but it appears to have satisfied most of the people most of the time.

When ANCC was established as a missionary training college in 1971, it lacked the ecumenical breadth and the academic credibility envisaged by the CBMS, but it was a deliberate attempt to provide a substantial programme of missionary preparation which was comprehensive in scope, addressed the needs of the whole person and the whole family, and directly related to the actualities of cross-cultural ministry in the contemporary world. To that extent it went some way to fulfilling the dream expressed at Edinburgh sixty years earlier.

7. Conclusion

7.1 Researching ANCC

In these final observations, we shall review the context in which the institutions, which eventually formed All Nations Christian College, were established (7.2). Thereafter, we shall examine the strengths (7.3) and weaknesses (7.4) of these colleges with regard to their staffing, purpose, programme and achievements. Finally we shall consider the challenges which faced ANCC after the retirement of Morris (7.5).

7.2 The context of ANCC

The twentieth century, in which these colleges emerged, developed and finally combined, witnessed enormous changes which had significant implications for those engaged in mission or the training of missionaries. Politically, the colonial empires of the European powers ceased to exist. Most of their former colonies and dominions achieved independence. Missionaries could no longer assume a right of access to their shores. Theologically, the authority of the Scriptures and the truth of the historic doctrines of the Christian church were challenged. Ecclesiastically, the search for Christian unity and the formation of the World Council of Churches resulted in a growing antipathy among evangelicals towards the ecumenical movement. Missiologically, the understanding of mission purely in terms of world evangelisation was questioned and rejected by many.

7.2.1 The political context

Mount Hermon Missionary Training College, Ridgelands Bible College and All Nations Bible College were all established in the first quarter of the twentieth century. They were founded at a time when the British Empire retained its integrity and much of its power. British missionaries enjoyed ease of access to many parts of the world and the protection of the British government when they arrived. The strength of the Empire supported their confidence in the superiority of Western religion and culture. Evangelical revivals on both sides of the Atlantic had encouraged their expectation of the rapid spread of the Christian faith throughout the empire and beyond.

As the years went by, hopes for the speedy Christianisation of the world was threatened by global conflicts and the disintegration of the British Empire. Two world wars, initiated among Western nations, raised questions about the superiority of Christianity, the religion of the West, over the other religions of the world. The disintegration of the empire deprived British missionaries of their ability to travel freely and safely within the continents of Africa and Asia.

The world in 1971, when ANCC was founded, was very different from that in which the antecedent colleges had been initially established. At the beginning of this period, British missionaries could go almost anywhere in the world with little problem. By the end of this period, many countries were closed to them and others placed significant restrictions on their activities.

7.2.2 The theological context

By the end of the nineteenth century, Charles Darwin's theory of evolution[1] was perceived by many as having undermined the trustworthiness and authority of the Bible. The writings of Julius Wellhausen[2] and others raised questions about the historicity of the Old Testament. Albert Schweitzer[3] had suggested that Jesus was mistaken about his own identity and God's purpose for his people. Many evangelicals were disturbed by the level of acceptance of these ideas in the mainline churches,. They grew increasingly critical of liberal scholarship and tended to withdraw into ghettos of evangelical isolation.

The founders of the three colleges were very conscious of this theological struggle and adhered closely to the historic tenets of the Christian faith. They rejected modern critical scholarship of the Bible and affirmed in their doctrinal statements the final authority of the Scriptures in all matters of faith and conduct.

As liberal scholars rejected some of their more extreme theories[4] and conservative scholars grew in stature and public recognition, evangelicals began to evaluate the findings of modern scholarship in a more positive light. The changing attitude of evangelicals is reflected in the curricula of the colleges over the years, and especially in the approach of positive critique that typified lectures given at ANCC at the end of this period.

7.2.3 The ecumenical context

John Mott longed to see the evangelisation of the world realised in one generation. He believed that the main obstacle in the way of completing that task was the disunity of the church. He worked tirelessly to bring Christians of different traditions together and encouraged the development of national Christian councils. The International Missionary Council derived its authority from these national Christian Councils, which in turn represented the denominations that were their constituent members. By contrast the three colleges under consideration were not supported by denominations, but by individuals and parachurch organisations, the missionary societies.

The spirit of ecumenism pervaded all the councils of the IMC and later the CWME in the WCC. It seemed obvious to many that a divided church could only give a divided witness. Some evangelicals, however, viewed the emphasis on ecumenism with growing disquiet, both because it seemed to threaten their independ-

1. C. Darwin, *The origin of species* (1859) and *The descent of man* (1871).
2. J. Wellhausen, *Die Geschichte Israels* (1878).
3. A. Schweitzer, *In quest of the historical Jesus* (1906).
4. See particularly H.H. Rowley's introduction to *The Old Testament and modern study* (1951) for his assessment of the changes in OT scholarship during the first half of the twentieth century.

ence and because it involved co-operation with some who held very different views of the Scriptures from their own.

7.2.4 The missiological context

The Edinburgh Conference of 1910 drew attention to the poor standard of training that missionaries received before leaving for the mission field. It appealed to churches and mission agencies to rectify the situation and to develop training programmes that provided academic, spiritual, moral and practical preparation for missionary candidates. In particular, it recommended the establishing on both sides of the Atlantic specialist colleges dedicated to the task of missionary training.

It was assumed that missionaries were being prepared to take the gospel of Jesus Christ to the far corners of the world. While they might be engaged in educational or medical work, their primary task was understood to be evangelism. John Mott had adopted the watchword of the Student Volunteer Movement, 'The evangelisation of the world in this generation,' as the guiding principle of his life. Those who attended the Edinburgh Conference understood mission primarily in those terms.

In the subsequent conferences of the IMC and the CWME, this understanding of mission was called into question. At the Jerusalem Conference of 1928, many called for a greater involvement by the church in issues of race relations, education and rural development. They believed that Christians could help establish the kingdom of God on earth by their participation in the improving of society. The Bangkok meeting of the CWME (1973) reminded Christians of their responsibilities towards the poor, the destitute, the oppressed and the hungry. Evangelicals, who produced their Lausanne covenant one year after Bangkok, acknowledged the rightful place of social action in the mission of the church, but expressed concern at the low priority given to evangelism within conciliar circles.

As the gulf between ecumenical and evangelical theology of mission widened, it became evident that the missionary candidates from the two groups were being prepared and sent out with a very different understanding of their essential task. Those from an ecumenical background saw their task primarily in terms of demonstrating the love of God through identification, through service, through involvement in the social and political conditions of those to whom they went. Those from an evangelical background understood their mission primarily in terms of evangelism. By 1980, however, some evangelicals had moved away from this narrow position and embraced a wider theology of mission, but most still wished to affirm the primacy of evangelism.

The discussion on the theology of mission had implications for the training of missionaries. Those who understood mission in terms of service and identification were quick to emphasise the importance of humility and cultural sensitivity, and the need for candidates to understand the political, economic and social environment in which they would work. These concerns were regularly expressed in the councils of the IMC and the CWME. But evangelicals were suspicious of the conciliar movement and uncertain of the extent to which they should get involved in issues of social and political action. They concentrated on preparing their missionary candidates for the tasks of evangelism and church-planting and were slow to introduce courses on cultural awareness, social development or political philosophy.

7.3 THE STRENGTHS OF ANCC AND ITS ANTECEDENT COLLEGES

Theological colleges and missionary training schools inevitably reflect the context in which they arise, and replicate the strengths and weaknesses of the constituency which they serve. ANCC and its antecedent colleges mirrored the virtues and failings of British evangelicalism during this period. There is the same personal piety and devotion to Jesus Christ, the same confidence in the Christian message and the same loyalty to the historic doctrines of the Christian faith. There is also the same criticism of liberalism, the same suspicion of the ecumenical movement, and the same reluctance to have fellowship with or learn from other traditions of the Christian Church.

The next two sections (7.3 and 7.4) focus first on the distinctive strengths of these institutions and then on their weaknesses. Their strengths are considered under six headings: the determinative influence of leadership (7.3.1); the composition of the staff (7.3.2); the adherence to biblical orthodoxy (7.3.3); the exclusive focus on missionary training (7.3.4); the commitment to holistic training (7.3.5); and the development of evangelical perspectives on mission (7.3.6).

7.3.1 The determinative influence of leadership

The history of these colleges clearly demonstrates the determinative role of institutional leadership in the emergence and development of effective training programmes. Mount Hermon Missionary Training College came into existence as a direct result of the vision, faith and energetic personality of Emily Whitfield, while Irene Crocker built faithfully on the foundations she had laid. The name of Mrs Howard Hooker is synonymous with that of Ridgelands Bible College. She founded the college, held it together after the early death of her husband, led it through a series of crises and continued as its principal for 42 years. She stamped her personality and authority on the college and, through her godliness and devotion to Christ, left a profound impression on those who were trained under her. But it is in the latter years of All Nations Bible College and the emergence of the united college that we see the influence that one individual can play in the shaping of an institution. David Morris changed not only the name, but the nature of the college. He recognised the need for a radical new approach to missionary training. He saw the value of co-educational training and the importance of preparing the whole missionary family. He realised that by combining their resources, a group of small colleges could offer greater breath and depth of training. He had not only the vision to see what was needed, but the perseverance and faith to see it through. He was able to attract together a group of gifted and like-minded men and women and, through the warmth of his own personality, weld them into a harmonious team. It is difficult to believe that ANCC could have become the institution it is today, if David Morris had not been appointed principal of ANBC in 1962.

7.3.2 The qualities and experience of the staff

None of those who served as successful principals in these colleges could have done so without the support of able and dedicated staff. Mrs Hooker was principal of RBC for over forty years, but it was her vice-principal, Dorothy Burton, a lady with the admirable gift of playing second fiddle well, who was seen by many as the 'heart of the college.' When ANCC was formed in 1971, Meg Foote was appointed as vice-principal under David Morris. Through her own experience as principal of Mount Hermon, together with her wise and measured counsel, she proved an invaluable colleague in leadership and made an enormous contribution to the development of the mixed college.

Morris took great care in the selection of staff. He sought those who would work well in a team, who were gifted pastorally, who related easily to people, and who were effective communicators. He also preferred to appoint staff who had been missionaries, on the grounds that successful practitioners would make good missionary trainers. While Morris did not discount the value of academic qualifications, he did not believe that they should be the primary consideration in the appointment of staff. The unity of the team which Morris created, and the success of the programme which he instigated, raises important questions about the criteria that are used in the selection of missionary trainers or any theological educators.

7.3.3 The affirmation of the role and gifts of women

In chapter two, we observed the significant role played by women, such as Anne Small, Florence Allshorn and Gwyneth Hubble, in the training of missionaries and the distinctive contribution they made to the discussion on how missionaries should best be trained. The stories of Mount Hermon and Ridgelands provide further examples of the particular qualities and insights women brought to missionary training: their understanding of the importance of human relationships; their sensitivity towards the pastoral needs and the personal development of their students; and their sense of realism about the challenges and frustrations of missionary life. When ANCC was formed, students had the benefit of a combined faculty. Women had the opportunity to learn from and be pastored by those who had been on the male staff of ANMC. Men learned to appreciate the pastoral insights, the teaching abilities and the academic gifts of the women lecturers, who had previously been at Mount Hermon and Rideglands.

Women had provided vision and leadership at both MHMTC and RBC. Although the possibility of appointing a man as principal was once considered at Mount Hermon, it was never implemented. Women continued to lead both colleges until the merger in 1971. In ANCC, the leadership was shared between the principal, David Morris, and a vice-principal, Meg Foote. The council sought to maintain an equal number of men and women on the faculty. The women enjoyed the same status as the men and taught the same range of subjects. In contrast to some evangelical colleges in the UK and the USA, where women were not allowed to lecture in the area of biblical or theological studies, no such restrictions were placed on the staff at ANCC.

The college gave equal recognition to the gifts and abilities of both men and women. It was particularly concerned to provide every opportunity for wives to take a full course of studies and prepare themselves thoroughly for the ministry to which they had been called. They were encouraged to work at their own academic level and to reach their full potential, which often meant they did better than their husbands. The presence of several married couples on the faculty also provided students with models of husbands and wives who had similar gifts and worked harmoniously and effectively together in ministry.

7.3.4 The adherence to biblical orthodoxy

ANCC and its antecedent colleges belonged to the conservative evangelical tradition. The initial colleges were strongly influenced by the Keswick Convention. Their doctrinal statements reflect an unequivocal commitment to the authority of Scripture. Viewed from one perspective, this clear doctrinal stance was an inherent strength of these institutions. The staff shared a common conviction about the basic doctrines of the Christian faith. The students had a clear understanding of their faith and went out with confidence in the power and universal relevance of the gospel.

From another perspective, their students lacked the benefit of learning from other traditions and interacting with those of different perspectives. Until the 1970s, there was little engagement with the ecumenical movement or contact with the leadership of the major Protestant denominations. Yet, the staff and students in each college came from a wide variety of denominations and represented a degree of evangelical ecumenism.

7.3.5 The exclusive focus on mission

Each college cited the training of missionaries as one of their priorities. The majority of MHMTC students went overseas. Many from ANBC had become missionaries. At RBC too, students had been prepared for ministry both at home and overseas. Morris's vision for the united college was to sharpen the focus on missionary training to the point where it was almost exclusively training people for cross-cultural ministry. Having this highly defined focus enabled the staff to narrow their training objectives and to design the curriculum with one end in view.

It is not easy to decide why the college grew so rapidly after 1971 and continued to draw an increasing number of applications. Part of the reason lay in the personality of the principal and the ethos of the community which he created. Part lay in the promotional ability of Martin Goldsmith, who travelled widely round the world and attracted many to come to the college. Part of the reason can be found in the educational practice of the college, which had replaced exams with continuous assessment. But perhaps the most significant factor in drawing people to study at the college was its exclusive focus on missionary training. This gave the college a clear and recognisable identity in the eyes of the Christian public. All Nations was perceived not as a Bible college but as an institution which specialised on training men and women for cross-cultural service.

7.3.6 The commitment to holistic development

Edinburgh 1910 recommended the incorporation of spiritual, moral, intellectual and practical training in programmes of missionary preparation. Subsequent missionary conferences endorsed this recommendation and stressed the importance of developing godly character and right attitudes. Those who wrote about missionary training and those who taught in missionary colleges also advocated the need for integrated preparation. They believed it was important to devote as much time to spiritual and character development as to academic learning.

MHMTC, RBC and ANBC were all committed to holistic training. Miss Crocker, writing in 1931, stated that the purpose of MHMTC was to foster spiritual growth, develop character, provide a thorough knowledge of the Scriptures and give practical experience of ministry. Miss Hooker at RBC wanted her students to develop a strong spiritual life, to gain a clear grasp of Christian teaching, to be transformed in their character and to undergo practical training in every aspect of Christian work. At ANBC, there was a similar emphasis on the same four dimensions of ministerial training – spiritual preparation, character formation, practical training and academic study. Although the academic level of the courses at these three colleges was not always high and their content was somewhat restricted, the programmes they offered were serious attempts at providing integrated courses to prepare the whole person for missionary service.

Each of these colleges viewed life in a residential community as the best context in which to provide such holistic training and foster such spiritual and personal growth. It was through the ordinary exigencies of daily life that the character of students could be observed. It was in their interaction with fellow students that they could learn to understand themselves, to cope with conflict and to improve their relational skills. The staff at these colleges believed that this aspect of missionary preparation required time. Character could not be diagnosed in a hurry. Changes of habits or attitudes could not be realised in a few weeks. Students might come to their colleges thinking they needed training, when their greatest need was transformation. The courses at these colleges were based on the conviction that a residential community provided a good context in which to encourage that transformation. Those who prepare missionaries for the twenty-first century and who may be tempted to provide shortened, non-residential programmes of training, would do well to reflect on the perspectives and practice of these early missionary trainers.

At ANCC the concept of holistic training was taken one stage further by the introduction of the tutorial system. This system was an adaptation and development of the one used at Oxford and Cambridge Universities. Whereas at Oxbridge, the role of tutor was largely confined to the academic realm, at ANCC the tutor became not only academic adviser, but also mentor, counsellor, pastor and prayer partner.

Through the tutorial system, character flaws could be addressed, progress in the spiritual life could be encouraged, guidance regarding the future could be discussed, and academic assignments could be planned which fitted the individual's personal needs.

7.3.7 The development of evangelical perspectives on mission

Initially, the colleges understood mission almost exclusively in terms of evangelism. The task of mission was to proclaim Christ so that others might come to put their faith in him. There was generally a pessimistic view of the state of the world and a heightened expectation of the return of Christ. There was a reluctance to devote much effort to social action as that seemed to detract from the primary task of proclamation, and it was strongly held that that society could only be transformed through the transformation of individuals by their conversion to Christ.

When the three colleges had merged, the staff realised that the time had come to re-examine this traditional understanding of mission. They did not abandon their commitment to evangelism, but they began to recognise that the responsibility of the church went beyond proclamation. They warmly welcomed the Lausanne Covenant (1974) with its emphasis on social action alongside evangelism. They studied the writings of ecumenical and Catholic missiologists and visited many of their institutions. They encouraged the students to read a wide cross-section of contemporary literature on mission.

The staff realised that the curriculum must relate to the perceived needs of mission in a post-colonial world. They were aware that the gospel could not simply be presented in Western dress, but must be contextualised appropriately within each culture. The introduction of the course on non-western theological developments was a significant step forward in the college programme. It enabled students to begin to understand how the Bible might be read and interpreted in different contexts.

The staff were also aware that more attention had to be paid to the doctrine of the church. Most evangelicals had a low ecclesiology and this was reflected in scant reference to the church in the early doctrinal statements of the three colleges. Evangelical missionaries tended to be unconcerned over the divisions of the Christian Church and to show little inclination to work with Christians who came from different traditions. In their enthusiasm to plant new churches, they were often guilty of ignoring churches that were already in existence. By introducing their own patterns of worship and church government, they were often guilty of ecclesiastical imperialism. The staff at ANCC were aware of these tendencies and sought to address them. They emphasised the importance of the doctrine of the church and its practical implications for missionary strategy.

7.4 The weaknesses of ANCC and its antecedent colleges

Having identified some of the intrinsic strengths of the training given at ANCC and its antecedent colleges, we must now turn to some of the weaknesses of their programmes. These relate to: the qualifications of their staff (7.4.1); their isolation from the ecumenical movement (7.4.2); the disadvantages of their educational theory (7.4.3); the weaknesses of the practical training (7.4.4); the omissions in the academic courses (7.4.5); and the limitations of their missiological perspective (7.4.6).

7.4.1 The qualifications of the staff

We have noted the strength and qualities of the staff and the unity that characterised their corporate life. We must now comment on their weaknesses.

First, the staff were uniformly caucasian. Although the students were being prepared for ministry in Africa, Asia and Latin America, there were no representatives from those continents on the faculty of any of these institutions. Biblical, theological and missiological courses were all taught by Western lecturers from a Western perspective. This only began to change in the united college when Martin Goldsmith, who came from a Jewish background, joined the staff and courses on Non-western theology were introduced into the syllabus. The staff, however, remained white and, with rare exceptions, British.

Secondly, in the early years, few if any of the staff had served as missionaries. None of the principals had worked overseas before the appointment of Mrs Fraser at MHMTC in 1960, Molly MacKenzie at RBC in 1961, and David Morris at ANBC in 1962. Morris sought to remedy this situation by appointing a succession of staff at ANCC who had overseas experience.

Thirdly, the staff did not have a high level of academic qualifications. Without doubt they were deeply dedicated to their task and their many fine qualities left a lasting impression on those who studied under them, but few of them had theological degrees and some of them were not university graduates. Even during the first ten years of the united college, none of the faculty held a doctorate, and the highest theological qualification anyone held was an MTh.

7.4.2 The isolation from the ecumenical movement

The unequivocal evangelical stance taken by the colleges was both a strength and a weakness. The strengths have been noted. The major weakness was that the colleges were isolated from other Christian traditions. All three colleges were suspicious of the ecumenical movement and, through the influence of Poole-Connor, ANBC was strongly antagonistic towards the WCC.

As a consequence, the three colleges were marginalised from the larger Christian community, and little known outside evangelical circles. Their training was sometimes not recognised by the mainline denominations. Alumni who wished to proceed to further education were often required to begin their theological course all over again. The students were not able to interact with, or learn from, Christians whose perspectives were different from their own. They did not learn to appreciate other forms of Christian worship and spirituality. In this respect, it was poor preparation for missionary work in Asia and Africa where, as they would discover, national church leaders were less concerned with denominational and doctrinal differences.

7.4.3 The disadvantages of the educational theory

In its commitment to train the whole family and train the whole person, ANCC set a high standard of integrated, holistic missionary preparation, but there was a price to pay. The tutorial system, which formed the centre piece of the training at the college, was extremely demanding in time. The staff found that if they devoted as much time to their students as they would wish, and as the system demanded, they would have little time for academic research and writing. This dilemma brought into focus a question of the college's identity – was its priority academic study or ministerial training? Every survey that has been conducted among students and alumni at ANCC has indicated that students came to ANCC to find practical training rather than pursue academic scholarship. On the other hand, the college was under increasing pressure from a few students and from the missionary societies to provide a higher level of academic training and to become a centre for evangelical missiological research. It became more and more difficult to resolve the tension between being a pastorally-centred, vocational training institution and a centre for academic research.

7.4.4 The weaknesses of the practical training

The practical nature of the course at ANCC constituted one of its major appeals. Students appreciated and enjoyed learning practical skills that would help them cope with the rigours of missionary life. The constant challenge, which the college faced and didn't always succeed in meeting, was to adapt the practical courses to meet the changing demands and opportunities of missionary work.

The students also appreciated the opportunity to gain practical experience in various aspects of Christian ministry through their weekly involvement in local churches. It was unfortunate that a college dedicated to training for cross-cultural ministry should be situated in a rural and almost totally monocultural context. In rural Hertfordshire, there were virtually no opportunities for students to meet, let alone minister to, people of different cultural backgrounds. This weakness was overcome in two ways. First, students were strongly recommended to gain several months experience overseas before coming to college. Secondly, all students were required to spend several weeks in a cross-cultural environment during one of the ministry placements which were essential components of the course. However, it remains true that the location of the college detracted from the efficacy of a training programme which was designed to prepare people for international ministry.

7.4.5 The omissions in the academic courses

In the early years, the colleges offered only a narrow range of academic subjects. Some of these, such as studies in English Literature, appeared to indicate a degree of confusion between the Christian faith and Western culture. They would not be regarded today as essential components in a programme of missionary training. After the Second World War, the curricula were extended to allow more time for the study of anthropology, comparative religion and contemporary issues. The course at ANCC was more comprehensive still, offering a wide range of theological, missiological, anthropological, ecumenical, religious and political subjects. Yet there were some surprising omissions. There was no course on medical missions although one third of the students belonged to the medical profession. There was no lecture series on development in spite of the urgent need for developmental projects in the newly independent nations of the non-western world. There was no course on urban mission in spite of the rapid process of global urbanisation. There was no course on leadership and management skills, an omission to which alumni repeatedly drew attention. Lectures were offered on the major world religions, but they suffered from the limitation of being taught by Christian lecturers rather than adherents of those faiths.

7.4.6 The limitations of the missiological perspectives

The extant literature of the colleges reveals no reference to the Edinburgh Conference, the IMC or the CWME. Their councils and staff seemed so suspicious of the liberal influences, which they saw as pervading these conferences, that they never gained any benefit from their deliberations.

The neglect of these ecumenical gatherings deprived the colleges of valuable insights into the task of mission and the training of missionaries that might have enhanced their own programmes. The meetings of the IMC and the CWME had highlighted a succession of desirable qualities in missionaries: humility, adaptability, sensitivity, a readiness to incarnate the gospel and a willingness to serve under national leadership. They had pointed out the rapid changes taking place in the world and the need for missionaries to be quick to adapt to those changes. They had drawn attention to changing patterns of missionary service and the increasing role which could be played by Christian professionals and short-term workers. They had affirmed the responsibility of the whole church to take the gospel to the world, and spoken of the need for Western missionaries to work alongside those from Asia, Africa and Latin America. They had challenged the view that saw mission only in terms of evangelism, and had raised the question of a possible missionary moratorium. While those within the conciliar movement were quick to make such observations and to respond accordingly, evangelicals lagged far behind. Had they been less suspicious of the movement and more ready to learn, the quality of training offered at these colleges could have benefited greatly.

The four colleges were located in Britain and were dominated by British students. Even in 1980, when the overseas students constituted the majority of the student body, the college remained predominantly Western in its ethos. Students coming from outside the West observed the cultural behaviour of Western Christians and were sometimes shocked by it. The staff at ANCC tried to inculcate appreciation of the customs and cultures of others and to challenge any suggestion of cultural insensitivity. But it may be questioned as to how far they were able to eradicate the incipient ethnocentricity of most Western students, or how successful they were in preparing them to work sensitively in international mission teams.

7.5 Challenges and expectations

When Morris retired in 1981, the council members of ANCC were faced with the task of finding a replacement. They were aware that the college was gaining increasing recognition as a missionary training school, not only in the UK, but also in other parts of the world. They decided to look for a principal with an international reputation as a missionary leader and statesman. In 1982, they appointed Dr Ray Windsor, the international director of InterServe, who came from New Zealand and had served for many years in India.

As Dr Windsor took over the helm and the college entered the last two decades of the 20th century, it faced a number of key challenges with regard to its future. These will be considered under the following headings: the appointment of staff (7.5.1); the size and composition of the student body (7.5.2); the issue of accreditation (7.5.3); the maintenance of the college's evangelical identity and its relationship to main line denominations and the ecumenical movement (7.5.4); and the continuing developing and updating of the college's missionary training programme (7.5.5).

7.5.1 The appointment of staff

Many students had criticised the college for its Euro-centricity. They pointed out that although all the staff were British (with the exception of Dr Windsor who was from New Zealand), the majority of students were not. They urged the council to appoint non-western staff. Some members of council questioned whether they were justified in inviting a lecturer from Africa or Asia to work in the UK, when their gifts and experience might be more urgently needed in their own country. On the other hand, they recognised that a reciprocal exchange of staff with an overseas college might solve the problem and prove beneficial to both institutions. All Nations would gain the benefit of a lecturer with a non-western perspectvie, while the ANCC staff member could fill the gap left by the visiting lecturer in his home country. A short-term solution, advocated by Dr Windsor, was the appointment of guest lecturers from the non-western world who would spend one term at the college. The council adopted this proposal but continued to seek more permanent appointments of non-western lecturers to the faculty.

Another dilemma facing the college at the beginning of the '80s was whether to appoint staff who were practitioners or academics. Morris had always chosen staff with field experience, pastoral gifts and communication skills. As a higher calibre of students were attracted to apply to the college, there was increased pressure to appoint staff with higher academic qualifications. If the college appointed faculty with extensive field experience but lower theological qualifications, the academic level of the course might not satisfy the demands of the brighter students. If the college opted for academics, there was a danger that the college would lose its distinctive ethos.

7.5.2 The size and composition of the student body

The success of the college brought its own problems. By 1981, the admissions office was receiving more than 1000 letters of enquiry every year from potential students. Many of these did not pursue their application after an initial enquiry and several others were not suitable for the course, but the college was still confronted with having more applicants than places. This was especially true in the case of single women and married couples. This inevitably raised the question as to whether the college should expand further. Already in the eyes of several staff members the college had grown too large (157 students in 1981), and was in serious danger of losing the atmosphere of a family community. Another response to the growing number of applications was to suggest the founding of a sister college in another part of the United Kingdom. A third option was to raise the selection criteria, demanding more experience in the secular world and in cross-cultural living prior to acceptance at the college. The danger of this proposal was that the age of students would rise at a time when many missionary societies were asking for younger candidates who were still full of enthusiasm and, arguably, more able to adapt to a new culture and learn a new language.

7.5.3 Accreditation

The dilemma concerning the selection of staff was part of a bigger issue facing the college. Since the amalgamation of the three colleges, the council and staff had spurned the idea of seeking academic accreditation. They were reluctant to commit the college to the demands and strictures of an external accrediting agency, fearing that might impact negatively the holistic nature of the course. At the same time they recognised that a minority of students did require an academic theological qualification for their future work. They were aware that the Cambridge Diploma for Religious Studies, the one external theological course which a small number of students pursued, was not altogether satisfactory for their needs. During the next decade the college had to grapple with the question of whether or not to seek accreditation. The staff had to weigh carefully the implications which it might have on the community and the training they gave.

7.5.4 Evangelical identity

Like its predecessors, ANCC was a theologically conservative institution. Evangelical churches and missionary societies were willing to send their missionary candidates there to study because of its unequivocal doctrinal stance. In the 1960s, there was little formal contact between the college and the major Protestant denominations or ecumenical institutions. In the united college, the staff became increasingly aware of the disadvantages of their isolation from the broader Christian community. They realised there were many things that their students could learn from the spirituality of other Christian traditions and the writings of ecumenical and Catholic missiologists. They were determined to maintain the evangelical tradition of the college, but to build bridges with the major denominations, with ecumenical organisations like the British and Irish Association for Mission Studies, and with other missiological institutions such as the Selly Oak Federation of Colleges, Birmingham.

7.5.5 Missionary identity

The staff faced the challenge of expanding their syllabus of missionary studies to address the issues which were being encountered by former students and were being discussed in wider missiological circles. These included the contemporary debates on the relationship between evangelism and social action, between proclamation and dialogue, between the gospel and culture. The staff also had to grapple with the legitimacy and limitations of contextualisation, the place of political action in contexts of oppression, and the challenges and insights of the feminist movement. They recognised the need to provide training in development work and urban ministry. They also wanted to initiate a course on medical missions, which among other issues, would examine the relationship between Western and traditional medicine.

Successive meetings of the IMC and CWME had pointed out the new structures of missionary service that were becoming apparent in the post-colonial age. They drew attention to the increasing contribution being made by short-term missionaries and to the strategic role that could be played by Christian professionals, who went overseas in secular employment. The college had to decided to what extent it could adapt or expand the existing courses to provide appropriate training for these new categories of Christian missionaries.

Morris rejoiced to witness the growth of the missionary movements in the developing world and the emergence of national missionary training centres. When he left in 1981, the staff at the college had to consider how they could best encourage this growing missionary movement and facilitate the growth of indigenous training programmes. Should the college continue to accept students from the Two-Thirds World? Was a college in the West the best place for them to train? Could the college course be adapted to address those issues that were relevant to those who would become missionary trainers in their own country?

Under the guidance of David Morris, ANCC had focused exclusively on developing a programme of holistic missionary training which prepared men and women for cross-cultural ministry. Morris was a convinced evangelical but he wanted the college to relate to and benefit from fellowship with the wider constituency of the Christian Church. He had been a missionary in a nation moving towards independence, and he wanted to develop a training programme which prepared candidates appropriately for their future service.

As was the case with the antecedent colleges, the large majority of students from ANCC went into cross-cultural ministry. The stringent selection process meant that there were few drop-outs in the middle of the course. Most appreciated their training and said they would choose ANCC again. This seemed to indicate that the college went some way to achieving its objectives. Morris had developed an effective pattern of training for Christian service in the world as he saw it. It remained to be seen how far the college would continue to adapt to meet the new challenges of political change, theological debate, and modern technology.

Photographs

Mount Hermon Missionary Training College

North Side, Streatham Common
(1921-1939)

Emily Whitfield
(Principal 1911-1927)

Irene Crocker
(Principal 1927-1961)

Ridgelands Bible College

Ridgelands, Bexley
(1943-1971)

Mr and Mrs Kenneth Hooker
(Founders, RBC)

All Nations Bible College

F.B. Meyer
(Principal 1924-1925)

Beulah Hill, Upper Norwood
(1923-1939)

H.S. Curr
(Principal 1925-1939)

Taplow Hill House
(1946-1964)

E.J. Poole-Connor
(Principal 1945-1948)

H.B. Bonsall
(Principal 1948-1952)

L.S. M'Caw
(Principal 1952-1962)

All Nations Christian College

Easneye, Ware
(ANMC 1964-1971, ANCC from 1971)

D. Morris
(Principal ANMC 1962-1971)
(Principal ANCC 1971-1981)

M.S. Foote
(Principal MHMTC 1965-1971)
(Vice-principal ANCC 1971-1981)

Appendices

Appendix 1: Doctrinal statement of ANBC (1926) and MHMTC (1930)*

* (as quoted in the Constitution, Purpose and Doctrinal Basis of ANBC, 1926, and in the Articles of Association, dated 28th March 1930)

(1) We believe in one God eternally existing in three persons – Father, Son and Holy Spirit.

(2) We believe that Jesus Christ was conceived of the Holy Spirit, born of the Virgin Mary; that He is very God and very man; and that all his teachings and utterances are true.

(3) We believe, that when the Lord Jesus Christ was crucified, He offered Himself as the representative and substitutionary sacrifice for the sin of the whole world, and that all who repent and believe in Him are justified on the ground of His shed blood, and that they constitute His church.

(4) We believe that the Body of our Lord which was crucified, was raised from the dead according to the Scriptures, and that He ascended into Heaven, and sitteth on the right hand of God as our High Priest and Advocate.

(5) We believe in the Second Coming of the Lord Jesus Christ, and that His return to the earth will be visible and personal in like manner as He went.

(6) We believe in the Holy Spirit the Lord and Giver of Life, Who proceedeth from the Father and the Son; that He spake by the Scriptures of the Old and New Testaments, and that He dwelleth in the believer.

(7) We believe that the Old and New Testaments are inspired of God, are historically trustworthy, and their teaching and authority final.

(8) We believe that man was created in the image of God; that he has sinned and thereby incurred, not physical death only, but also that spiritual death which is separation from God: that all human beings are consequently born with a sinful nature, and on reaching the period of moral responsibility, become sinners in thought, word and deed. We believe in the necessity of regeneration by the Holy Spirit, in order that man may enter the Kingdom of God, and that the evidence of this new life should be manifested in the daily walk.

(9) We believe in the resurrection of the just and the unjust, the eternal blessedness of the redeemed in Christ, and the eternal punishment of those who have ignored or rejected the offer of salvation.

Appendix 2: Examination in medicine (ANBC, 1927)*

* (MRANs August, 1927)

(1) Give a list of diseases which commence with a sore throat.
How would you distinguish a case of Diptheria from follicular Tonsillitis?
(2) Describe the complications which may occur in a case of Scarlet Fever.
(3) Give an account of the signs and symptoms of Typhoid Fever during the third week.
(4) How would you treat a case of Lobar Pneumonia?
(5) Describe the onset, course and treatment of a case of dry Pleurisy.
(6) What precautions would you take to protect yourself in a tropical climate against:

(a) Smallpox
(b) Typhoid
(c) Malaria?

(7) Give an account of the early symptoms of Tuberculosis of the lungs.

Appendix 3: Curriculum of MHMTC (1930)*

* (Taken from *Two Years' Course*, 1930)

Synthetic Bible Study:
Pentateuch, Historical books, Prophets and Poetical books
The Gospel and Acts, Epistles and Revelation

Constructive Criticism:
The origin, transmission and unity of the Bible
Inspiration and authority
The making of the New Testament
OT prophecy

Homiletics:
Practical training in public speaking
Personal work and visitation
Conduct of meetings

Studies in the New Testament

Doctrinal studies:
The biblical view of man, The biblical view of sin
The person and work of the Holy Spirit

Church History:
Church history 1 – the early period
Church history 2 – the Reformation

Characteristics of Christian experience:
Biographies of A.J. Gordon, Hudson Taylor, George Muller
The writings of William Law, Samuel Rutherford, John Newton and John Bunyan

Bible biographies:
Joseph, Elijah, Nehemiah, Abraham, Peter, Paul

Missionary studies:
Missionary problems
History of missions
Missionary methods
Comparative religion

Miscellaneous studies:
Experimental difficulties in the Christian life
Memory control
Dispensational Bible Studies
Spiritual lessons from the Prayer Book

Appendix 4: Curriculum of ANBC (1935)

The English Bible:
General introduction to the Old Testament, Pentateuch
OT History and Prophecy, OT Poetry and Wisdom
General introduction to the New Testament
The Gospels, Acts and the Pauline epistles
The General epistles and Revelation

Expository lectures:
Matthew 5-7, Romans 1-8, 1 Peter
The Tabernacle, Amos, Psalm 119

Christian doctrine:
The doctrines of God, the person and work of Christ, the Holy Spirit and the Trinity
The doctrines of man, sin, salvation, the church and eschatology

Church history:
The rise of Christianity, The rise of the Papacy
The Renaissance and the Reformation, The Counter Reformation
The Huguenots and the Camisards, The Wesleyan revival and foreign missions

English Literature:
Chaucer, Shakespeare, Spencer and Milton
The classical school, The great prose writers, Byron to Tennyson

Medical courses:
Elementary anatomy and physiology
Elementary surgery and First Aid
Elementary medicine and hygiene

Technical training:
Building, carpentry
Metal work, printing
Book-keeping, linguistics

Miscellaneous studies:
English composition
Preacher's classes
Missionary addresses
Comparative religion

More advanced courses in Biblical Studies, Christian Doctrine, New Testament Greek and Elementary Hebrew were also available for students who required a third year in training.

Appendix 5: Missionary societies*

* (Societies which accepted missionary candidates from ANBC during the period 1923-1939, *ANMR* Nov 1939)

Baptist Missionary Society
Bible Churchmen's Missionary Society
"Brethren" Missionaries
China Inland Mission
Eastern Bolivian Mission
European Christian Mission
India Gospel League
Japan Railway Mission
Maranhao Mission (Brazil)
North Africa Mission
New Hebridies Mission
Regions Beyond Missionary Union
Russian Missionary Society
Sudan Interior Mission
Zambesi Industrial Mission

Barbican Mission to Jews
Bolivian Indian Mission
British Jews' Society
Church Missionary Society
Egypt General Mission
Evangelical Union of South America
Japan Evangelistic Band
Lakher Pioneer Mission
Mildmay Mission to Jews
North Angola Mission
Poona and Indian Village Mission
Russian Gospel Movement
South American Missionary Society
Worldwide Evangelisation Crusade

Appendix 6: Doctrinal statement of ANCC (1970)*

* (as expressed in the Memorandum and Articles of Association, dated 24th September 1970)

The objects of the Association shall be conducted in obedience to the divine command to preach the Gospel to all peoples and in accordance with the fundamental truths of Chistianity, as revealed in Holy Scripture, including:

(a) The unity of the Father, the Son and the Holy Spirit in the Godhead.
(b) The sovereignty of God in creation, revelation, redemption and final judgment.
(c) The divine inspiration and infallibility of Holy Scripture, as originally given, and its supreme authority in all matters of faith and conduct.
(d) The universal sinfulness and guilt of human nature since the fall, rendering man subject to God's wrath and condemnation.
(e) Redemption from the guilt, penalty and power of sin only through the sacrificial death (as our Representative and Substitute) of Jesus Christ, the incarnate Son of God.
(f) The resurrection of Jesus Christ from the dead.
(g) The necessity of the work of the Holy Spirit to make the death of Christ effective to the individual sinner, granting him repentance toward God and faith in Jesus Christ.
(h) The indwelling work of the Holy Spirit in the believer.
(i) The one holy universal Church, which is the Body of Christ, and to which all true believers belong.
(j) The expectation of the personal return of the Lord Jesus Christ.

Appendix 7: Assignments (ANCC, 1971-1981)*

* (selected from *Bible Study Assignments and other work* 1971-1981)

* Give an account of the Christian doctrine of the Trinity, its biblical foundation and historical formulation. What difficulties are likely to occur in seeking to present this truth to the particular religious and cultural context in which you expect to work, eg Islam, Judaism, Hinduism, Western Materialism?

* On the basis of your own detailed study of the Acts of the Apostles, seek to deal with the following questions:

a. What are the main milestones in the spread if the Gospel as recorded in Acts?
b. What differences in the form and content of the message are caused by the varying audiences in Acts?
c. How valid is it to make Paul's "missionary methods" as seen in Acts normative for today?

* EITHER Contrast the nature of Revelation in Islam with the Christian doctrine,
OR Discuss the possibility of incarnation in Hinduism or re-incarnation in Buddhism and compare it with the Christian doctrine of the Incarnation of Christ,
OR Compare the views of authority found in Judaism and Christianity,
OR Study the Christian doctrine of the Communion of the saints, considering carefully its biblical basis. Are there similar ideas in Primal religions?

* Discuss ways in which culture can condition our understanding and communication of the gospel and its outworking.

* What are the social implications of James and how would you apply this to world situations today?

* Give a critique and/ or summary of ONE of the following:

Introduction to the science of missions – J.H. Bavinck
Contemporary missiology – J. Verkuyl
Witness to the world – D.J. Bosch

* You are expected to read and be able to expound to your tutor one book on theology written from a non-Western background, e.g.

No handle on the cross or Waterbuffalo theology – K. Koyama
Theology of pain – K. Kitamori
An introduction to Indian Christian theology – A.J. Boyd
New Testament Eschatology in an African background – J.S. Mbiti
African Traditional Religion – E.B. Idowu
Theology of liberation – G. Gutierrez
Marx and the Bible – J.P. Miranda

Appendix 8: Student numbers 1971-1980

	1971	1972	1973	1974	1975	1976	1977	1978	1979	1980
Women	58	58	56	54	57	57	58	58	62	70
Men	34	34	32	30	32	34	33	32	39	31
Marrieds	36	38	40	46	46	46	62	66	56	56
Total	128	130	128	130	135	137	153	156	157	157

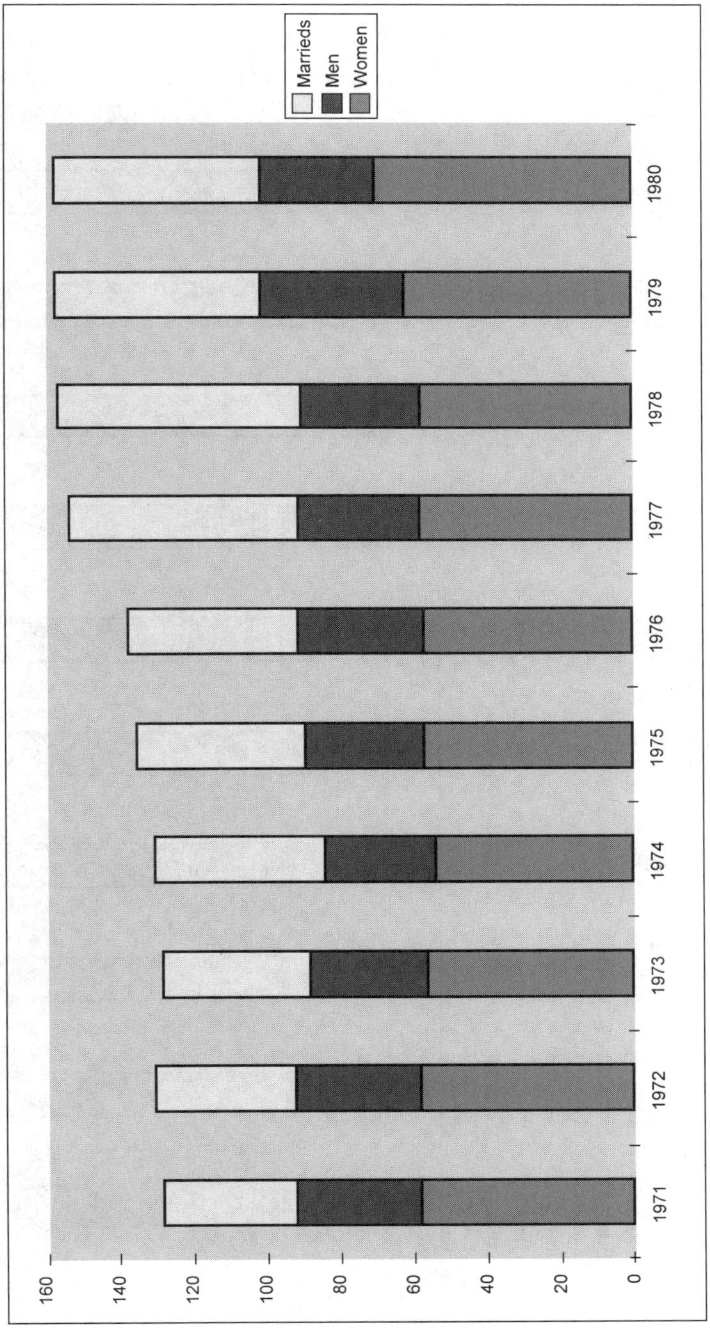

Appendix 9: Student nationality 1971-1980

	1971	1972	1973	1974	1975	1976	1977	1978	1979	1980
UK	110	106	100	98	102	98	97	88	91	75
Europe	14	16	16	16	13	19	25	29	29	47
Asia	2	5	5	7	8	9	5	14	17	13
Africa	2	2	5	5	7	7	20	20	14	15
Other		1	2	4	5	4	6	5	6	7
Total	128	130	128	130	135	137	153	156	157	157

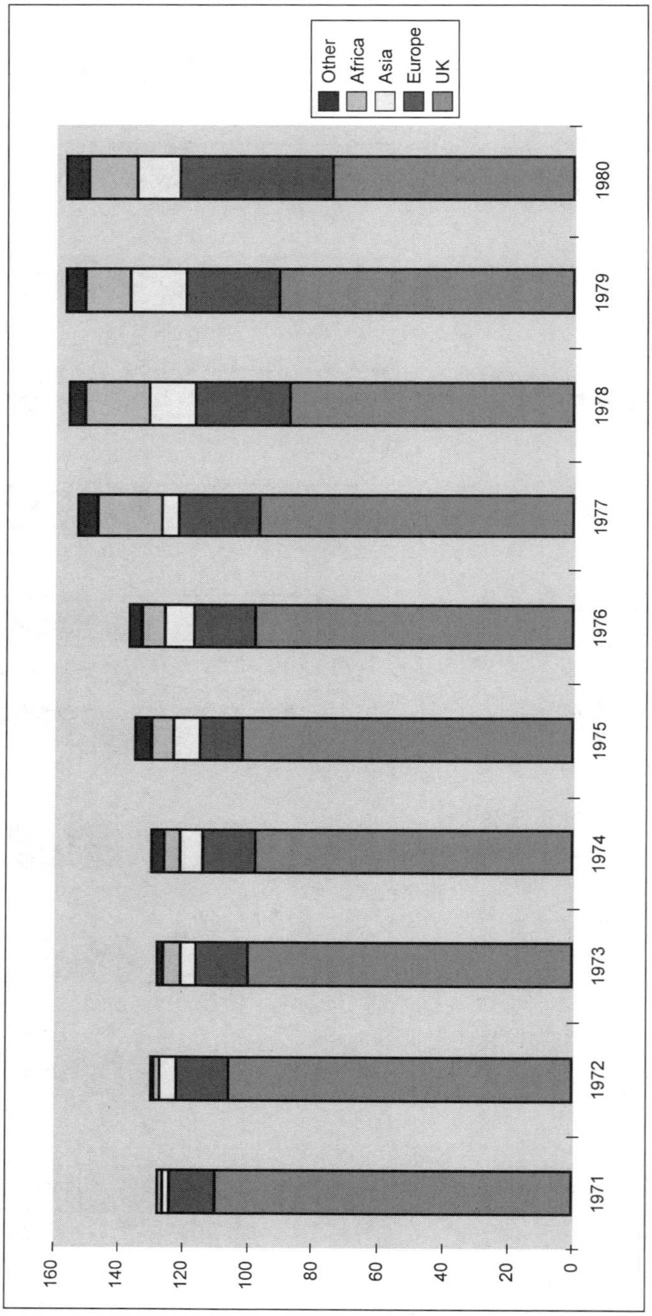

Appendix 10: Student denomination 1971-1980

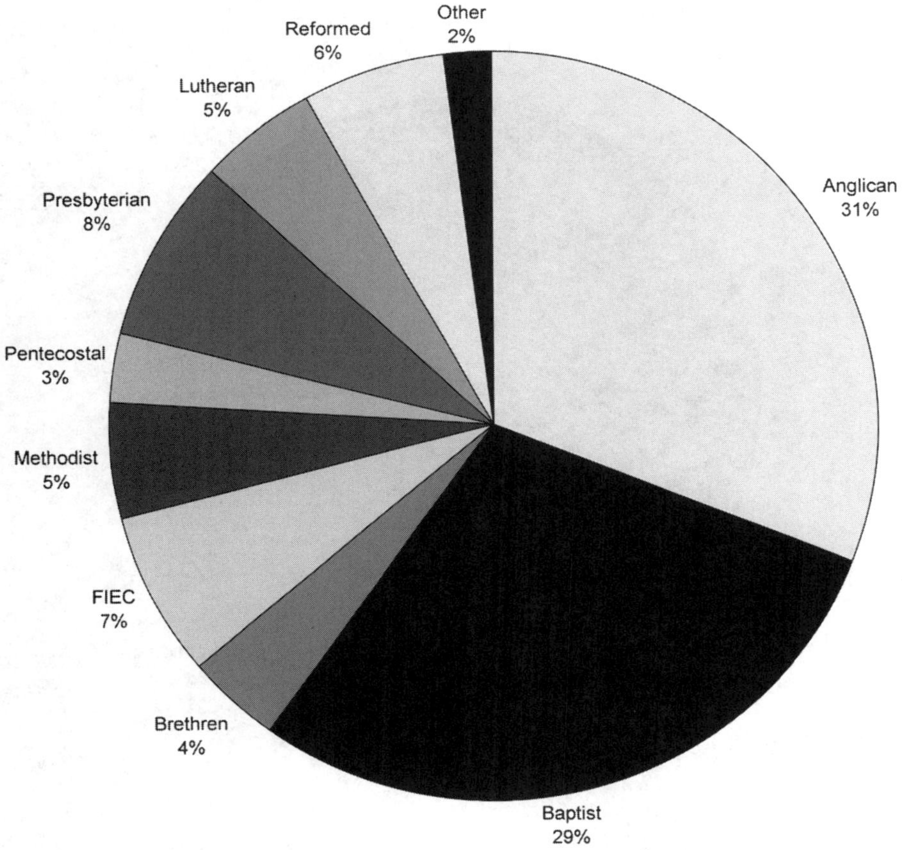

Appendix 11: Student professions 1971-1980

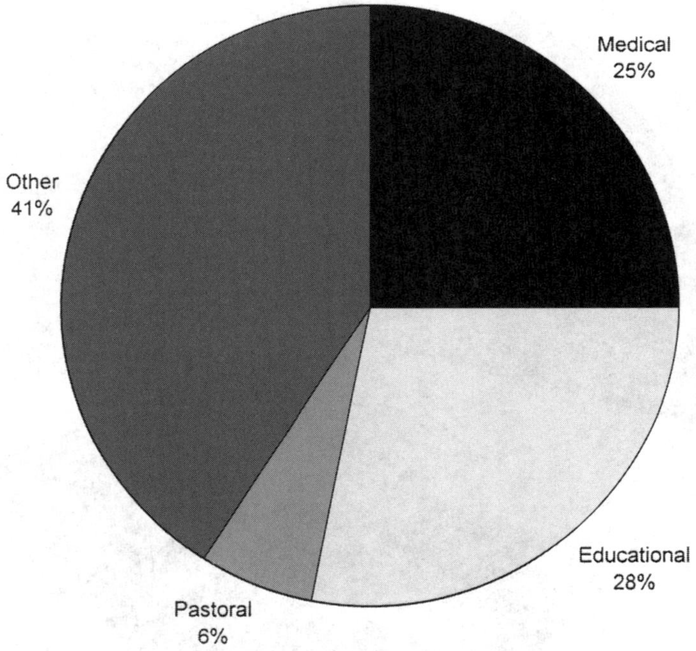

Appendix 12: Fields of service 1971-1980

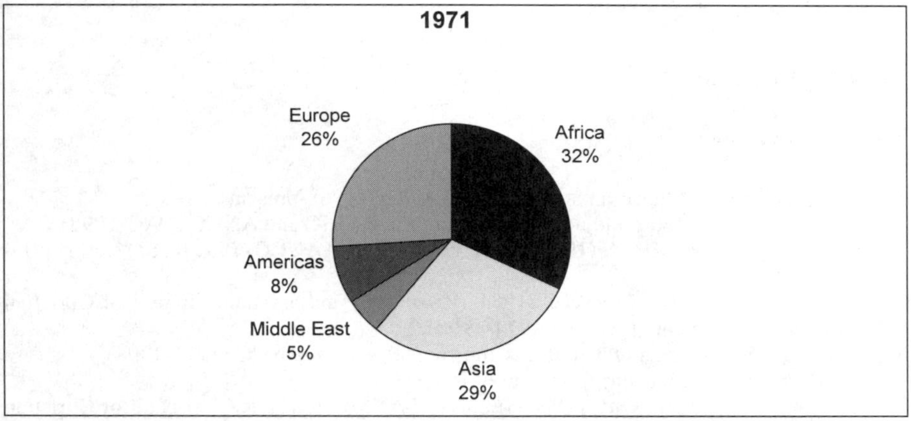

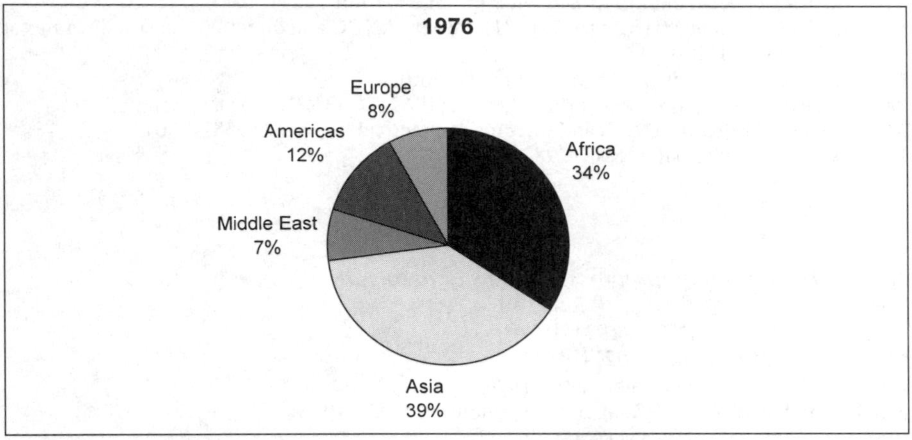

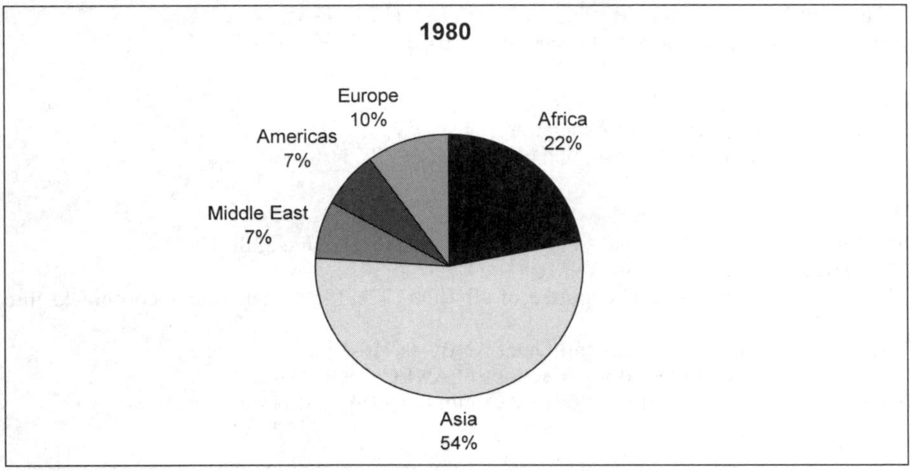

Bibliography

1. PRIMARY SOURCES

1.1 Oral sources

Mr. S. Bruce, tutor and librarian at ANMC and ANCC (1968-present).
Rev. Dr. R. E. Davies, tutor and director of studies at ANMC and ANCC (1963-1998).
Ms. M. Foote, principal MHBC (1965-1971), vice-principal ANCC (1971-1981), acting principal ANCC (1981-2).
Ms. R. Giesner, student at MHMTC (1954-1956), tutor and assistant director of Christian ministries department at ANCC (1974-1990).
Mr. M. Goldsmith, tutor and head of missions department of ANCC (1971-1994).
Mrs. D. Harman (née Johnson), principal of RBC (1966-1971).
Rev. R. Hunt, student at ANMC (1964-6), tutor of ANMC and ANCC, director of Christian ministries department (1973-87), vice-principal (from 1987).
Rev. M. Jones, tutor at MHBC (1967-1971), tutor at ANCC and director of pastoral studies at ANCC (1971-1986).
Mrs. M. Mackenzie, principal of RBC (1961-1966).
Dr. D. Morris, principal ANMC (1962-1971) and ANCC (1971-1981).
Mr. T. Paget, warden of ANCC and director of practical courses (1958-1990).
Dr. R. Windsor, principal ANCC (1982-1985).

1.2 Archival material:

1.2.1 Minutes, annual reports, articles of association

MHMTC

Annual reports of MHMTC (1921-1926)
Minutes of staff meetings (1922-1925)
Declaration of Trust (December 31st, 1924)
Minutes of Trustees and Management Committee (1927-1973)
Register of students of MHMTC (1927-1972)
Minutes of Mount Hermon Missionary Union Ltd. (1946-1964)
Balance sheets and statement of accounts at MHMTC (1930-1970)

RBC

Memorandum and Articles of Asociation (1928)
Minutes of the Executive Committee of RBC (1960-1971)

ANBC

The Memorandum and Articles of Association of ANMU (June 22th, 1920)
The minutes of the Council of ANMU (1923-1962)
Minutes of the Executive Committee of ANBC (1922-1953, thereafter incorporated into ANMU)
The minutes of the Student Committee of ANBC (1946-1962)
The minutes of the Student Body Meetings of ANBC (1946-1962)
The minutes of the Student Evangelistic Committee of ANBC (1946-1962)

ANMC
The minutes of the Council of ANMU (1962-1971)
The minuites of the Student Committee of ANMC (1962-1971)
The minutes of the Student Body Meetings of ANMC (1962-1971)
The minutes of the Student Evangelistic Committee of ANMC (1962-1971)
Reports of the Vacation Campaigns of ANMC students (1962-1969)

ANCC
Proposals for discussion and amendment for the proposed missionary training campus (1967)
The minutes of the Formation Committee of MHMTC, RBC and ANMC (1969-1970)
The Articles of Association of ANCC Limited (1971)
The minutes of the Council of ANCC (1970-1982)
The minutes of the Council of ANMU (1971-1973)
The minutes of the Student Committee of ANCC (1971-1981)
The minutes of the Student Body Meetings of ANCC (1971-1981)
The minutes of the Student Evangelistic Committee of ANCC (1972-1981)
Reports of the Vacation Campaigns of ANCC students (1972-1978)
Submission of ANCC to the Council for National Academic Awards for accreditation as an institution (1985)

1.2.2 Curricula, lecture notes

ANCC, *Timetables and assignments work sheets* (1971-1981).
Crocker, E., *Lectures of all books of the Bible* (MHMTC, 1935-1936).
—, *Lectures on the person and work of the Holy Spirit* (MHMTC, 1936).
Oliver, E., student at ANBC, hand-written lecture notes (1934).
Sayer, J., *Lectures on constructive criticism* (MHMTC, 1934-6).
Tett, W., *Diary of ANBC students on evangelistic trek to Maldon and Braintree, Essex* (1936)
Titterton, C. L., *Comparative study of the various religions of the countries of the world* (MHMTC, 1934-6)

1.2.3 Student records, surveys

Records of students at MHMTC (1926-1971)
Records of students at RBC (1920-1971)
Records of students at ANBC (1923-1959)
Register of students at ANMC (1962-1971)
Register of students at ANCC (1971-1981)
Student Evaluation questionnaire, conducted by D. Foster in 1982.
Survey of alumni of all three colleges, conducted by R. Hunt in 1993/4.
Survey of RBC alumni, conducted for this dissertation in 1997.

1.2.4 Unpublished material

Correspondence with D. Morris (principal, ANMC 1962-1971 and ANCC 1971-1981), Miss. M. Foote (principal, MHMTC 1965-1971, vice-principal ANCC 1971-1981, acting principal 1981-1982), Mrs. M. MacKenzie (principal RBC 1961-1966), Mrs. D. Harman (principal RBC 1966-1971).
Letters sent out by G. Thomas, Hon. Secretary of ANBC, to supporters, Feburary 14 1922 and July 15 1932.
Personal reflections by D. Morris, nd.
Principal's record and notebook, D. Harman (1966-1971).
Private notes of D. Morris, dated February 18th, 1998.
Twelve keys to missionary training, handwritten notes by D. Morris, c. 1980.

1.3 Published material

All Nations Bible College (1959-1960)
All Nations Bible College for the training of missionaries (1947)
All Nations Bible College Brochure (1953)
All Nations Bible College Bulletin (1961-1962)
All Nations Christian College Newsletter (1975-1981)
All Nations Christian College Syllabus (1971)
All Nations Missionary College Syllabus (1965)
All Nations Missionary College Syllabus (1967)
All Nations Missionary College Syllabus (revised 1969)
All Nations Missionary Review (1900-1920)
All Nations Missionary Review, new series nos: 2-15 (1947-1952)
A brief history: 1923-1958 (Taplow, ANBC, 1958)
The men of All Nations: 1923-1958 (Taplow, ANBC, 1958)
Missionary Review of All Nations (1921-1940)
Missionary Review of All Nations, supplement (1925-1935)
Missionary Review of All Nations, new series no: 1 (1947)
Mount Hermon Outgoings (1922-1929)
News from All Nations (1955-1958)
Outgoings, new series (June 1940-June 1957)
Outgoings (Autumn 1957-Summer 1966)
Outgoings (annual 1967-1971)
Ridgelands College Record (London, Queensgate Press, 1924-1938)
Ridgelands calling (London, Marshall, Morgan & Scott, 1933)
The story of Easneye (Ware, UK, ANCC, 1975)
The story of Easneye (Ware, UK, ANCC, 1997)

2. SECONDARY SOURCES

Cooper, A., *It shouldn't happen to a missionary!* (Ware, ANCC, 1993).
Ferris, R. W., 'All Nations Christian College,' in: *Renewal in theological education: strategies for change* (Wheaton, Billy Graham Center, 1990), pp. 99-106.
Fullerton, W. Y., *F. B. Meyer: a biography* (London, Marshall, Morgan & Scott, 1930).
Goldsmith, M., *Life's tapestry: reflections and insights from my life* (Carlisle, Paternoster, 1997), pp. 170-184.
Taylor, W. D. *Internationalising Missionary training* (Exeter, Paternoster, 1991).

'Adorning doctrine,' in: *The Christian* (July 5 1934), p.19.
'The All Nations Bible College,' in: *The Christian* (July 14 1932), p. 20.
'Ambassadors of the Divine Government,' in: *The Christian Herald* (January 19 1957), p. 8.
'ANBC Anniversary,' in: *The Christian* (August 23, 1935), p. 11.
'ANBC trekkers,' in: *The English Churchman* (August 31 1956), p 395.
'Answering the call,' in: *The Christian* (July 15 1937), p. 17.
'Bible colleges affiliate,' in: *The Christian* (May 31 1928), p. 7.
'College old boys tell of missionary experience,' in: *Hertford Mercury* (May 30 1966), p. 5.
'Criticism of modern living: Bible weekend at Taplow,' in: *Maidenhead Advertiser* (April 15 1955), p. 3.
'Delhi next stop,' in: *Church of England Newspaper* (April 14 1967), p. 9f.
'From Harlow to jungle mission,' in: *Harlow Citizen* (March 26 1965), p. 1.
'The fruit of a woman's indominable faith,' in: *Life of Faith* (February 23 1938), p. 167ff.
'The missionary is shaking off his jungle image,' in: *Bristol Evening Post* (January 29 1965), p. 7.

'Outreach to six villages,' in: *The Christian* (February 3 1967), p. 13.
'Preparing for service,' in: *Life of Faith* (February 19 1936), p. 9.
'The school of the prophets,' in: *The Christian* (May 11 1933), p. 29.
'Spreading the faith from Taplow,' in: *Maidenhead Advertiser* (April 25 1958), p. 6.
'Taplow convention,' in: *The Christian* (May 30 1958), p. 1.

3. General sources

Allen, R., *The spontaneous expansion of the church and the causes that hinder it* (London, World Dominion Press, 1927).
Allshorn, F., *The notebooks of Florence Allshorn* (London, SCM, 1958).
Armitage, C., *Reaching for the goal; the life story of David Adeney – ordinary man, extraordinary mission* (Wheaton, OMF, 1993).
Baba, P., 'Frontier mission personnel,' in: A. Starling, ed., *Seeds of Promise* (Pasadena, William Carey Library, 1981), pp. 114-123.
Baillie, J. 'The theological course as a preparation for the missionary,' in: *IRM* (1939), pp. 535-548.
Barclay, O., *Evangelicalism in Britain* (Leicester, IVP, 1997).
Bassham, R.C., *Mission theology 1948-1975: years of worldwide creative tension, Ecumenical, Evangelical and Roman Catholic* (Pasadena, William Carye Library, 1979).
Bavinck, J.H., *An introduction to the science of missions* (Philadelphia, Presbyterian & Reformed Publishing Co., 1960).
Bebbington, D.W., *Evangelicalism in modern Britain: a history from the 1730s to the 1980s* (London, Unwin Hyman, 1989).
Board of Missionary Preparation, *The specialised training of missionaries* (New York, 1919).
Bosch., D.J., *Witness to the world: the Christian mission in theological perspective* (London, Marshall, Morgan & Scott, 1980).
—, *Transforming mission: paradigm shifts in theology of* mission (New York, Orbis, 1991).
Brereton, V.L., *Training God's army: the American Bible school 1880-1940* (Indianapolis, Indianapolis University Press, 1990).
Brewster, N.N., 'The need of a missionary training institute,' *Methodist Review* (1902), pp. 507-602.
Brierley, P., *Survey of British Missionaries* (London, Marc Europe, 1986).
Britt, W.G., 'Pretraining variables in the prediction of missionary success overseas,' *Journal of Psychology and Theology* 11 (1983), pp. 203-212.
Brown, E., 'The legacy of Florence Allshorn,' *IBMR* 8 (1984), pp. 24-28.
Castillo, M., 'Missiological education: The missing element in mission strategy,' *Asia Pulse* 7:2 (1973), pp. 2-5.
CBMS, *Report of the annual conference* (London, Edinburgh House, 1912-1978).
Church of England, *The report of a joint committee of enquiry on recruitment and training of ordinands and clergy for service overseas* (London, Church Information Board, 1957).
Church Missionary Society, *First C.M.S. summer school report* (London, 1904).
Cobbs, L.R., 'The missionary's call and training for foreign missions,' *Baptist History and Heritage* 29 (1994), pp. 26-35.
Conn, H.M., and S. F. Rowen, *Missions and theological education in world perspective* (Farmington, Associates of Urbanus, 1984).
Copland, E.B., 'Historical notes concerning missionary preparation during the period 1910-1952, ' in: *The church's preparation in today's world* (Hartford, Kennedy School of Missions, 1954).
Cummings, D., 'Programmed for failure: mission candidates at risk,' in: *EMQ* 23 (1987), pp. 240-246.
CWME, *Bangkok Assembly* (Bangkok, CWME, 1973).

Davis, J.M., 'The preparation of missionaries for work in the post-war era,' in: IRM 33 (1944), pp. 241-253.
Dipple, B., 'To teach overseas: preparations for missionary work,' in: *Journal of Christian Education* 36 (1993), pp. 37-42.
Dixon, J.B., 'Unrealistic expectations: the downfall of many missionaries,' in: *EMQ* 26 (1990), pp. 388-393.
Douglas, J.D. (ed.), *Proclaim Christ until He comes: International Congress on World Evangelisation in Manila* (Lausanne, LCWE, 1990).
Elliot-Binns, L.E., *The evangelical movement in the English Church* (London, Methuen, 1928).
Elliston, J.E., *Christian relief and development: developing workers for effective ministry* (Dallas, Word Publishing, 1989).
Ferris, R.W., *Renewal in theological education: strategies for change*, (Wheaton, Billy Graham Center, 1990).
—, ed., *Establishing ministry training: A manual for program developers*, (Pasadena, William Carey Library, 1995).
Fiedler, K. *The story of faith missions* (Oxford, Regnum, 1994).
Foreign Missions Conference of North America, *Conference on missionary preparation* (New York, 1922).
—, *Preparation of missionaries for Africa* (New York, 1935).
Foster, J., 'Missionary training for the post-war world,' in: *IRM* 33 (1944), pp. 361-367.
Fountain, D.G., *E.J. Poole-Connor: 1872-1962* (Worthing, Walter, 1966).
Fullerton, W.Y., *F.B. Meyer: a biography* (London, Marshall, Morgan & Scott, 1930).
Gairdner, W.H.T., *Echoes from Edinburgh, 1910: an account and interpretation of the World Missionary Conference* (New York, Fleming H. Revell, 1910).
Gardner, L.M., *A case study examination of missionary terminations* (Denver, Conservative Baptist Seminary, 1984).
—, 'A practical approach to transitions in missionary living', *Journal of Psychology and Theology* 15 (1987), pp. 342-349.
Goldsmith, M., *Life's tapestry* (Carlisle, OM, 1997).
Gollock, G.A., *Candidates in waiting: a manual of home preparation for foreign missionary work* (London, CMS, 1907).
—, *The call and preparation of the missionary in the light of the modern situation* (London, Edinburgh House, 1921).
—, *An introduction to missionary service* (London, Milford, 1921).
—, 'The present outlook on the preparation of missionaries,' in: *IRM* 14 (1924), pp.383-402.
Goodall, N., ed., *Missions under the cross: addresses delivered at the enlarged meeting of the committee of the International Missionary Council at Willingen, in Germany, 1952; with statements issued by the meeting* (London, Edinburgh House Press, 1953).
Hardman, J.T. and R.K. Orchard, *Two minutes from Sloane Square: the Conference of the Missionary Societies of Great Britian and Ireland 1912-1977* (London, Edinburgh House, 1977).
Harley, C.D., *Preparing to serve: training for cross-cultural mission* (Pasadena, William Carey Library, 1995).
Harrison, P.W., *Preparation for missionary service* (New York, Student Volunteer Movement for Foreign Missions, nd)
Hedlund, R.E., 'Missionary training in the Indian context', in: R. E. Hedlund and F. Hrangkhuma, eds., *Indigenous missions in India* (Madras, Church Growth Research Center, 1980).
Henderson, A., 'A historical review of missions and missionary training in the Churches of Christ,' in: *Restoration Weekly* 35:4, (1993), pp. 203-217.
Hendrix, E.R., *The call and qualifications of a missionary* (Nashville, Missionary Training School, 1905).
Higden, E.G., *Missionaries for new days* (St Louis, Bethany Press, 1956).

Hodge, A., 'Training of missionaries for Africa: the Church Missionary Society's Training College at Islington, 1900-1915,' in: *Journal of Religion in Africa* 4:2 (1971), pp. 81-96.

Hodgkin, H.T., 'The special preparation of missionaries,' *IRM* 1 (1912), pp. 108-119.

Hogben, R., *In training: A guide to the preparation of the missionary* (London, Inter-Varsity Fellowship, 1946).

Hooton, W.S. and J. Stafford Wright, *The first twenty-five years of the Bible Churchmen's Missionary Society: 1922-1947* (London, BCMS, 1947).

Houghton, A.T., *Preparing to be a missionary* (London, Inter-Varsity Fellowship, 1956).

Hubble, G., 'Reasons for missionary training,' in: *IRM* 52 (1963), pp. 257-265.

Hunt, R.G., *An evaluation of the adequacy and effectiveness of a cross-cultural missionary training programme, with particular reference to ANCC* (Ware, ANCC, 1995).

International Council of Accrediting Agencies, 'Manifesto on the Renewal of Evangelical Theological Education,' in: *Evangelical Review of Theology* 8:1 (1984), pp.136-143.

IMC, *The Jerusalem meeting of the IMC*, Vols. II, III, VI and VII (1928).

IMC, *The world mission of the church* (1938).

IMC, 'The place, function and training of the future missionary' in: *Findings and recommendations of the IMC, Tambaram, Madras, India, 1938* (London, I.M.C., 1939).

IMC, *Report to the assemblies of the IMC and the WCC* (1961).

Jones, M., 'Preparation for missionary service: Training for work in a new culture', *Christian Brethren Review* 36 (1985), pp. 31-38.

Jongeneel, J.A.B., *Philosophy, science and theology of Mission in the 19th and 20th Centuries: a missiological encylcopaedia.* Parts I and II (Frankfurt am Main, Peter Lang, 1995 & 1997).

Jonson, J., 'Missionary education and pre-service training for the universal church,' in: *IRM* 56 (1967), pp. 418-428.

Kane, H., *The making of a missionary* (Grand Rapids, Baker Book House, 1975).

Keyes, L.E., *The last age of missions: a study of Third World missionary societies* (Pasadena, William Carey Library, 1983).

Latham, R.O., *God for all men* (London, Edinburgh House, 1964)

Latourette, K.S., *A history of the expansion of Christianity,* 7 vols. (Chicago, Zondervan, 1976).

Latourette, K.S. and W.R. Hogg, *Tomorrow is here* (New York, Friendship Press for IMC, 1948).

Lee, D. Tai Woong, *A missionary training programme for university students in South Korea* (Deerfield, Trinity Evangelical Divinity School, 1983).

Lefever, H.C., 'The preparation of missionaries 1910 and 1960,' in: *IRM* 49 (1960), pp. 281-290.

Lennox, W.G., *The health and turnover of missionaries* (New York, The Foreign Missions Conference, 1933).

Long, P.B., *Discipling the nations: training Brazilians for inter-cultural mission* (Pasadena, Fuller Theological Seminary, School of World Missions, 1981).

Loong, T., 'Training missionaries in Asia,' *Evangelical Review of Theology* 14 (1990), pp. 168-178.

Lyman, E., *Preparing missionaries for intercultural communication: a bi-cultural approach* (Pasadena, William Carey Library, 1985).

Mackenzie, F., 'A problem in missionary preparation,' in: *IRM* 10 (1920), pp. 439-443.

Maclennan, K., *Twenty years of missionary co-operation* (London, Edinburgh House Press, 1927).

Martin, H., *Fifty years of Carey Hall* (Birmingham, Council of Carey Hall, 1962).

Mayers, M.K., 'Training missionaries for the 21st century,' in: *EMQ* 22:3 (1986), pp. 306-319.

McKinney, L., *Cultural attunement of programmed instruction: individualism-group and expository-discovery dimensions* (Michigan, Michigan State University, 1973).

—, 'Selected annotated bibliography for missiology: missionary education.' in: *Missiology* 21 (1993), pp. 107-111.
Mercer, H.S., 'The missionary call and how to state it', *The first C.M.S. summer school report* (London, CMS, 1904), pp. 225-238.
Morgan, E. R., 'Missionary vocation and training,' in his *Essays catholic and missionary* (1928), pp. 233-252.
Morgan, H., *Who'd be a missionary?* (London, Patmos, 1965).
Mott, J.H., *International cooperation: its possibilities, its costs and its realisation* (London, Edinburgh House, 1921).
Moyer, K.E., *A study of missionary motivation, training and withdrawal (1932-1952)* (New York, Missionary Research Library, 1957).
Murray, J.L., 'Missionary preparation in America: its development and present outlook,' *IRM* 15 (1925), pp. 586-597.
Myklebust, O.G., *The study of missions in theological education: an historical inquiry into the place of world evangelisation in western Protestant ministerial training with particular reference to Alexander Duff's chair of evangelistic theology,* 2 vols. (Oslo, Egede Instituttet, 1955 and 1957).
Neill, S.C., *The Christian character* (London, Lutterworth, 1955).
—, *A history of Christian missions* (London, Penguin, 1986).
Newbigin, L., 'Cross-currents in ecumenical and evangelical understandings of mission', in: *IBMR* 6:4 (October 1982), pp. 146-151.
Newbolt, M.R., 'Training of missionaries,' in: *Missionary question* (1918), pp. 98-119.
Northfield, H.D., 'The training of men missionaries,' in: *IRM* 46 (1957), pp. 59-67.
Orchard, R.K., ed., *The Ghana assembly of the IMC* (London, Edinburgh House, 1958).
Pedersen, N.N., *Study of missionary withdrawal 1933-1952* (Methodist Board of Missions, nd).
Petty, O.A., ed., *Home base and missionary personnel* (New York, Harper and Brothers, 1933).
Piggin, S., *Making evangelical missionaries 1789-1858: the social background, motives and training of British Protestant missionaries to India* (London, Sutton Courtenay Press, 1984).
Poole-Connor, E.J., *Evangelicalism in England* (London, FIEC, 1951).
—, *The World Council of Churches: whence and whither* ? (London, FIEC, 1962).
Pocock, M., 'A recruiter's view of missionary training,' in: *EMQ* 21:4 (1985), pp. 409-412.
Ransom, C. W., ed., *Renewal and advance* (London, Edinmburgh House,1948),
Reed, L.E., *Preparing missionaries for intercultural communication: a bicultural approach* (Pasadena, William Carey Library, 1985).
Rivers, W.H.R., 'Anthroplogy and the missionary,' in: *IRM* 10 (1920), pp. 208-213.
Rogers, C.M., 'One world: an implication for missionary training,' in: *IRM* 34 (1945), pp. 306-314.
Rouse R. and S.C. Neill (eds.), *History of the ecumenical movement* (London, SPCK, 1967).
Rowlandson, M.L., *Life at the Keswick Convention: a personal recollection* (Carlisle, OM, 1997).
Sargent, D.N., *The making of a missionary* (London, Hodder and Stoughton, 1960).
Selly Oak Colleges, *Selly Oak Journal* 1-10 (Birmingham, Selly Oak Federation, 1984-1989).
Smith, D. P., *A new approach to missionary orientation* (London, Oxford University Press, 1961).
Soper, E.D., 'The study of religion in the training of missionaries,' in: *IRM* 12 (1922), pp. 406-422.
Stewart, M., *Training in mission: St Colm's College, Church of Scotland* with foreward by Lesslie Newbigin (Edinburgh, St Andrew's Press, 1972).
Student Volunteer Movement, *The call, qualifications and preparation of candidates for foreign missionary service* (New York, Student Volunteer Movement for Foreign Missions, 1901).

Taber, C.A., 'The training of missionaries,' in: *Practical anthropology* 14 (1967), pp. 267-274.
Taylor, W.D., ed., *Internationalising missionary training: a global perspective* (Exeter, Paternoster Press, 1991).
Tidball, D.J., *Who are the evangelicals: tracing the roots of today's movement* (London, Marshall Pickering, 1994).
Ward, T.W., *Living overseas: a book of preparations* (New York, Free Press, 1984).
—, 'Educational preparation of missionaries: a look ahead', in: *EMQ* 23 (1987), pp. 398-404.
Webster, D., *What is a missionary?* (London, Highway, 1955).
—, *In debt to Christ* (London, Highway, 1957).
Weddell, S., 'Missionary training in North America,' in: *IRM* 33 (1944), pp. 368-375.
Welch, J., 'The missionary training of medical missionaries,' in: *IRM* 29 (1940), pp. 262-269.
Whiteman, D.L., ed., 'Preparation for cross-cultural mission,' in: *Missiology* 21 (1993), pp. 3-75.
Williams, T., *Together in Mission* (Bangalore, World Evangelical Fellowship Missions Commission, 1983).
Williamson, M., *Have we no right?* (London, China Inland Mission, 1958).
Wittenbach, H.A., 'The training of a missionary', in: *IRM* 49 (1960), pp. 405-410.
Wolcott, L.T., 'Missionary training: the communal non-academic orientation,' in: *IRM* 49 (1960), pp. 401-404.
World Council of Churches, *Statement from a consultation on the preparation of missionaries* (New York, WCC, 1964).
World Missionary Conference, *Report of Commission V* (1910).
Yates, T. , *Christian mission in the twentieth century* (Cambridge, CUP, 1996).
Ziffer, W., 'Missionary pre-service training: some observations,' in: *IRM* 58 (1969) pp.195-203, 292-301.

4. Encyclopedias, dictionaries

Biograpical dictionary of Christian mission, ed. G. H. Anderson.
Concise dictionary of the Christian world mission, eds. S.C. Neill, G.H. Anderson and J.F.B. Goodwin. (Nashville and New York, Abindgon Press, 1971).
Dictionary catalogue of the Missionary Research Library New York (Boston, G.K. Hall and Co, 1968). 17 vols..
Dictionary of the ecumenical movement, eds. N. Lossky et al. (Geneva, WCC, 1991).
Directory of foreign missions: missionary boards, societies, colleges, cooperative councils, and other agencies of the Protestant churches of the world , eds. E.B. Strong and A.L. Warnshuis (New York and London, IMCl, 1933).
Directory of schools and professors of mission, ed. J. A. Siewert (Monrovia,Ca: Marc, 1995).
Encyclopedia of mission: descriptive, historical, biographical, statistical, eds. H.O. Dwight, H.A. Tupper and E.M. Bliss (New York and London, Funk and Wagnalls, 1904).
Encyclopedia of modern Christian missions: the agencies, ed. B.L. Goddard (Camden, Thomas Nelson, 1967).
World Christian Encyclopedia: a comparative study of Churches and religions in the modern world AD 1900-1000, ed. D.B. Barrett (Nairobi, Oxford, New York, Oxford University Press, 1980).
World directory of missionary training centres, ed. R.V.J. Windsor (Pasadena, William Carey Library, 1995).

Samenvatting

De zendingsbeweging van de westerse protestantse kerken, die tijdens de negentiende eeuw in een stroomversnelling was gekomen, ontving een sterke stimulans van de Wereldzendingsconferentie, die in 1910 in Edinburgh werd gehouden. Mannen en vrouwen werden opgeroepen om de zending in te gaan en men verwachtte dat het aantal westerse zendelingen binnen dertig jaar zou verdrievoudigen.

Tegelijkertijd werd erkend dat degenen die uitgezonden zouden worden, voldoende geschoold moesten zijn. Eén van de acht commissies van de Edinburgh conferentie besprak in het bijzonder de kwestie van de zendingsopleiding en vroeg aandacht voor de behoefte aan meer gespecialiseerde voorbereiding van zendelingen op hun werk en op hun specifieke zendingsveld.

Ondanks de nadruk die in Edinburgh en op de daarop volgende internationale zendingsconferenties gelegd werd op een grondige voorbereiding, werden de meeste zendelingen nog steeds uitgezonden met weinig of geen gespecialiseerde opleiding. Het gebrek aan voldoende scholing leidde op het zendingsveld vaak tot ernstige problemen en tot vroegtijdige terugkeer van werkers naar hun vaderland. Kerkleiders en zendingsorganisaties maakten zich zorgen over het grote aantal mislukkingen en gaven onvoldoende scholing aan als één van de hoofdoorzaken van het onaanvaardbaar grote verlies aan werkkracht in de zending.

Het doel van deze studie is om de eenheid en de verscheidenheid te bestuderen van de zendingsopleiding zoals die tussen 1911 en 1981 op vier evangelische instellingen (*colleges*) in het Verenigd Koninkrijk werd aangeboden en om te zien welke lessen kunnen worden getrokken uit de verschillende opleidingsmodellen. De context van deze studie is de overgangsperiode van het kolonialisme naar het post-kolonialisme en de groeiende tegenstelling tussen de evangelische en de oecumenische beweging.

Drie van de vier bestudeerde instellingen werden opgericht tijdens het eerste kwart van de twintigste eeuw. Mount Hermon Missionary Training College werd in 1911 gesticht om vrouwen voor dienst overzee op te leiden. Ridgelands Bible College werd in 1919 opgericht om vrouwen te scholen voor christelijke dienst, zowel in eigen land als overzee. All Nations Bible College werd in 1923 geopend als een interkerkelijke opleiding voor mannen, die voor de zending naar het buitenland wilden gaan. De drie instellingen fuseerden in 1971 tot één instituut, het All Nations Christian College.

Deze studie beschrijft de geschiedenis en de ontwikkeling van deze instituten, hun dogmatische positie en de specifieke kenmerken van hun opleiding. Er wordt een kritische beschrijving gegeven van de verschillende bestanddelen van hun programma en onderzocht wordt in hoeverre zij geestelijke voorbereiding, karaktervorming, theoretische scholing en praktische voorlichting gaven. Verder wordt de nationaliteit, kerkelijke achtergrond, diploma's en de daarop volgende bediening van hun studenten in kaart gebracht.

Het laatste hoofdstuk bespreekt de politieke, theologische, oecumenische en missiologische context, waarbinnen deze instellingen werden opgericht en ontwikkeld. Het evalueert de sterke en zwakke punten van deze opleidingen. De aandacht wordt gericht op hun veranderende houding ten opzichte van de oecumenische beweging en de ontwikkeling van hun missiologisch denken. Tenslotte wordt aangegeven welke lessen er getrokken kunnen worden door hen, die, in de westerse of in de niet-westerse wereld, betrokken zijn bij de opleiding van zendelingen voor zending in de eenentwintigste eeuw.

(Vertaald door Marja Kerr & Magritha Jongeneel)

Index of personal names

Curriculum vitae

David Harley was born in Chalfont, England in 1941, the son of an Anglican vicar. He studied classics and theology at Cambridge University and Trinity College, Bristol. He was ordained in the Church of England in 1966 and served a curacy in a parish in North London. From 1970 to 1978, he and his wife, Rosemary, worked with an Anglican missionary society in Ethiopia and in the United Kingdom. From 1978 to 1993, he served on the faculty of All Nations Christian College and in 1985 he was appointed principal. In 1993, he joined the staff of Crosslinks (formerly the Bible Churchmen's Missionary Society, an Anglican missionary agency founded in 1922) and in 1996 he became dean of the Discipleship Training Centre in Singapore. He is currently teaching missions at Trinity Theological College in Singapore, while continuing his work as a missionary training consultant. His doctoral dissertation (DMin) from Columbia International University was on missionary training in the Two-Thirds World. He has three married children.